dowment that distributes the fellowships known simply as "the Guggenheims." There is a chapter on Harry F. Guggenheim, present head of the family, and also information on a few members of the clan with "aberrations and scandals common to most families and especially to those who can afford their more expensive manifestations."

Highlighting the book are numerous examples of Guggenheim support of men and ideas that have made history: Jimmy Doolittle, pioneering in blind flying in the 20's; Charles A. Lindbergh's cross-country flights made to demonstrate the safety of air travel; Theodor von Kármán, the brilliant space scientist, brought to America by a Guggenheim foundation; Robert H. Goddard, whose work with rockets was supported for ten years almost solely by Guggenheim money.

Seed Money—based partly on the recollections of contemporaries, but chiefly on patient scrutiny of the voluminous Guggenheim family files—is a thorough and absorbing book; the story of a benevolent and civic-minded dynasty such as could occur only in this country. Appendix, index, photographs.

Milton Lomask, biographer and specialist in American history, spent more than two years writing the story of the Guggenheims and their foundations. He is the author of *Andrew Johnson: President on Trial,* and has also written many biographies and stories for children.

SEED MONEY:

The Guggenheim Story

Meyer Guggenheim and His Seven Sons

On the facing page is a reproduction of the portrait which hangs in the partners' room of Guggenheim Brothers. Meyer Guggenheim (February 1, 1828 – March 15, 1905) is seated at the center of the table.

Reading from left to right, his sons are:

Benjamin, October 26, 1865 – April 14, 1912
Murry, August 12, 1858 – November 15, 1939
Isaac, June 7, 1854 – October 10, 1922
Daniel, July 9, 1856 – September 28, 1930
Solomon, February 2, 1861 – November 3, 1949
Simon, December 30, 1867 – November 2, 1941
William, November 6, 1868 – June 27, 1941

On the wall is a picture of Simon Meyer (1792–1869), the founder of the family in America and father of Meyer Guggenheim.

Library of Congress catalog card number 63-22088
First Printing, 1964

Published simultaneously in Canada by
Ambassador Books, Ltd., Toronto
Manufactured in the U.S.A.

SEED MONE

The Guggenheim Stor

by Milton Lomask

FARRAR, STRAUS AND COMPANY
NEW YORK

The institution known as a "foundation" is
the best means yet invented to make
the resources of the past serve the future.

HENRY ALLEN MOE,
Former President
The John Simon Guggenheim Memorial Foundation

Foreword

During the two decades beginning in 1924 five philanthropic foundations were established by members of the American Guggenheim family. Four of them were set up as permanent and are still functioning, and although the fifth, the Daniel Guggenheim Fund for the Promotion of Aeronautics, terminated its activities more than thirty years ago, its influence is still being felt.

This book is the story of the Guggenheim foundations and of the Guggenheim family. It is also a story of some of the many productive individuals whose work the foundations have helped bring to fruition—

Of Jimmy Doolittle, for example, taking a giant step toward the conquest of the problems of blind flying for aviators in the 1920's.

Of Charles Lindbergh, touring the country during the same period in a demonstration of the then little appreciated potentialities of travel by air.

Of the Baroness Hilla Rebay von Ehrenweisen, alternately convulsing and alarming the art world of the 1940's with her novel ideas of how the Guggenheim Museum should be run.

Of Frank Lloyd Wright, architect of the present Museum, battling with everybody in the course of designing and bringing into existence probably the most discussed and certainly the most controversial building since the rise and fall of the Tower of Babel.

Of Hungarian-born Dr. Theodore von Kármán, brought to America by a Guggenheim foundation to assist in making this country pre-eminent in the development of astronautical theory.

Of Dr. Henry Allen Moe, as principal executive officer of the foundation that distributes the Guggenheim fellowships, pointing out the value of private giving to a skeptical congressional investigating committee in the early 1950's.

And of Dr. Robert H. Goddard, "Father of Modern Rocketry," carrying on the pre-World War II experiments that laid the scientific basis for the age of space.

Since there were Guggenheims before there were Guggenheim foundations, the story opens with the family. And since the Guggenheims started their life in this country as penniless Jewish immigrants, it opens in a ghetto—in a ghetto, however, far different in appearance if not in spirit from the onetime *Judenstrassen* of such European cities as Worms and Frankfort-on-Main—in a ghetto surrounded by open country and roofed by the spreading trees of a small farming town in a scenic corner of Switzerland.

Contents

SEED MONEY:
The Guggenheim Story

I

In Switzerland's Green Ghettos

Much of the little knowledge we have of the ancestors of the American Guggenheim family is available because in 1740 Johann Casper Ulrich, pastor of the Fraumünster or Cathedral of the Holy Virgin—then as now the second most important church in Zurich, Switzerland—decided to take his wife to the baths at the nearby town of Baden. To Frau Ulrich the trip was necessary. She was a sufferer from arthritis. But to her scholarly husband the indolent life of a small health resort was less than satisfactory. To entertain himself he began making visits to two neighboring villages standing side by side in the Surbtal—a green and picturesque valley formed by a little stream called the Surb —and bearing the names of Lengnau and Ober-Endingen.

For Pastor Ulrich to occupy himself in this manner was noteworthy. In 1740 Lengnau and Ober-Endingen, or Endingen as it is now known, were the ghettos of Switzerland and at that time their Jewish occupants were widely regarded as not quite fit company for decent Christians.

Pastor Ulrich had his reasons. One was that as a seminary student he had acquired an interest in rabbinical studies and it had come to his attention that among the some five hundred Jewish residents of Lengnau and Endingen was one Jakob Guggenheim, a *parnas* or elder of the synagogue and a *lamden* or scholar, versed in rabbinical lore. Another was Pastor Ulrich's frequently voiced hope that in the Surbtal communities he might find ways of luring some of the Israelites from what he regarded as the "darkness" of their ancient faith into the "light" of Protestant Christianity.

That he succeeded with his first mission is a matter of record. He was charmed by Parnas Guggenheim. Soon he, the parnas and the rabbi of the congregation jointly serving the two communities became good friends. As for the pastor's proselyting ambitions—in these, too, he achieved a limited success. In the course of a rush of events which shook the profoundly religious Jews to their roots, he persuaded Joseph Guggenheim, a son of the parnas, to leave his wife and children to live as a Christian convert in Zurich. On the whole, however, it would appear that the pastor's proselyting efforts worked in reverse. He became an ardent champion of the Jews. He worked for them, traveled for them, spoke for them, and in the last year of his life he published his *Collection of Jewish Narratives.* One of the first books from a Christian pen to depict the Jews with fairness, it contains the fullest known history of Swiss Jewry prior to 1760 and many glimpses into the life and personality of Parnas Jakob Guggenheim and other members of a family whose American descendants were to achieve fame first as the creators of a mining empire and later as the founders of five unusual foundations.[1]

At Sixteen Minutes to Three

According to old-timers of the Surbtal, the Lengnau[2] and Endingen to which Pastor Ulrich repaired generations ago were not too different from the slightly larger villages confronting the visitor today. Symbolic of the area's unchangingness is the clock high on the stately façade of the Lengnau Synagogue. Its hands stand at sixteen minutes to three. And thus they have stood for the last seventy-seven years.

Since no railroad serves the two villages, the modern traveler, coming as Pastor Ulrich did from Baden, approaches them by private car or bus. His route is along a graveled highway that spills gradually into the valley, to wind through rich pastureland broken by orchards planted to pear and apple and an occasional vineyard. This quiet northeast corner of Canton Aargau is not mountain country, but it has its charms. Carefully tended vegetable gardens run straight up the hillsides, their neat rows of celery, endive, and cabbage growing practically at right angles to the incline. Here and there a typical Swiss farmhouse appears, with its thick stone walls, its masses of geraniums and margarites in the window boxes on every casemented sill, its barn and home under the same pantiled roof with its high ridge and broad overhang. Lengnau, reached first, signals its presence with a flash far over to the traveler's right where the sun strikes the white walls of one of the town's two inns.

The traveler by bus disembarks at an open platform on the banks of the Surb, at this point a swift and narrow stream, its clear waters swarming with a black fish called Foralla. Immediately across the highway, at the foot of the steep hill crowned by a 250-year-old Catholic church, is a two-story building, finished in pink stucco and consisting of several apartments, a combination beauty parlor and barbershop and, in a recently added one-story extension alongside the main street of the village, a *Metzgerei* or butchershop. Local tradition tells us that in the old days this building, Number 64,* sheltered the home and tailor shop of Simon, who with his son Meyer was to found a Guggenheim dynasty in the New World.

The main part of Lengnau is across the Surb to the north. On the far side of the bridge the principal street widens to encircle the *Dorfplatz,* a triangular-shaped park shaded by birch and chestnut trees. At its broad northern end is a tie rail for horses and cattle, a wagon scale for weighing livestock at steer auctions, the town's main commercial activity.

Near the *Dorfplatz* are most of the public and business establishments. A large new building houses the school and the town offices, a smaller and older one the postal, telephone and telegraph facilities. There is a second inn, a second butchershop, a grocery, a feed-and-grain store, a scattering of cafés where the townspeople drink beer and play *Jass,* a card game that, when American music first invaded Lengnau via the jukebox, gave rise to the conviction among the villagers that they were listening to something produced by a *"Yass-band."*

Directly across from the *Dorfplatz,* on the east, stands the synagogue. Once this structure was a busy religious center, but

* In 1903 Number 64 underwent considerable modernization, but townspeople say it still retains its original lines.

the Jewish population of the Surbtal has dwindled profoundly since May 15, 1877, when Switzerland's "Emancipation Law" extended full citizenship to its Jews and put an end to ghetto life. Today, in Lengnau, which has a population of some 1400, there are less than sixty Jews. Of these only three live in the town proper. The remainder are residents of the Schweizerish Israelitish Altersasyl, a home for the aged, given to the community in the early part of this century by the Guggenheim family. In Endingen, the other one-time ghetto a few kilometers to the west, the change has been even more pronounced. In that village, now the larger of the two, only one Jewish family remains of the more than fifty that formerly lived there.

Throughout the Surbtal are mute reminders of its ghetto days. In Lengnau many of the homes along the curving side streets date back to the seventeenth century, with little that is modern about their exteriors save an infrequent advertisement, plastered on the front of barn or home, urging the populace to smoke *Stella Filtra* or *Trink Coca-Cola, die Limonade Gazeuse*. Although practically all of these older houses are now inhabited by Christians, some still display the *mezuzahs* affixed to their entranceways years ago by their former Jewish tenants. A small piece of parchment inscribed with texts from Deuteronomy, rolled up inside a metal or wooden case and nailed in a slanting position to the right-hand doorpost, the *mezuzah* symbolizes the desire of the orthodox Jew to consecrate his home to God and to invoke God's blessing upon it. Near the *Dorfplatz* is a row of old multiple dwellings. Each of these has two entranceways—one into the hall serving the first-floor apartments, the other into the hall and stair to the apartments above—an arrangement adhered to in the ghetto days when the Christians of Lengnau refused to come and go from their homes across the same thresholds as those used by their Jewish neighbors.[3]

A Shrinking Homeland

Lengnau was the first of the two villages to attract Jewish residents, and throughout the ghetto era the Jews of Lengnau liked to think of themselves as a little better than those of Endingen. This situation gave birth to jokes among the Endingen

A view of the main street of Lengnau, Switzerland, birthplace of Simon and Meyer Guggenheim. The building in the center of the photograph is the synagogue.

Jews. One of them, loosely translated from the Yiddish in which it was spoken, was that "if the Jews of Lengnau were as good as they think they are, none would be living there because they would all be in Heaven."

How any came to be there at all is a development that goes back to the Middle Ages when in many parts of Europe the Jews were the victims of discriminatory laws and of gross indignities. In 1348 and 1349—with the Black Death sweeping the continent —Swiss mobs, seeking to blame the pestilence on the Children of Israel, were guilty of excesses seldom if ever exceeded until the tragic days of Nazi Germany. One reads of the governing authorities in Swiss cities trying to protect their Jewish residents only to be overruled by a rabble bent on killing, plundering, burning, suffocating, and otherwise torturing them in the name of Christianity.

Beginning in 1384, the story of the Swiss Jews is the story of a constantly shrinking homeland as first one and then another of the cantons decreed their expulsion.

These actions were dictated by the evolving economics of the time. During the pre-Reformation centuries many of the laws of Switzerland, as was true of those of most European countries, were issued in conformance with ecclesiastical law as this was formulated by the ecumenical councils of the Roman Catholic Church. In the eyes of the early Church fathers usury, taken to mean the lending of money at any rate of interest whatsoever, was viewed as a sin—a view based partly on the general principles of New Testament teaching, but chiefly on certain direct proscriptions on usury in the Old Testament.[4] In the beginning the ecclesiastical ban on usury applied only to clerics. Later, in the ninth century, it was extended to laymen, and in the thirteenth century the Church gave legal cognizance to an already existing situation by specifically exempting Jews from its ban with the proviso that they must refrain from what the Church described as "grave and excessive usury."

In Switzerland and elsewhere these pronouncements had the effect of giving the Jews a monopoly on moneylending for several generations. During the late thirteenth century, however, this monopoly began to crumble as the result of several developments.

One was the emergence of trade, in the modern sense, bringing with it the then relatively new concept of money as capital. Obviously for capital to be available where needed, those in a position to lend must be allowed payment for the use of their money. This economic reality was brought home to the Church when one of its orders, the Franciscans, began setting up pawnshops for the poor, only to discover that these could not be maintained unless a reasonable charge were placed on the loans made. Finally, during the eighteenth ecumenical council (1512-17), also known as the Fifth Lateran, the Church removed its prohibition on usury.

In Switzerland the response to this development took the form of a series of laws which not only permitted Christians to exact interest but in some instances took care to designate such action as "not sinful." Concomitant with these changes the confederacy underwent a population explosion, with some three million people scrabbling to feed themselves by primitive agricultural techniques on the soil of a land of which 25 per cent consisted of scenic but untillable mountains, glaciers, lakes and rivers.

Once the Jews lost their monopoly on moneylending, they ceased to be so important to Swiss commerce. It then became expedient for the cantons, mindful of their population problems, to throw them out. By the opening of the fifteenth century they could live only in those sections known as provinces—territories that had no governments of their own but were jointly owned by two or more of the thirteen cantons then comprising the Swiss confederacy.

One of these provinces was the Earldom of Baden, later—1803—to become a member of the confederacy as Canton Aargau. For two and a half centuries all of the earldom was open to the Jews, but in 1776 they were restricted to the two Surbtal communities. Thereafter, all the other provinces having meanwhile expelled their Jewish residents, Lengnau and Endingen became the ghettos for the whole of Switzerland.[5]

"So no one's feelings will be hurt"

Among the possessions of the American Guggenheims is a yellowing sheet of paper on which has been written in German script a tribute to one of their Swiss ancestors. Framed and under glass, this memento hangs now in the Partners' room of the New York offices of the old firm of Guggenheim Brothers. Accompanying it is a typewritten English translation, quaint with misspellings and reading as follows:

Samuel Guggenheim

On the 25th of July, 1818, fire broke out in Wyle, in the Canton of Zurich. A whole house soon enveloped in flames, and made the hurriedly arrived people shudder. But, oh! two peacefully sleeping children were still within the building. The cries of anguish of the congregated populace of the town and the cracking of the flames and smoke woke the little ones from their sweet slumber, apparently only to die the sleep of death. Who can command the flames? Who can save the little ones? A Hebrew, Samuel Guggenheim of Largan [Lengnau], Canton Aargan [Aargau], Switzerland, a man full of presence of mind and honest courage, rushed into the blazing house, graps [grasps] both children and carries them triumphantly through the terrible heat and smoke to safety.

The Samuel referred to was the uncle of the Meyer Guggenheim who with his father was to found the American family. For this we have the word of the *Universal Jewish Encyclopedia.* What neither the encyclopedia nor Pastor Ulrich nor any other authority can tell us, because it is lost in the impenetrable past, is by what routes and for what reasons the Guggenheims first came to Lengnau in the closing years of the seventeenth century. About all that can be said with assurance is that at some point, in the course of their prior wanderings, they must have settled near Heidelberg in a German village then known as Guggenheimb, now Jugenheim, lingering there long enough to acquire the family name.[6]

In Lengnau, the Guggenheim family line is traced by official documents. The oldest is dated 1696 and alludes to *"der Jud Maran Guggenheimb von Lengnau."* Maran was either the grandfather or the father of Parnas Jakob, the friend of Pastor Ulrich.

The parnas had four sons, although in the official records no mention is made of the one called Joseph, presumably because he abandoned the faith of his fathers. Born sometime in the 1720's and educated at the Talmudic Academy in the Alsatian town of Metz, Joseph returned to Lengnau while still in his teens. Passionate, temperamental, brilliant, he soon became a beloved if somewhat erratic community leader. He doted on theological argument, loved mulling over first and last things. Pastor Ulrich, noting these predilections, made the most of them. He persuaded the authorities to let Joseph visit freely at the Ulrich home in Zurich, a city ordinarily open to Jews only during certain hours of the day. From Halle, Germany—center then of a world-wide Protestant mission to convert the Jews—the pastor obtained armloads of pamphlets. These he placed in Joseph's hands, along with a copy of the New Testament in Yiddish.

The young man wavered. Sensitive, high-strung, torn between the pastor's arguments and loyalty to his people, he twice fell ill of a severe mental disorder. Sixteen years passed before he finally made known his intention of embracing Christianity in due time. For two more years he and the pastor kept the decision a secret between them. Its revelation precipitated a violent break between the Surbtal Jews and their Christian friend. The Jews accused Ulrich of a breach of hospitality; and when Joseph fell ill the first time, the Pastor raised counteraccusations. In a letter to the Governor or *Landvogt* of the Earldom of Baden, he asserted that the young man was not ill at all. The Jews, he charged, were simply spreading the impression that he was ill in an effort to head off his conversion. In the same letter, Ulrich charged Joseph's kinsmen with a "conspiracy of murder." He contended that they stood ready to destroy the young man rather than see him become a Christian. In the end, the pastor won, but only after the long and turbulent quarrel had involved half a dozen rabbis in Germany, two succeeding *Landvogts* of Baden, and practically all of the higher officials of Zurich.

Of Parnas Jakob's other sons, the most colorful was Isaac who during his long life in Lengnau—eighty-four years—accumulated a substantial fortune as a moneylender. In Isaac's day, as throughout most of the ghetto era, the Surbtal Jews enjoyed considerable autonomy in the management of their affairs. Subject only to the *Landvogt* of Baden, they existed within the two villages as a communal entity, separate from that of the gentiles.

In local judicial matters, civic as well as religious, their rabbi sat as judge. No Christian court except the high court at Baden had jurisdiction over them. They named their own civic and religious leaders, built and operated their own schools, maintained their own cultural and charitable institutions. Off and on Isaac served as *Kozin* or treasurer of the congregation, and so large was his fortune that in after years the Surbtal Jews referred to all wealthy men as *Kozin*.

It is not difficult to picture Isaac in his older years: a bearded patriarch, clad in kaftan and skullcap and surrounded by his large family, sufficiently aware of his own dignity—a trait that we will encounter among his American descendants—and sufficiently stern of demeanor to cause the townspeople to speak of him not as "Old Isaac" but as "Old Icicle."

When he died on August 12, 1807, the bulk of his estate, valued at about 25,000 florin, consisted of a large trunk which was promptly sealed by the president of the congregation. On September 15 it was ceremoniously opened in the presence of Rabbi Raphael Ris, the elders of the congregation, and the heirs, including the children and grandchildren of Old Icicle and his wife, Rachel, who had preceded him in death.

Among the contents of the trunk was an envelope containing 830 gold and silver pieces. The remaining objects, some two hundred in all, were items which Old Icicle had accepted as collateral on debts. These included seventy-two plates, a mortar, a frying pan, two kneading pans, a Sabbath lamp, a ewer with "basin for washing hands," a brass coffee pot, four featherbeds, nineteen sheets, fifteen towels, eight nightshirts and an infant's potty. The true value of these items lay in the right to collect on the 117 outstanding debts they represented, all but a small fraction of which were eventually made good. Since Old Icicle's will did not specify how the collection rights were to be distributed, this was done by casting lots under the direction of Rabbi Ris. The Rabbi suggested the procedure, as he said, "so no one's feelings will be hurt." In addition certain other sums were distributed among the heirs, along with donations of 100 florin to the congregation, 50 to the Society for Nursing, 50 to the Brides' Dowry Fund, 200 to Rabbi Ris for supervising the disposal of the legacy, and 10, twice the usual sum, for "his sermons in the House of Mourning."[7]

As Old Icicle had been the leader of the family in his generation, so his oldest son, Meyer, was the leader in his. Born on January 24, 1749, Meyer on April 9, 1775, was married to Vögel (surname unknown) from the German town of Gailengen. To Meyer and Vögel were born eight children, four sons and four daughters. One of them was that Samuel who rescued the youngsters from the burning house in Wyle. Another was that Simon who in his fifty-fifth year was to leave Lengnau to inaugurate the Guggenheim dynasty in America.[8]

Thanks to a Woman

Because Lengnau and Endingen were villages, roofed by trees and surrounded by open country, they lacked the crowdedness and the smell of such historic ghettos as the "Jew Streets," of Worms and Frankfort-on-Main. They were true ghettos nonetheless. Their inhabitants were not even second-class citizens. They were "Alien Protection Fellows," a designation that made them little more than serfs of the *Landvogt* of Baden. To retain their homes they were required at intervals, every sixteen years after 1696, to purchase from the *Landvogt* a document known as the "Safe-Conduct and Patronage Letter."

In 1732 Parnas Jakob was one of two delegates sent by the Surbtal Jews to a session of the Diet of the Swiss Confederacy. Their task was to listen while the *Landvogt* of Baden or his representative read an expulsion order filled with reasons why the Jews should be banished from his province. It was then the delegates' turn. They answered the arguments and corrected the misrepresentations in the expulsion order, interlarding their pleas with flowery tributes to the person of the *Landvogt*. All this was words, words, words. In the end the "Safe-Conduct and Patronage Letter" was renewed in return for a price which the *Landvogt* set and which, it can be assumed, was as high as the stern and subtle authority dared make it.

Indeed, the Surbtal Jews paid heavily for the right of managing their own affairs and of doing a limited amount of buying and selling in specified sections of Switzerland. A melancholy irony pervaded their situation. Traditionally a largely agricultural people, descendants of the sheepherders and tillers of the soil described in the Old Testament, they were permitted to live in two little country towns but were forbidden to engage in farming. Wherever they traveled beyond the borders of the ghetto, they paid the Jew toll. Special taxes, a long list, were imposed upon them. Men of military age paid a fee for the privilege of not serving in an army which was not permitted to accept them anyhow, even when they volunteered, as many did. From time to time an individual was served with an expulsion order, always with the understanding that it could be abrogated for a price. In 1754 this happened so often to one of the richer Guggenheims as to suggest that this procedure, like the frequent renewal of the Safe-Conduct and Patronage Letter, was a kind of blackmail.

Making a living was not easy. Only a small number of occupations—among them moneylending, peddling, and tailoring—were open to the Jews. Such buying and selling as they were allowed to do was limited to movable goods. They were not permitted to possess real estate other than their own homes. In 1702 this decree brought Parnas Jakob and his brother Schmaul before the high court in Baden on a charge of possessing a vineyard on Wettinger Hill on the outskirts of that town. The brothers' plea was that they had accepted the property as collateral on a debt and their creditor had defaulted. Prior to 1776 the Jews could engage in livestock trading but the Safe-Conduct and Patronage Letter of that year compelled them to get rid of all livestock by selling it at prices favorable to gentile buyers. The 1776 Letter featured other new proscriptions. For the first time the number of Jewish households in the two villages was limited to the existing figure, 108. Moreover, the Jews were forbidden to enlarge their houses or to alter the exteriors of them. In the years that followed—years highlighted by the French Revolution, the rise of Napoleon, and changes in the political structure of Switzerland—the proscriptions on the Surbtal Jews were lightened, but the process was a slow and gradual one.

Too slow, in the opinion of the Lengnau tailor, Simon Guggenheim, a small, intense man with brooding eyes in a rugged face, third oldest of the four sons of Meyer Guggenheim and grandson of Old Icicle. The late 1840's found Simon dreaming of following in the footsteps of other Surbtal Jews who in recent years had emigrated to America.

Since his birth in 1792, Simon had witnessed improvements in the lot of his people. Throughout the same period, however, Switzerland had suffered economic reverses. There were the famine years of 1817 and 1818, depressions in the aftermath of the Napoleonic Wars. Unlike his grandfather, Simon had not prospered. He could dream of going to the New World but he had not the wherewithal to make the journey.

Thanks to a woman this handicap was overcome. In 1836 Simon's wife, Schafeli (Eva), had died after bearing him six children—a boy who was named after his grandfather, Meyer, and five girls, one of whom had died in childhood. In the late 1840's Simon remarried. His second wife was Rachel Weil Meyer, the forty-one-year-old widow of Isaac Benedict Meyer of Lengnau and the mother of three sons and four daughters. Rachel had a little money; enough, it would appear, to secure passage for the two families, fourteen persons in all.

In 1847 the Simon Guggenheims and the Rachel-Meyer Guggenheims packed their belongings in sacks and carpetbags and left Lengnau for nearby Koblenz. A sailing vessel bore them down the Rhine to Hamburg. A sloop, whose suffocating darkness young Meyer would often remember with a mild shudder in later years, carried them across the Atlantic. On a sunny morning in 1848, three months after the departure from Lengnau, their ship nosed into the Delaware River. From there they saw for the first time the spires of Philadelphia, a city that had numbered Jews among its population since the American Revolution and before, but which since its founding by the Quakers in 1681 had never known the existence of a ghetto.[9]

II

For Seven Sons, One Business

The Guggenheims began their life in the New World as thousands of immigrants before them had begun it, without money, without knowledge of the language, with nothing in their favor except that challenging and heady thing called freedom. They found a home, perhaps with the help of fellow countrymen who had preceded them to Philadelphia. Where it was located is not known, but it couldn't have been elegant and it was certainly crowded.

Simon and his twenty-year-old son Meyer went to work as peddlers. Early every Monday morning, for years, they left home, bent under packs bulging with pins and needles, stove and furniture polish, scraps of lace, shoe strings and spices—Simon to trudge the streets of Philadelphia itself, Meyer the rutted lanes of the Pennsylvania anthracite country. They returned, packs lighter and purses heavier long hours later, in the case of the father, but not until sundown of the following Sabbath, in the case of the son.

But the purse was never heavy enough for Meyer. Short, slender, well-featured, with thick brown curls and traces of the refinement of Parnas Jakob and other scholarly ancestors in his bearing, Meyer learned quickly the facts of American life.

Before he could master the language, he realized that every time he got ten cents for an item purchased from a manufacturer, he was giving seven or eight of it back to its maker. Lumping his sales, he found that he was working at least two-thirds of each day for the manufacturer, only one-third for himself.

How was this situation to be reversed?

Having uncovered the problem and put it into question form, Meyer was a bloodhound on the trail to the proper answer. Obviously he must put something of himself into one of his products. But which one? Which of his wares was unsatisfactory as it was, in need of improvement?

A warm smile and willing ears at countless front doors elicited complaints from voluble housewives. The stove polish he was selling: it was effective, they conceded, but it dirtied their hands.

Answer to the problem in sight—almost. First he must grapple with another fact of American life—the division of labor. Before the stove polish could be re-created into something equally efficient but inoffensive, it had to be analyzed. That called for an expert—a reflection that took Meyer one morning to the Bethlehem, Pennsylvania, home of a German friend, a chemist.

"Please to analyze this polish," we can imagine him saying in his imperfect English. "See what ingredient in it soils the hands and then replace it with one that is just as good but doesn't." And perhaps he added, "There's a fee in it for you."

The chemist analyzed the polish, altered it, and pocketed his fee, if any; and Meyer's father withdrew from the street to manufacture the new stove polish at home while Meyer himself, taking again to the lanes of the coal country, sold it in increasing quantities at a nice profit for the first, but not the last, family firm to be created by the American Guggenheims.[1]

Family Unity and Discord

Young Meyer's memories of the filthy vessel that had brought him to the New World were not altogether unpleasant. Aboard ship he had fallen in love with fifteen-year-old Barbara, third oldest of his stepmother's four daughters. She was a beauty, if we may trust the reminiscences of the last of her sons—with "unusually fair skin," eyes that were brown in some lights and "soft warm gray" in others, and auburn hair "that burned in the sun."

In 1852 she and Meyer were married at Keneseth Israel Synagogue in downtown Philadelphia and went to live in a small house in suburban Roxbury. During the next two decades they became the parents of eleven children, all of whom were to live to adulthood except Robert, twin of Simon, who died in his ninth year of injuries suffered in a fall from a horse and complicated by what appears to have been a ruptured appendix.

Practically every third child was born in a different house, most of them in Philadelphia proper. Each house was a little larger and in a little better neighborhood than its predecessor, for Meyer prospered. The profits from his improved stove polish went into other products. These in turn went into others as he moved gradually from door-to-door salesman, to manufacturer (of stove polish, lye, and bluing) to shop-owner, to commission merchant on a small scale to spice merchant on a large one, to importer—with the assistance of a partner—of fine lace and embroidery from Saxony and his native Switzerland. By 1869, when his father died, he was sufficiently well off to be a regular five-dollar-a-year member of the Jewish Foster Home Society. By 1871 his affluence had become so evident that the family's newly acquired physician, called in to sign the birth certificate of that year, took care to spell the name "Guggenheim" instead of "Gougenheim," "Guggenheimer" or any of the other whimsical approximations of previous and less-impressed physicians. By the following year the Meyer Guggenheims were living on the eastern, or almost fashionable, side of Philadelphia's North Sixteenth Street, and by 1884 they had moved across to its western, or socially impeccable, side.

Between 1854 and 1873 the children arrived at regular two-year intervals: first a quartet of boys—Isaac, Daniel, Murry and Solomon; then a girl—Jeannette; then another male quartet—Benjamin, Simon, Simon's twin and William; and finally—Rose and Cora.

Meyer and Barbara complemented one another as parents. He was the stern father, quick with the hairbrush; she the comforting mother, always on hand to hug away the sting. He was given to taciturnity, she the one to talk and be talked to. He made the rules, she winked at them. He set his children examples of thrift and industry, she of self-sacrificing care. He commanded their respect first, their love second; she their adoration. If home wasn't the democratic chaos so popular with ensuing American generations, it at least had a realistic balance of authority with understanding, of discipline with affection.

Meyer pushed his sons to activity, especially the older ones. So long as they remained at home, they had chores. As rapidly as possible he shoved them out of the house, into the business. Often business and schooling were combined, as in the case of Dan who at seventeen was in Switzerland, working in lace and embroidery, learning German and at the same time completing his education. By 1880 four of the boys were working practically full time with Guggenheim and Pulaski, as the importing firm was known, even after Pulaski stepped out, leaving Guggenheim in sole possession.

Not everything Meyer started came to fruition. He had the continental love of melody. Untrained himself, he set out to make musicians of his children. Instruments were purchased and the hour of 6 A.M. set aside for daily practice in the cellar, the later hours of the day being pre-empted by household duties, schooling and business. Alas for Meyer's hopes. Except for Sol, who was to become a cellist of less than startling skill, there wasn't a grace note of musical talent among the children, nor any interest in developing it. Fortunately—for them—the cellar walls could not contain the dissonance. Residents along North Sixteenth Street, having achieved nothing by neighborly complaints, summoned the police, whose arrival at chez Guggenheim one summer morning released the young musicians from their torment and banished forever Meyer's dream of spending his declining years soothed by the strains of an orchestra composed of his own offspring.[2]

The Winds of Success

There would come a day in the autumnal years of Meyer Guggenheim when, having become a millionaire and what the press called a "mining magnate," he would exhibit his wry smile as he harkened to the flattering words of a distant relative. The relative had called on him for business reasons, had lingered to exchange family gossip. As the two of them were making their good-byes, "Meyer," said the visitor, "before leaving, I must say something that I've been meaning to say to you for some time. I must express my admiration for the way, beginning with nothing, you have risen financially—and all by the use of your own good head."

At this point the head in question was being shaken. "No, cousin," was Meyer's rejoinder. "I didn't make my money with my head. I made it by getting hold of good things and sitting on them. So you see, I do not owe my prosperity to my head at all, but to another extremity entirely."

The story has the merit of calling attention to a penchant for a convivial joke which Meyer appears to have indulged frequently in the presence of family and close friends, much less frequently, if at all, in the competitive world of business where early in life he learned the value of preserving an impassive façade reminiscent of Old Icicle of Lengnau. As fact, the story is less convincing since obviously a man who began his career by the strenuous use of still another extremity, his legs, did not "sit" his way to fortune.

He worked at getting rich. He made up his mind to do so the minute he landed on American soil and took his first breath of the only free air he had ever known. The run-of-the-mill motives can be assumed. In addition he was driven—and sustained—by an undeviating desire to establish during his lifetime a commercial enterprise with sufficient possibilities for growth to keep his sons busy—and interested—long after he had gone. Hence his repeated changes of occupation during the early Philadelphia years, his practice, as his son William would phrase it, of tacking "now here, now there, to allow the winds of success to blow full upon his sail." Close friends vented censorious clucks, asserting one to the other that Meyer Guggenheim harbored a streak of instability. It was obvious that he lacked common sense, as witness his habit of abandoning one business after giving himself barely enough time to learn its tricks, to plunge into another about which he knew nothing at all. If Meyer was aware of these animadversions, he remained undisturbed. "He kept books of small neat figures," to quote William, "and he knew that every change he had made had improved his financial status. . . ."

But making a living was one thing. Creating a business that would absorb the energies of a whole new generation of Guggenheims was something else. The wholesaling of spices would not do. Its horizons were too limited. The importing of lace and embroidery gave promise of serving his purpose. That it was inherently expansive had already been proved by another immigrant, Alexander Stewart, who years before had built a small dealership in Irish lace and linens into a mercantile empire. Moreover the importing business was international. There were positions abroad to which the sons could be sent, and the onetime Swiss ghetto-dweller believed that in his youth a man should rattle about the world, knocking off his provincialism and acquiring a perspective on wine, women, and other fundamentals.

Quite likely Meyer would have settled for lace and embroidery had he not received a visit one day in 1881 from his white-bearded Quaker friend, Charles H. Graham, Philadelphia groceryman and speculator in western mineral lands. There are so many versions of what happened at this conference that only one thing can be said with assurance. When it was over, Meyer had parted with $5,000 (or $25,000; the versions differ) and was approximately one-third owner of two lead-and-silver mines, the A.Y. and Minnie, located in California Gulch on the outskirts of the wildly booming mining town of Leadville, Colorado.

A few weeks later Meyer himself was in California Gulch, under a shed perched on the steep slope of Iron Hill, 10,000 feet or more above sea level, 40 feet above the clattering torrent of the Arkansas River, looking down a dark hole—and not too pleased with what he saw. Or rather with what he heard when a stone was dropped into the 70-foot shaft. The A.Y. Mine, as his partner-superintendent Sam Harsh insisted, might have a great future; but for the present it was flooded. So was the Minnie. To "unwater" them—Meyer's term—took time and money, thousands of dollars of it from his own pocket. During the anxious months that followed there must have been times when he wondered if he were not throwing good after bad. Indeed he has been pictured during this period as breaking out in his wry smile on hearing that a Leadville merchant was stocking up on Guggenheim and Pulaski embroideries, and growling to himself, "And that's about all I'll get out of Leadville."

But it wasn't all. The "winds of success" were still blowing full on Meyer's sail. On a hot August Friday, in his Philadelphia office at Front and Arch streets, he slit open the envelope of a telegram from Superintendent Sam Harsh to find inside not the usual plea for more money but the announcement of a "rich strike," a bonanza! The A.Y. mine, unwatered at last, was producing 15 ounces or $19.35 worth of silver per ton, plus valuable amounts of lead. Its companion hole, the Minnie, would soon "come in." By 1888—the year in which the Guggenheims pulled stakes in Philadelphia, shifted their headquarters to No. 2 Wall Street in New York City and began liquidating their lace and embroidery business—Meyer had long since banked the first million of what was to become the largest fortune ever made from mining and its companion industries.

How it was made need not detain us long. For one thing, our chief concern here is with how it was spent, the foundations it was to make possible. For another, the business saga of the Guggenheims—how Meyer's sons multiplied Meyer's millions manyfold—has been often and ably chronicled elsewhere.

It all happened very fast; the quarter-century which started in 1881 just about embraces the Grand Business Era of the Guggenheims. The same can be said of the larger development of which it was a part, the American Industrial Revolution, that swift phenomenon that was ushered in by the Civil War and was only just beginning to taper off in the wake of World War I. The Industrial Revolution, like the Guggenheims, has had its chroniclers. Many of them, finding more to condemn than to praise, have excoriated it as the "great barbecue," the "Gilded Age," the age of the "Robber Barons," of "frenzied finance," of "big bad money" and "conspicuous consumption."

Unquestionably its outrages, its tastelessness, its tragedies and its waste were grandiose. But so were its accomplishments. In 1860 only a little more than a billion dollars was invested in American manufacturing and the country had only half a million industrial wage-earners. Less than fifty years later, capital investment in manufacturing had risen to more than $12 billions, the number of industrial wage-earners to five and a half million.

During the same half-century the value of America's manufactured products escalated to $14 billion a year, fifteen times the total at the beginning.

Given these indices of growth, it is not difficult to appreciate the statement of the historian, Allan Nevins, that the Industrial Revolution is "one of the most spacious, interesting and important areas of American history." In Nevins' opinion all the evidence on it is not yet in. Neither, necessarily, is the final judgment.

"Everyone," Nevins has written, "who looks at the record of industry and commerce from the Civil War to the First World War sees that the economy underwent the most sweeping transformation. A business world of small, weak, highly competitive units gave way to a world of concentration, efficiency, and highly organized power. This transformation involved a long process of destruction and reconstruction . . ." but, in the long run, the "constructive aspects of the transformation . . . were more important than the destructive; the development of new wealth far outweighed the waste of existing wealth." Nevins concedes that as late as 1910 there was reason to suspect that our Industrial Revolution had "proceeded too fast," but today, he argues, "this view appears dubious. Had our pace been slower, our achievement weaker," he concludes, "had we not created so swiftly our powerful industrial units in steel, oil, textiles, chemicals, electricity and the automotive vehicles, the free world might have lost the First World War and most certainly would have lost the second."

The Guggenheims made their contribution, a substantial one, to the great transformation. In doing so they played the game pretty much as the bulk of the American people at that time appeared to believe it had to be played if the desired goals were to be attained. In other words, they stepped on toes because, as Nevins has observed, "Great business aggregations are not built without frustrating, crushing or absorbing multitudinous small enterprises." It is only fair to add that the Guggenheims were among the first industrialists to sense the coming change in the moral climate of the American economy and to give some recognition to the rights of organized labor and to accept some responsibility for the welfare of their employees. At first this recognition and this acceptance were mostly in words, but as early as 1914 the matching deeds were beginning to materialize.

Another credit can be awarded, without reservation. Meyer Guggenheim was a square dealer. He believed in square dealing and he passed that belief on to his sons, who implemented it even as they endeavored to implement many of their father's business principles. Ever since Meyer and his own father started manufacturing their improved stove polish in a grubby corner of Philadelphia, the name Guggenheim has been synonymous with honesty in the business world. We come upon an example of it in the fall of 1906, shortly after the Guggenheims had taken an option on a Canadian silver development called Nipissing. Early reports from experts were that there were "all kinds of money for all kinds of people" in the Nipissing vein. On the market "Nip" stocks soared—and then plummeted as further researches revealed that the vein pinched off, was limited and essentially of little value. At this point the Guggenheims, having already lost $2,300,000 on the deal, withdrew from it, simultaneously serving notice that they would reimburse the hundred and fifty investors who had purchased Nip stocks through their company.

According to Medley G. B. Whelpley, New York financial consultant and one-time partner in a Guggenheim company, some investors took advantage of the situation by sending in and letting the Guggenheims reimburse them for stock they had purchased, not through the Guggenheim company, but on their own. Whelpley remembers telling Solomon Guggenheim that this was happening. He remembers Solomon giving him a bewildered look and saying, "Come now, Medley. No one would do a thing like that!" Whelpley remembers also a conversation in the 1930's with Montague Norman, governor of the Bank of England. "The Guggenheims are more Christian than the Christians," Norman told him. "They stand up to their obligations even if those are not in writing, even when they're merely implied. I feel they are more to be relied on than other people."[3]

The Tree and the Branches

On the day Meyer Guggenheim learned that the A.Y. and Minnie were going to pay off, he knew he had found what he was looking for: a business of such amplitude that there was reason to believe it would enlist and hold the attention of his sons and perhaps of their sons, too. On this conviction he proceeded, first organizing a company through which the family's expanding interests could be handled.

He called the company, incorporated in 1882, M. Guggenheim's Sons. That's what it was. Meyer himself never became a member of it, although for many years he exerted a pervasive influence on its affairs. Its partnerships were open only to his sons, each of them, from the day he became a member, receiving the same percentage of interest.

A business associate questioned this policy. "Is it fair," he wanted to know, "to ask the older and seasoned boys to work for no greater reward than that set aside for the younger and greener ones?"

Meyer prefaced his response with the well-known smile. "True," he admitted, "when the younger ones first come in they are more bother than they are worth. During this period the older ones must carry the load. But in time all that changes. The day arrives when the older ones wish to retire. Then the younger ones must carry the load. Besides, let us not forget the wives! If the wife of one partner hears that the partner-husband of another is making more money, trouble follows."

Meyer's faith in his sons was not misplaced. "Rarely unto the branches of the tree," Dante wrote centuries ago, "doth human worth mount up. . . ." In this regard, the elder Guggenheim was blessed. Five of his sons were able businessmen and the second oldest, Daniel, was a born leader and initiator, shrewd, daring and inventive.

Bernard Baruch—onetime "boy wizard" of Wall Street, chairman of the board that mobilized American industry for World War I, elder statesman ever since—can remember "Mr. Dan" in some detail. Reminiscing in the ninth decade of his own full life, Baruch describes him as "one of the three small men I've known

Solomon R. Guggenheim.

—the others were Sam Gompers and Henry Davidson—who sat taller than most men stand. I see Dan yet, a little fellow sitting in a big chair and dominating the entire room from it. Physically small, you understand, but big in spirit, he was a man who, as Thomas Fortune Ryan once remarked, bored with an auger, not with a gimlet. He was no double-dealer, no bargainer. His appearance?" The question induces Baruch to close his eyes for a reflective pause. "Pleasing is the best single word, I believe," he decides after a time. "Piercing eyes"—they were greenish-blue, more greenish than blue—"strong features and wonderful teeth, wonderful smile. Other attributes? Courage and charm in about equal amounts, I would say."

In the commercial heyday of the Guggenheims, Baruch as a then rising young stockbroker on Wall Street, was always pleased whenever his business took him to 71 Broadway where the Guggenheims were headquartered for many years. He saw a good deal of the brothers in those days, remembers most of them well.

Isaac, the first-born: "Taller than the others," he says, "and perhaps the best-looking, but their inferior as a businessman. He was a good man, Isaac was, but overly conservative and I doubt if he would have gone too far on his own. As a member of the group, he was fine. He made his contribution. He was steady and reliable and he had a great tolerance for detail."

Murry, the third oldest of the brothers: "Extraordinary—definitely so; but quiet, very quiet."

Solomon, the fourth: "When courage was given out, Sol was sitting in the front pew. He was left-handed, incidentally. I remember him pounding the table with that left hand. Come to think of it, Sol was always pounding away at something. He had very pronounced ideas, and when he decided to do something, he insisted on doing it his own way and would brook no interference."

Simon, the sixth: "Good company. We fished and golfed together. He was small, charming, quiet, and had courage."

As for the others—Benjamin, the fifth oldest of the sons, and William, the youngest, "I didn't know them very well," Baruch says. "My impression, however, is that so far as the business was concerned neither of them made a lasting dent." (A correct enough statement. People who accumulate wealth also accumulate legends about themselves, and one of the most persistent about the Guggenheims is that to the very end their enterprises were staffed by a solid phalanx of seven energetic brothers. As a matter of fact, Benjamin and William pulled out of the business in 1901, after which, although both continued to be carried on the rolls of the family firm for sentimental reasons, they went their separate ways.)

So much for one man's memories of the Guggenheim brothers, the branches of the tree that was Meyer, who with their father set out in the late nineteenth century to erect a mining empire. One of their first discoveries was that the new business raised a problem similar to one the elder Guggenheim had met and solved in his early Philadelphia days. Just as Meyer, having discovered that most of his peddling profits were going to the manufacturer, became a manufacturer himself, so in 1888 he and his sons, having discovered that most of their lead and silver profits were going to that middleman of mining, the smelter, became the owner of their own half-a-million-dollar smeltery in Pueblo, Colorado. Other smelteries followed, the first of them in Mexico, and in 1895 the Guggenheims built a large refinery at Perth Amboy, New Jersey. Having placed themselves astraddle the secondary aspects of their business, they set the stage for expanding the basic ones by establishing in 1899 a separate mine-finding organization popularly known as Guggenex (for Guggenheim Exploration Company).

The creation of Guggenex inaugurated the first grand era of the Guggenheims: the era in which Meyer's sons became, in the jargon of the press, first the "silver princes," then the "smelter overlords" and finally the "copper kings"; the era in which they roamed the globe in search of profitable holdings, stripping the hillsides of Nevada, Utah and New Mexico of copper porphyries; developing tin mines in Bolivia, gold mines in Alaska, diamond fields in Africa, rubber plantations in the Belgian Congo, copper mines and smelteries in Mexico and copper mines and nitrate fields in Chile. "It was the Guggenheims," says Baruch, "who made mining an investment."

In the same year that saw the birth of Guggenex, H. H. Rogers, financial genius associated with Rockefeller's Standard Oil, cast a baleful glance at the omnisciently traveling brothers and proceeded, with associates, to establish ASARCO—the American Smelting and Refining Company—a huge trust composed of eighteen member companies and designed to monopolize the smelting industry in America.

By this time the Guggenheims were too strong to be simply bought off or forced out of business, as such a trust might buy off or force out an independent with only one or two smelteries to his name. The Guggenheims not only had their mines and smelteries and their big refinery, they also had contracts—practically exclusive ones—with the best outlets for selling metals in Europe. Besides, there were so many of them. It was said that what one Guggenheim missed, another was sure to think of; what one forgot, another was sure to remember. "While you're outsmarting six of them," a competitor moaned in the days when all of the brothers were active in the business, "the seventh is already two jumps ahead of you."

Since the Guggenheims couldn't be pushed out, they had to be got rid of by being gobbled up, which is to say, invited to join ASARCO. It was the old routine of " 'Come into my parlor,' said the spider to the fly," only in this instance the fly was wise to the game. The Guggenheims politely declined the invitation and continued to decline until 1900, by which time—thanks to a spate of astute maneuvers—they were in a position to wage a battle for control. The initial year of their adherence to ASARCO was marked by a running skirmish of courtroom arguments and boardroom ploys, from which Meyer Guggenheim's sons emerged some $43 million richer and in what amounted to full control of the smelting colossus that had been set up to engineer their commercial demise.

The "Copper Kings" phase of the saga began, for all practical purposes, in 1906 with the development of Kennecott in Alaska, followed in 1907 by the opening of the Braden mine in Chile and climaxed in 1910 by the acquisition of the fantastically productive Chuquicamata, also in Chile. Six years later, in 1916, Guggenex disappeared as an entity for the time being and the old firm of M. Guggenheim's Sons—then as now located high in the

Equitable Building at 120 Broadway—was reorganized, taking on a non-Guggenheim as one of the partners for the first time and receiving the name of Guggenheim Brothers, the name its present successor continues to hold.[4]

There are other chapters to the story, but they belong more to tomorrow than to yesterday. They have to do with the nitrate fields still being worked by the Guggenheims in Chile—with continuing tin operations in Asia—with experiments, so far inconclusive, aimed at developing a superior method for sewage disposal and a cheaper method for producing the rocket fuel called hydrazine—with the revival in 1959 by Harry Guggenheim of the old mine-hunting firm of Guggenex. These undertakings may contain the seeds of a great industrial growth in the future, but as for the past—with the sale of the fabulous Chuquicamata copper mine of Chile to Anaconda for $70 million on March 1, 1923, the curtain may be said to have come down on the Grand Business Era of the American Guggenheims.[5]

III

Victorians, Puritans and Playboys

In 1937 there came to the Guggenheims, as it must to all prominent people, the shock of seeing themselves the subject of a book. The perpetrator of this villainy, a collective biography called *The Guggenheims,* was Minnesota-born Harvey O'Connor, author also of biographies of the Mellons, the Carnegies, the Rockefellers and the Astors. In his caustic account of the Guggenheims' industrial ascent, O'Connor, long associated with the labor movement as a journalist and publicity writer, left no doubt but that his sympathies were on the side of the unions and the independent mine- and smelter-owners caught up in the struggles involved. Having forthrightly exposed his bias, he set forth a sobersided tale that found favor with the critics who were impressed by the care with which the author had done his research and the restraint with which he touched on the Guggenheims' peccadilloes, those sins, aberrations and scandals common to most families and especially to those who can afford their more expensive manifestations.

Few members of the family shared the critics' enthusiasm. None was less pleased with O'Connor's work than Mr. Dan's only daughter, Gladys Eleanor. An attractive and delightfully feminine woman—level-headed and civic-minded, traits which O'Connor took care to record—Gladys was married in 1914 to the late Roger Williams Straus, president for many years of ASARCO and son of the Oscar Solomon Straus who was Theodore Roosevelt's Secretary of Commerce and Labor and the biographer of Roger Williams. A woman of executive ability, long prominent and active in political and philanthropic circles, Gladys Straus has had an unusually constructive life. During the Second World War she was the only woman on the eleven-member food commission set up for New York state by Governor Thomas Dewey. Her job was an educational one. By lectures and over the radio, she helped keep some 800,000 women informed on how to obtain the most nutriment for their families under the stringent food-rationing program of the war years. Mrs. Straus is a past vice president of the Women's National Republican Club, and since 1961 has been a vice president on the board of Mt. Sinai Hospital in New York City. Both of her sons have had distinguished careers. Oscar II is currently in charge of mining operations for Guggenheim Brothers, and Roger Williams, Jr., has been instrumental in the development of the publishing firm, Farrar, Straus and Company, of which he is president.

Gladys Straus' criticisms of O'Connor's biography of her family was directed chiefly at the author's practice of frequently putting words into the mouths and thoughts into the minds of his historic characters without benefit of documentation. So annoyed was Mrs. Straus at the author's fictional picture of Mr. Dan looking over a Yukon mining property and "thinking a lot of schoolboyish thoughts that couldn't possibly have crossed my father's mature mind" that she seriously considered bringing suit. She abandoned the idea, however, on the advice of an attorney who pointed out that the only certain outcome would be publicity for "that dreadful book."

An ironic reaction has been registered by another member of the family, Harold Loeb, oldest of the three sons of Rose, the tenth born of the eleven children of Meyer and Barbara Guggenheim. Novelist, economist and founder-editor of the magazine *Broom,* one of the first and most important of the avant-garde art and literary magazines of the 1920's, Loeb—now a strapping and good-looking man in his early seventies—describes himself as "on the wrong side of the track as Guggenheims go." His explanation is that although his mother was a Guggenheim and was married to a Wall Street broker, her sons have never had access to anything like the resources open to main-line members of the family. "Perhaps for that reason," says Loeb, "perhaps for others, there was a time when I was 'anti-Guggenheim.' All that

Daniel Guggenheim.

changed, however, after I read O'Connor's biography. I figured that if an old socialist like O'Connor could find nothing worse to say about my businessmen-uncles than appears in his book, they must have been a pretty good lot."

Perhaps the most unforgettable reaction was that of Solomon Guggenheim, who took issue with the chapter in which O'Connor describes Meyer Guggenheim in his peddling days as traversing the coal country of Pennsylvania with a "bent" back. "Nonsense!" Solomon has been quoted as saying. "My father always walked straight. Besides, he had a horse and buggy!"*

Censorious as O'Connor was where the Guggenheims' business practices were concerned, he was not proof against their personableness. In a recent letter he admits to "a sneaking affection for the Guggies," and in his book this feeling emerges at several points. He has especially kind words for Meyer, to whom he attributes "modesty, simplicity, scrupulous honesty," agreeing with the statement of a contemporary that the father of the seven brothers was "a man who got ahead without walking over the graves of others." High praise for an old capitalist from an old socialist.[1]

The Old Capitalist

Meyer Guggenheim was seventy-three in 1901, that being the year when his sons seized control of ASARCO and stepped forward in seven-league boots as it were to make themselves top dogs of the associated worlds of smelting and mining. We can "see" the old man as he was that year, since it was along about then that he sat, or rather stood, for the portrait which hangs, along with those of his father and five of his sons—Isaac, Daniel, Solomon, Benjamin and Simon—against the walnut paneling of the spacious Partners' room in the New York offices of Guggenheim Brothers. It shows a small, white-haired man, his triangular face with its snub nose and straight brows flanked by the noble muttonchops of a Dundreary. The full lips are firmly

* Solomon Guggenheim's facts are correct. Although his father started his peddling career on his feet, he eventually saved enough to purchase a horse and cart.

shut and composed as is fitting, or at least in those days was considered fitting, to a formal portrait. But there is a faintly humorous cast to the wide and deep-set eyes, much as if the wry smile, displaced from its accustomed resting place, had taken temporary lodgment there. In spite of the ramrod stiffness of the pose, the implausibly perfect alignment of every article of apparel, the portrait manages to exude an aura of contentment and repose.

Certainly Meyer had reason to be content as he approached the twilight of his time. He had lived long enough to see his goal achieved, his sons ensconced in an enterprise of heroic proportions. Naturally, as his years piled up, he had become increasingly more willing to relinquish the reins into their capable hands. He had his hobbies now. He dabbled in stocks, mulled over current events, read history, attended the opera, especially light opera, having a fancy for Gilbert and Sullivan. He enjoyed these pastimes up to a point, but his passion was horses. Nothing pleased him more than to drive a pair of trotters along Riverside Drive, then known as the Speedway of New York.

His grandson, Harry Frank Guggenheim, who was born in 1890, remembers him "rolling about town in a runabout with a footman," always dressed in a Prince Albert coat. According to Baruch, the coat was "usually white" with the dust that fell from the old man's perpetual cigar, for unlike his sons, Meyer was inclined to be indifferent to his personal appearance. Son William remembers that when at summer resorts his daughters chided him about this, he put them off with one of two replies. If it was a resort to which the family had been before, "Oh, what's the difference?" he would say. "Here everybody knows me"; and if it was one to which they had not been before, "What does it matter? Here nobody knows me."

Grandson Harry remembers the "community stable"—"community" in that it was used by all members of the family—that stood in the vicinity of the New York home of Meyer and Barbara at 36 West 77th Street, just off Central Park, in a quiet and unpretentious neighborhood. Apparently old Meyer had no prejudices against newfangled modes of transportation, for Harry also remembers being driven around the block one evening in his grandfather's newly acquired electric car, "in form just like an old hansom cab, even to having a place for the driver above and to the rear."

The evening of the Jewish Sabbath was family night at 36 West 77th Street. The sons and daughters gathered, bringing their wives and husbands and the younger members of their own enlarging families. Most of them had only a few steps to come. Sol and Will, not yet married, lived at home whenever they were in the city. Murry and family were at 35 West 76th, directly to the rear, with a gate in the fence linking the back yards. Two of the girls lived with their husbands in adjoining houses on West 70th. Dan and family were also on West 70th for a time, moving later to West 54th into a house near to that of John D. Rockefeller, Sr., whom Harry remembers as ringing the Guggenheim doorbell at 8:30 one morning, with the explanation, "I just thought I'd drop by to be neighborly."

Harry has vivid memories of his grandfather's house, which stood just south of and facing the American Museum of Natural History across the street. It had a red-stone front with a bay window. Inside was a long hall with an ornate hatrack. Alongside the hall and extending far beyond its length were a front parlor, middle parlor, rear parlor and dining room, all in a string. For music there was a player piano in the front parlor. It was called the "Angelus," brand name (Harry believes) of the first such piano ever made.

Another piece of furniture impressive to a small boy was a white statue ("quite a forbidding looking object, really") that adorned a pedestal in the front parlor. At the Friday night gatherings Harry's pal was his slightly older cousin, Edmond, Murry's boy. "We were inclined to be unruly," Harry recalls. "One evening, just horsing around, we broke one of the little fingers of the statue by accident. After that, each Friday evening, we broke another finger on purpose. One night we bestowed our attention on a new silk hat belonging to Uncle Isaac. He had left it on the hall rack. We played games with it. Then we put what was left of it back on the rack and hid in the portieres to see Uncle Isaac's expression."

Harry no longer remembers his uncle's reaction. He does remember Grandfather Meyer's wrath. The old man ruled that henceforth the young cousins must come to the house separately, one of them—and one only—being allowed in every other week.

There was no religious significance to these Friday-night gatherings. Like so many Jews from the Old World, Meyer and Barbara, falling in love with their adopted country, had resolved to make themselves inconspicuous parts of it. To this end they had divested themselves of the orthodoxy of their elders, had become Reformed Jews and members of fashionable Temple Emanu-el, then on Fifth Avenue at 42nd Street. Meyer's contributions to the Temple and to various Jewish charities and educational institutions were generous, but he was inclined to regard them as merely the fulfilment of a civic duty. His attendance at temple was desultory, that of his wife only slightly less so.

Once or twice a week the Old Capitalist took the Elevated downtown to spend a few hours at a roll-top desk reserved for him in the office of M. Guggenheim's Sons. Baruch tells of an incident, presumably connected with one of these visits. In its Grand Era, M. Guggenheim's Sons was the lodestone of every grizzled sourdough or free-lance mining engineer itching to get his hands on a little financing for this or that get-rich-quick scheme. One day a skinny, wild-eyed character of this genre managed to get past the burly ex-policeman who stood guard at the Guggenheim gate, past the receptionists and secretaries behind him, into the private office of Mr. Dan.

Mr. Dan was not alone. Sitting behind the extra desk in the room was old Meyer, his smile in evidence as he took in the drama. The visitor was an excited little man. He spoke in German, his arms flailing. He wanted to sell Mr. Dan a new smelting process, and the more Mr. Dan shook his head, the more the little man flailed.

"But with this new process," he argued, "you will soon have control of all the copper on earth."

Mr. Dan shook his head.

"But the control of copper," the little man shouted, "will bring you control of all the other metals."

Another headshake.

"And once you have control of all the metals," the little man screamed in his whirring German, "you will become a Colossus, the richest and most powerful man in the world."

At this juncture Meyer leaned across his desk. *"Und dann?"* he inquired, pulling at his sidewhiskers and meaning, of course, "and after that, where do we go?" or "so what?"

Barbara enjoyed her old age much as her husband did, although she was troubled by prolonged spells of poor health. She suffered from diabetes, and this in a day before insulin was known. In 1900 her illness worsened and on March 20 of that year, at the age of sixty-seven, she died and was buried in the mausoleum which son William had designed for the family the year before in Salem Fields, Jamaica, Long Island. "No mother," biographer O'Connor writes, "was ever more sincerely mourned."

Five more years, almost to the day, remained to Meyer. They were not without event. A forty-five-year-old woman, Hanna McNamara, brought suit against him for $100,000, charging breach of promise and claiming that the two of them had been intimate off and on for twenty-four years. Meyer denied everything, even denied that the woman had been a domestic in his house, as she claimed. Nothing came of the action. In 1904 the old man was weak and unwell and on Thanksgiving Day he submitted to the third in a series of operations. He refused to go to a hospital, refused an anesthetic. As the operation began he asked one of the nurses to play a record on the phonograph, called for a cigar, and alternately puffed and winced his way through the ordeal.

The operations did not have the desired effect. The old man was still weak and suffering from a bad cold when, in March of 1905, he left New York for a vacation in Palm Beach. There, on March 15, death came quietly to Meyer Guggenheim in his seventy-eighth year.

Grandson Harry remembers the heavily attended funeral in New York, the long cortège as it left Temple Emanu-El and headed for Salem Fields. He and Cousin Edmond found themselves alone in one of the horse-drawn carriages. "Its side windows," says Harry, "had solid black screens that could be pushed up, so just as the procession reached Long Island—having crossed the East River by ferry—Edmond and I slipped out and scooted off to have a beer and a sandwich at the nearest saloon."

The suspicion arises that the Old Capitalist would have had trouble suppressing his wry smile at these disrespectful antics.[2]

The Victorians

The death of Simon Guggenheim in 1869 ended the first generation of American Guggenheims, and the death of his son Meyer in 1905 ended the second. Since Meyer's day, many twists and turns have overtaken the thinking of the American people about marriage and living in general, and in the behavior of third- and fourth-generation Guggenheims we find some of these twists and turns reflected.

In moral attitude, Meyer's seven sons were chips off the old block. Harold Loeb speaks of them as "Victorians." "All of the brothers," he says, "were well aware of their dignity. They wore high hats on Fifth Avenue longer than other men did and they always dressed impeccably in the best J. Pierpont Morgan manner. Mind you, they were not Puritans. A Puritan tries to live up to his moral code. To a Victorian the chief thing is to keep up appearances."

There were no divorces among the brothers, except in the case of William. Generally speaking, each of them, including William after his second journey to the altar, gave his wife the proper respect and affection, endeavored to be a good father, comported himself with decorum in public—and did pretty much as he pleased in private, which is to say in whatever private life he allowed himself outside of the home. A business associate remembers Solomon lunching at a Wall Street club and soberly lecturing his tablemates on the care and feeding of mistresses, concluding his remarks with the admonition that "when the time comes to part, it is of the utmost importance to provide generously for the lady in question."

There were exceptions to the Victorian pattern. Murry, for example. Loeb describes him as "uxorious" about his wife, the former Leonie Bernheim of the wealthy, silk-making Bernheims of Mulhouse, Alsace. "I doubt very much," Loeb says, "that

Murry ever so much as gave another woman more than a passing glance." Similarly William, after making his second and permanent marriage, was "dominated" (Loeb's expression) by his "big, dark, buxom wife," the former Aimee Lillian Steinberger of New York, until at a late date the two of them agreed to live apart.

Will, to be sure, was an exception on all scores. Most of the Guggenheims have shown a genius for making history. Will was one of the few to bother writing it. In 1934 he brought out through his own firm, the Lone Voice Publishing Company, what was actually an autobiography, although it was issued in the third-person biographical form with William using the pen name of Gatenby Williams.

A certain pathos breathes from Will's *William Guggenheim*. It is plain, as Loeb has said, that the youngest of the brothers was "just one too many." Overwhelmed by his more effectual seniors, he devoted the better part of his adult energies to *being* an exception. He longed to stand out both from the small crowd (his brothers) and the large crowd (his race). Describing his own appearance as a mature man, he notes with relish that all of the brothers "except Benjamin and himself, were dark," adding that a person seeing his own "light complexion and the cast of his features . . . would not have surmised his Semitic ancestry."

He was born in Philadelphia on November 6, 1868, on Franklin Street, a happenstance that Will would find prophetic in view of his subsequent admiration for the career of Benjamin Franklin. Even as a lad, he wrote of himself, he exhibited "traits that distinguished him from all the others." He was more scholarly than they, more fond of books, more sensitive to the innerness of things. "Few pause for beauty in the quest of gold," he would mourn, apropos of his later managerial duties at sundry Guggenheim mines and smelteries. Notwithstanding his "differences," he enjoyed a pleasant enough boyhood. He built a kite "of clothes-line props, which in a strong wind would lift him clear of the ground." Always smaller than average, he got into fights, often taking on boys "pounds better than his weight." He played "rugger" and cricket and attended public school where his high grades were the despair of his brothers and the delight of his favorite teacher, a Miss May, who would often keep him along with her after school, during which sessions she would pause occasionally in the act of correcting papers to lean over and give her pet a kiss. Will's ingenuous comment on this hanky-panky is that it gave him at an early age an awareness "of the charm he was capable of exerting on older people."

After public school came college, about four years in all, during which he studied in general science, chemistry and metallurgy at the University of Pennsylvania. One of Will's earliest and longest-lasting loves was for elocution. In his youthful days he dreamed of going on the stage, a dream that passed even "as passed his brother Simon's desire to be a streetcar conductor" when Will realized that his destiny, like that of his brothers, was "to evolve . . . in the mining camps of Colorado and the mountains of old Mexico." As a matter of fact, his active participation in the family business was almost as short-lived as his dream of being an actor. It began in 1887 with a two-months apprenticeship in the laboratory and assay office of the A.Y. and Minnie mines, and was terminated by his own wish in 1901. Thereafter, sometimes alone, sometimes with Benjamin, the other maverick of the brothers, he fribbled at a number of commercial enterprises, none successful, eventually eschewing business to devote the remainder of his life to philanthropy, to the International Benjamin Franklin Society and other patriotic study clubs, and to the writing and publishing of poetry, philosophy, treatises on economics and politics, and popular song lyrics bearing such titles as "Jubilee" and "Crumbs of Love."

His "autobiography" is of interest if only for his occasional comments on the way the brothers worked together. Writing of the family business as it stood shortly after the opening of the first smeltery, Will notes that each "of the brothers was capable in his own way and the division of labor among them followed the lines indicated by their various talents. Isaac, the oldest, acted as treasurer, taking care of bank loans and credits. Daniel, the most ambitious of them, was the organizer and negotiator; . . . Murry, with a natural taste for statistics, handled and sold the metals. Solomon, the 'good fellow' of the family, became the popular contact man. Simon, affable and easygoing, devoted his attention to the purchase of ores. . . ."

There is no mention in the autobiography of what must have been an emotional turning point in Will's life, a contretemps which had its beginnings on November 30, 1900, when he showed up in Hoboken brandishing a marriage license. The bride was Grace Brown Herbert, a California divorcée who had been living in New York for the previous six years. Will's father and the four oldest brothers took one look at Grace—pretty, soft-faced and blond—recognized her at once as the "fancy girl" of a prominent New Yorker, concluded that Will had been "taken," and confronted him with an ultimatum: Get rid of her, or be disowned.

Poor Will! His powerful brothers were presenting him with the opportunity of a lifetime, the chance to assert himself once and for all. He muffed it. Grace got a divorce and $78,000 in lieu of monthly alimony payments of $500. It wasn't enough. Eight years later, having undergone another marriage and an annulment thereof, she sought to annul the divorce on the grounds that it had been obtained by fraud, since neither she nor Will was a resident of Illinois at the time it was granted in Chicago, the Guggenheims having taken the matter to the Midwestern metropolis in a futile effort to keep it out of the New York newspapers. Grace's suit to annul the divorce alarmed them. If she succeeded, William and Aimee, married since 1904, would be living in bigamy and their first, and as it turned out only child, one-year-old William, Jr., would be illegitimate. There were court hearings, first in New York, then in Chicago. The headline-producing wrangle dragged on until February 24, 1913, when a Chicago judge refused to set aside the divorce decree, asserting that often-married Grace had not come into court with clean hands but simultaneously agreeing with her that neither she nor Will had been a "bona fide resident" of Illinois when the divorce was handed down. Its procurement by the Guggenheims, therefore, "was an outrage against the laws of the state of Illinois and a fraud upon the Circuit Court in Cook County."

In 1916 Will brought suit against the five brothers still active in the family business, seeking to recover what he claimed were profits due to him as the result of mining ventures in Chile. The matter was settled out of court. How much Will got is not known. What is known is that from 1923 on he was the one-half beneficiary, with his wife, of a million-dollar trust fund set up by his brother Simon, apparently with the assistance of some of the other brothers.

After Will and Aimee separated, amicably and without legal action, Will maintained bachelor quarters in an unpretentious three-room apartment on the first floor of Number 3 on New York's Riverside Drive. During the closing decade of his life he reverted to his old love, the theater, taking on a succession of showgirls as protégés. One of them revealed that Will met her while she was playing in *Ballyhoo* at the Forty-fourth Street Theater. "I was reading a copy of *The Literary Digest,*" she informed reporters, "and that caught his eye."

When Will died on June 27, 1941, he left his entire fortune to "Miss America" of 1929, "Miss Connecticut" of 1930, and two other former showgirls. It was first reported that the girls would "share and share alike" in more than a million dollars, but subsequent court action brought out that since his retirement from business in 1901, Will had gone through close to five million. By the time his widow asked and received the percentage due her under New York State law, Will's winsome protégés divided up a modest $5,229.00.[3]

Another exception to the Victorian pattern was Benjamin, who was in his late twenties when he became engaged to Florette Seligman. Florette's proud banking family went to some pains to make it clear to their relatives abroad that Ben was a member of the smelting family and therefore immensely wealthy. Hence the cable from the American to the European Seligmans, its sly misspelling originating with the sending office: "Florette engaged Guggenheim smelt her."

Ben didn't give a hoot about appearances. Harold Loeb says, "Of all the brothers he was the most extravagant in his amorous divagations, even introducing them into his own home." After his marriage to Florette in 1894, Ben had a succession of mistresses, most of them "openly arrived at," and ranging in glitter from a red-headed registered nurse, employed in his own household, to a marquise of Paris.

"He wasn't as handsome as the other brothers," says Loeb, "but women were drawn to him, partly because of his warm smile but principally, I suspect, because he really liked women, they sensed that he did and women like to be liked." The most famous of Ben's three daughters, art-collecting Peggy Guggenheim (born Marguerite), describes her childhood in her father's New York home as darkened by parental quarrels over his philandering and only slightly lightened by the frequent presence in the house of two of the odder of her Seligman kinsmen—an aunt who was "an incurable soprano" and "an inveterate gambler," and an uncle who ate nothing but charcoal.

Many and gamey are the tales about Ben. Harry Guggenheim was only fourteen or fifteen when Uncle Ben undertook to give him some advice. "Never," said Ben, "make love to a woman before breakfast for two reasons. One, it's wearing. Two, in the course of the day you may meet somebody you like better."

Born in Philadelphia during the year that saw the end of the Civil War, Ben was the first of the brothers to go to college, entering Columbia in 1882. He didn't like it. Neither did he like what he considered the "gloomy" offices downtown where his older brothers juggled profit-and-loss statements and huddled with their father in business conferences. Fortunately for Ben, Meyer Guggenheim was now in mining, and since the older sons were needed to take care of what remained of the lace and embroidery business, Meyer decided to send the younger ones West.

Ben, leaving Columbia without completing his course, was the second to go, becoming general manager of the smeltery at Pueblo in 1888. Later, he came back East to oversee the construction of the refinery at Perth Amboy and to become the family representative there. When Guggenex was organized, Ben, along with brother Will, objected to the decision to let non-Guggenheims into the family's exploration ventures, and in 1901 he and Will disassociated themselves from the family business. After that Ben, like Will, engaged in various enterprises on his own.

Harry Guggenheim remembers meeting his uncle by accident on the streets of Paris on the morning of Tuesday, April 9, 1912. Ben had been in Europe for the last three months, but he informed his nephew that he was leaving for home the following day. "He took me to lunch," says Harry, "and talked with me for a long while. It flattered me that, with so many errands to do on his last day in Paris, he was willing to give me so much time."

On the next day Ben was off to Cherbourg where, between seven and nine that evening, he went aboard ship for what was to be the maiden voyage of a 46,328-ton luxury liner, recently built by the White Star Line and touted as the supreme triumph of modern engineering, a "ship that God Himself couldn't sink." In the dark early hours of the following April 15, Benjamin Guggenheim was dead, one of 1,517 men and women to perish[4] with the *Titantic* in the 28-degree waters of the iceberg-clogged Northern Atlantic. His last moments were noble, as Walter Lord makes clear in his unforgettable etching of the ship in its death throes, *A Night to Remember.* As 651 children, women and men, in that order, were crowded into an inadequate number of lifeboats, Ben cast aside the lifebelt and sweater that a steward had tearfully compelled him to put on and quietly dressed for the inevitable in his evening clothes. He ordered his valet, one of the eight aboard the palatial liner, to do the same. His last known act was to place a note in the hands of a woman as she entered one of the lifeboats. "If anything should happen to me," it read, "tell my wife I've done my best in doing my duty."

In the wake of the disaster a rumor arose and found its way into print. It was that among the survivors was a lady who had registered herself as "Mrs. Benjamin Guggenheim," although actually she was Ben's mistress. To this day the rumor pops up in books touching on the Guggenheims. It seems to be a case of a man's reputation living after him, for in the official report on the *Titanic* disaster issued by the Committee on Commerce of the United States Senate there is no "Mrs. Benjamin Guggenheim" on the passenger list of the doomed vessel.[5]

In one respect all of the brothers—even William, after his divorce—adhered to the Victorian standard. Each married a woman of his own race and of comparable social background.

Isaac was seventeen, and for the time being in business for himself, when in 1876 he married seventeen-year-old Carrie, daughter of Jonas Sonneborn, a New York dealer in fancy goods. Loeb remembers Carrie as "a little, red-haired woman with excess energy." She survived by eleven years her husband who died in 1922 while traveling in Europe.

Dan was married in 1884 to Florence Shloss of Philadelphia—"a sweet woman and a lovely hostess" is Loeb's memory of her; Solomon in 1895 to Irene Rothschild, daughter of a New York merchant; and Simon in 1898 to Olga Hirsch, daughter of a New York realty operator and diamond merchant.

Of the seven brothers, Sol was the longest-lived. Since his death in 1949, at the age of eighty-eight, the "life and times" of the third-generation Guggenheims have belonged to history.[6]

The Neo-Puritans

Few traces of Victorianism can be found among the fourth-generation members of the American Guggenheim family. The pattern has been one of multiple marriages and divorces, with most of the marriages to men and women outside the Jewish faith. Mistresses? Only one on the record. "We marry the girls," Harold Loeb has said. "It's the Puritan in us."

In spectacular contrast to the accomplishment of Meyer and Barbara, the ten of their children who survived to adulthood had small families; only twenty-four children in all—ten sons and fourteen daughters. Moreover, among the offspring of the seven brothers, males were so scarce as to arouse concern among those members of the family eager to keep the name of Guggenheim in the family business.

Ben, Sol and Isaac had daughters only. Will's only child, William, Jr., was never in good health and died in 1947 at the age of thirty-nine, leaving behind William III, a married young Yale alumnus interested in radio engineering.

Simon and his wife became the parents of two sons: John Simon, born in 1905, and George Denver, born two years later. John Simon died in 1922 following a mastoid operation; George Denver—long a victim of ill health—in 1939, by his own hand. As for Edmond, Murry's only son, since his retirement from Guggenheim Brothers in 1923, his only major business connection has been that of a director of Kennecott Corporation. For the most part he has devoted himself to golf and other sports, and since the death of his father, to his duties as president of the Murry and Leonie Guggenheim Foundation.

To Mr. and Mrs. Dan were born two boys, Meyer Robert in 1885 and Harry Frank in 1890. One of Harry's most wistfully voiced remembrances of his childhood is that M. Robert was his mother's favorite—perhaps because the older boy was the first-born of her three children, perhaps because of the often-remarked-on tendency of a mother to favor the son who gives promise of becoming the family cutup.

Certain it is that in those parts of the world where M. Robert lived and played during his seventy-four years, his devotion to the arts of pleasure is still a topic of conversation. He began his adult life with four years at the Columbia School of Mines followed by a few years in various executive positions with the Guggenheim firms. Work, however, had no charms for him. "Every wealthy family," M. Robert declared at an early age, "supports at least one gentleman in leisure. I have elected to assume that position in mine." He was out of the family business before World War I. Thereafter such commercial connections as he assumed for varying intervals received only a margin of his attention, the bulk of which he expended on prize dogs and jumping horses, racing cars, hunting, and high society.

He began World War I by going overseas as a lieutenant with the 69th Regiment, ended it as a major, with his superior dubbing him "the best general's aide in the United States Army." M. Robert liked the companionship of army men. After the war he was much seen in military circles, eventually achieving the rank of colonel in the Reserves. In 1925 he was graduated from the Army War College and from 1932 to 1935 he served on the staff of the War Department.

In 1953 he was named American ambassador to Portugal. A year later he was back home, having become *persona non grata* to the Portuguese government. M. Robert's own version of this event, as given at the time to an American businessman in Lisbon, is that during an official dinner he dropped a teaspoon down the front of a Portuguese lady's dress. This much of the incident was an accident, and might have been forgiven had M. Robert

Simon Guggenheim.

not made the mistake of trying to retrieve the spoon with his own hands.

There were four marriages. The first, to Grace Bernheimer in 1905, was terminated by divorce ten years later with Grace receiving custody of the two children, Daniel II, who died in 1925, and M. Robert, Jr., now a resident of California and a trustee of the Daniel and Florence Guggenheim Foundation.

The second marriage, taking place in the same year as the divorce, was to Margaret Weyher of Scranton, Pennsylvania, a horsewoman. Margaret was a Roman Catholic, so M. Robert obligingly changed his religion. New York reporters, sensing a story in this situation, converged on the St. Regis Hotel where M. Robert's father was then living. They got their story, although it was not the stormy one they had expected. "I'm delighted," Mr. Dan said calmly. "My son has always been a very bad Jew. I hope they'll make a good Catholic of him."

Good or bad, M. Robert did not remain a Catholic long. In 1928 Margaret got a Paris divorce and a week later M. Robert was married to Elizabeth Eaton of Babylon, Long Island, New York, this time in a Lutheran church. Now home was an estate in Babylon, next door to that of August Belmont. There M. Robert and his third wife raised horses and dogs. The stable was known as Firenze; so was the kennel. Firenze, of course, is the Italian name for Florence, the name of M. Robert's mother; and in M. Robert's youth his father's Italian-style summerhouse on the New Jersey coast had borne the name which M. Robert would later apply not only to his Long Island stable but also to a small kennel in Jersey, to a large estate in Washington, D.C., and to the five yachts which he owned from time to time. Like his second wife, M. Robert's third was a horsewoman, a spirited one who dazzled her friends by jumping 230 fences in a single day. In winter the Guggenheims deserted Long Island for the social life of warmer Washington, D.C. There Elizabeth substituted fast cars for horses.

Boon companions, she and M. Robert, it would seem, but not boon enough. Divorce came in 1938 and M. Robert hastened to Miami Beach to pay court to Mrs. William Bird Van Lennep of Philadelphia, whose estranged scholar-husband had disappeared for the time being into the recesses of the British Museum. Born Rebecca De Loatch Pollard and the daughter of a Norfolk, Virginia, real estate man, "Polly," as Mrs. Van Lennep was known to her friends, was dainty, blond and discrete. When M. Robert asked her to be a guest on his yacht, she asked permission to bring along a girl friend as chaperone. M. Robert reluctantly agreed. When he proposed marriage, she asked time to talk things over with her husband in England before making a decision. Again M. Robert reluctantly agreed. In England there was a reconciliation; but after returning to the States, Polly changed her mind, got a divorce and married M. Robert.

For four years they lived on the Colonel's 170-foot Krupp-built white cruiser, one of his five seagoing *Firenzes,* sailing to California and back for their honeymoon and later docking in the Potomac for the Washington social season. During the week following Pearl Harbor, the Navy Department requested the cruiser, and the Colonel and his fourth wife bought a thirty-six-room Norman-style mansion on a rolling stretch of land along the flanks of Rock Creek Park. With its well-like great hall, its stately living room—soon refurnished with Georgian paneling brought from England—its breeze-swept porches and tree-shaded lawns, the new house was perfect for entertaining. In the years that followed, Polly Guggenheim became one of the popular hostesses of the Federal capital, where party-giving ranks only a little lower than government and tourism among the native crafts. For three months each winter the M. Robert Guggenheims moved south to "do the shooting season" on the Colonel's 1400-acre plantation, Poco Sabo, 38 miles below Charleston on the Ashepoo River.

Petite, fair-haired and soft-spoken, Polly—now Mrs. John A. Logan of Washington—remembers her late husband as "loving it all." M. Robert, she says, "enjoyed what he had, enjoyed enjoying it and loved entertaining his friends." As a host he had only one fault. "He was blunt," Polly says. "He lacked that seventh sense that some people are born with and some aren't, and Bob just wasn't. He was forever telling people exactly what he thought of them, and some people, you know, are offended by that sort of thing. He didn't mean it, of course. It was only his way of being funny. His old friends understood and didn't mind, but we always had so many guests and there were always new ones among them. My job at the end of every party was to go around pouring salve on hurt feelings."

It is unlikely that another word of criticism about the Colonel has ever passed Polly's lips. "So many bad things have been said about him," she says. "I feel it is my duty to bring out the good things. He was a wonderful friend, a wonderful companion. He was kind to the point of being impractical. Most wealthy men, you know, worry about their deductions—for taxes, that is. Not Bob. He never gave such things a thought. He was the soul of generosity."

Three years after M. Robert's death, his generosity would bring his name back into the headlines, with the Federal government seeking to collect $169,548 in taxes which it claimed he should have paid on $800,000 in gifts—cash, jewelry and "a comparatively modest home in Georgetown"—to "an unidentified woman friend."

Polly was in Washington Hospital Center, under treatment for a heart condition, when on the evening of Monday, November 16, 1959, her husband collapsed while boarding a taxi in Georgetown after having dined with a friend there. He died en route to a hospital and was buried on the following Friday in Arlington National Cemetery. A picture in one of the Washington obituary pages showed a balding, white-haired gentleman with winglike brows and neat mustache, his wide and sensual mouth still further extended by a puckish grin.[7]

IV

There Is No Guggenheim Foundation

In 1938 American newspaper readers were entertained by a syndicated cartoon which depicted an amply proportioned matron stepping into "Madame Francine's Corset Shoppe" and saying to the startled saleslady, "Have you one of those Guggenheim foundations I've heard so much about?"

What was true in 1938 is still true and has been since the establishment in the 1920's of the first of the five foundations—one temporary, the others permanent—founded by members of the Guggenheim family. For almost four decades these organizations, in the words of the lady of the cartoon, have been much "heard . . . about." To be sure, when the first of the Guggenheim five was set up in 1924, any foundation was news because at that time there were less than two hundred such organizations in the United States. As late as 1937 when the last of them came into existence, the national total was still under five hundred. But even today, with over ten thousand foundations in operation and more coming along at the rate of two hundred a year, the Guggenheim five continue to attract a large amount of public attention.[1]

The reasons for this appear to be as varied as the activities, many of a pioneering nature, which these endowments have helped to put under way.

Since the inception of the John Simon Guggenheim Memorial Foundation in 1925, its fellowships have furthered the careers of thousands of scholars, scientists, authors, artists, and composers and historians of music. Among them have been such well-known figures as Arthur H. Compton in science, Senator Paul H. Douglas in economics, Robert Penn Warren in fiction, Leonard D. White in history, Douglas Southall Freeman in biography, Stephen Vincent Benét in poetry, and Aaron Copland in music. Seven holders of Guggenheim fellowships have received the Nobel Prize, thirty-one the Pulitzer.

In the late 1920's the Daniel Guggenheim Fund for the Promotion of Aeronautics made news with its efforts to help put on its feet the then struggling aviation industry. There were headlines when, under the auspices of the Fund, Lieutenant (now Lieutenant General) James H. Doolittle took a big step toward conquering the problems of blind flying; more headlines when Charles A. Lindbergh, fresh from his historic transatlantic solo flight, toured the United States for the Fund in a giant demonstration of the airplane's potentialities, still more when the Fund brought to the United States the Hungarian-born scientist, the late Theodore von Kármán, whose work in this country was to help give it a dominant role in the development of the theoretical aspects of aeronautics and jet propulsion.

When in 1929 the newly organized Murry and Leonie Guggenheim Foundation began the construction of a dental clinic for the children of New York City, its program received a grateful welcome from the dental profession. Where dental science is concerned, one of its leaders remarked, "Nothing has been done of such magnitude for the public health."

For more than a decade, on the eve of World War II, the oldest of the Guggenheim five, the Daniel and Florence Guggenheim Foundation, was almost the sole supporter of the experiments of a quiet New England professor, Robert H. Goddard—experiments that were to install Goddard in the history books as one of the architects of the space age and "The Father of Modern Rocketry."

And in 1959, with the opening of the art museum designed by the late Frank Lloyd Wright, the youngest of the group, the Solomon R. Guggenheim Foundation, presented to New York City and the world probably the most discussed and certainly the most controversial building since the rise and fall of the Tower of Babel.[2]

Which Does What

Newspapers frequently speak of "The Guggenheim Foundation." Actually, there is no such organization, and the existence of a number of foundations bearing the family name sometimes creates confusion as to which does what. People often ask the Solomon R. Guggenheim Foundation for application blanks for the fellowships issued by the John Simon Guggenheim Memorial Foundation; or the John Simon for catalogues of the art exhibits sponsored by the Solomon R.; or the Murry and Leonie Guggenheim Foundation for programs of the free band concerts underwritten by the Daniel and Florence Guggenheim Foundation; or any one of the four permanent foundations for information concerning the now-liquidated Daniel Guggenheim Fund for the Promotion of Aeronautics.

Obviously a guide is of the essence, and to be brief about it, the Guggenheim five and their identifying characteristics are:*

1. *The Daniel and Florence Guggenheim Foundation,* founded in 1924 by the late Mr. and Mrs. Daniel Guggenheim. Although this organization has helped a variety of undertakings, today it devotes most of its funds to the aerospace sciences.

2. *The John Simon Guggenheim Memorial Foundation,* founded in 1925 by the late United States Senator Simon Guggenheim and his wife. This is the foundation which awards the fellowships, popularly known as "the Guggenheims," to men and women of "high intellectual and personal qualifications who have already demonstrated unusual capacity for productive scholarship or unusual creative ability in the fine arts."

3. *The Daniel Guggenheim Fund for the Promotion of Aeronautics,* a self-liquidating organization founded in 1926 by Daniel Guggenheim to provide for aviation, at a critical period in its infancy, "immediate, practical and substantial assistance. . . ." It began operations in January of 1926, ended them in January of 1930.

4. *The Murry and Leonie Guggenheim Foundation,* founded in 1929 by the late Mr. and Mrs. Murry Guggenheim, chiefly,

* Further data about the foundations is given in the Appendix beginning on page 291.

although not necessarily exclusively, to promote dental science. This is the organization which operates the Guggenheim dental clinic for children in New York City.

5. *The Solomon R. Guggenheim Foundation,* founded in 1937 by the late Solomon R. Guggenheim to encourage art and art education. It operates the Guggenheim Museum.

Seed Money

Offhand it would seem that the Guggenheim five have nothing in common but diversity, but a closer look uncovers at least two shared attributes.

One is an emphasis on the individual. The John Simon gives its funds only to individuals, and Henry Allen Moe, its principal executive officer for many years, has quoted with approval the statement of Dr. Clifford Ambrose Truesdell III, a Guggenheim fellow, that while today's man-made satellites are put together and sent aloft by "great, smoothly functioning teams of workers," the concepts underlying this accomplishment are based on "the work of a handful of men, scattered over a continent and a century—men who were willful, uncompromising, quarrelsome, arrogant, and creative."

While the John Simon is the only member of the five that makes grants exclusively to individuals, the others do so in a more limited way. Many gifted individuals—"willful, uncompromising, quarrelsome, arrogant, and creative"—loom large in their histories. Harry Guggenheim, now president of two of the foundations, has said that "my father and his brothers," meaning the four men chiefly responsible for the Guggenheim five, "believed that what counts with a foundation is not how much it spends but what results it gets, and our experience has been that the way to get results is to hunt for and support, not institutions of brick and mortar, but men with ideas."

The other attribute common to all of the foundations is their adherence to what Harry has termed the "seed money" principle. The phrase explains itself. Ever since the formation in 1866 of the Peabody Fund, first of the modern philanthropic endowments, it has been found good practice for such organizations to support projects which give promise of being so valuable to society that once they have received an initial "leg up" they can be counted on to support themselves or to attract support from government or private industry.

A clear example of this appears in the records of the Fund for the Promotion of Aeronautics. In 1928 this temporary endowment set up in California a small, experimental weather service, which proved so effective that it was taken over by the Federal government to become the prototype of the national air weather service now conducted by the United States Weather Bureau. The Fund's "leg up," the seed money put into its regional air weather service, came to slightly more than $27,000. Today the government spends at least that many millions yearly on its countrywide successor.[3] In the story of the Guggenheim five, featured in the chapters to come, we will encounter several other examples of the seed money principle in action.[4]

V

Harry Guggenheim and the Universal Highway

The first of the Guggenheim endowments, chronologically, was the Daniel and Florence Guggenheim Foundation, established by Mr. Dan and his wife in 1924; but the first to catch the public fancy was the Daniel Guggenheim Fund for the Promotion of Aeronautics, established by Mr. Dan two years later.

Much of the effectiveness of the Fund was the result of its timeliness. It came into being in an hour when America's aviation industry, languishing since the close of the First World War, was in need of a booster. America had provided the birthplace for the modern phase of aeronautics—a development dating from December 17, 1903, when above the sand dunes of Kitty Hawk, North Carolina, Wilbur and Orville Wright succeeded for the first time in history in putting a heavier-than-air machine into sustained flight. In the First World War, American combat pilots had given a good account of themselves. But in the years immediately after the armistice, the hoped-for development in America of a passenger-and-freight-carrying commercial airplane industry was slow in materializing.

In the mid-1920's this country was lagging far behind the rest of the world. In England, Imperial Airways Ltd., a government-subsidized amalgamation of three private lines that had been going strong since 1920, was making daily flights across the Channel to Paris, Brussels and Amsterdam, carrying passengers, freight and mail. In Germany no less than thirty transport lines, soon to be combined into the subsidized Deutsche Lufthansa, were in operation. Even little Belgium had Sabena, its national airline; had had it since 1923. Comparatively the United States had next to nothing: a few small, irregular and isolated domestic transport lines and a transcontinental mail route conducted by the Federal government.

American pilots were confined for the most part to flying the mail or to barnstorming about the country, earning a precarious living by selling rides and doing stunts at county fairs. Lindbergh unreels a picture of his own barnstorming days in his books, *We* (1927) and *The Spirit of St. Louis* (1953): the old Negro woman asking him how much he would charge to take her up to Heaven and leave her there; the Illinois farmer, sounding off with his version of a standard joke of the period, "I feel just like my dad [about airplanes]. He says he just a'soon fly in one of 'em as long as he can keep one foot on the ground. Haw-haw-haw!"; the gawking fair and carnival crowds pelting the young aviator with such questions as why was there a hole in the radiator of the plane, how often did its wings fall off and were they made of leather? An amusing tintype, but the mournful gist of it is that in the mid-1920's the generality of Americans regarded the stick-wielding pioneers of aviation as mountebanks and the industry they were straining to build as a source of casual entertainment.

True, its potentialities were the subject of many a public speech, but they were also the butt of many a private joke. In his novel *The Big Money,* that acid word-portrait of the boom-bust decades after World War I, John Dos Passos has one of his characters—a War Department-type army general—conceding that "all this work with flyin'-machines is very interestin'. . . . But speakin' as a military man, gentlemen, you know some of us don't feel that they have proved their worth. . . . Experiment is a great thing, gentlemen, and I don't deny that perhaps in the distant future—" At which juncture there is an interruption from another unforgettable Dos Passos character, Dick Savage, a public relations man. "In the distant future," Savage echoes the skeptical general with a laugh. "The trouble with us is we are in the distant future and don't know it"

As Dan Guggenheim set about establishing the aeronautical fund, he was under no illusion that where aviation was concerned

America was "in the distant future." In what was then a mere germ of an industry, however, he envisioned a new source of wealth for a country to which he felt indebted for having permitted him and his immediate forebears to live with a freedom and a dignity that had been denied to his more remote forebears in Europe.

For years he had been on the outlook for some form of charitable endeavor that would properly express his gratitude to a country he loved. For a period, in 1912, he had toyed with what he described in a letter to his second son, Harry, then in England, as "philanthropic work in connection with agricultural colleges." A short time later he abandoned this idea. "I find the field already so very well covered," he wrote Harry, "that I could not be of use. . . ." With agriculture off the agenda, he turned to the problems of American working men. "The 'poor devil' and the rich devil," he reminded his son, "are far, far apart; one has too much and the other, too little. Some equalization can take place by providing for the employee's welfare at his work." What Mr. Dan had in mind, he wrote Harry, was the establishment of a group of experts "to make a thorough study of what is being done in all parts of the world for the workman's welfare and to make suggestions of a practical nature. . . ." In a matter of months this idea, too, had been discarded, the older man dispatching to the younger a copy of a recent act of Congress calling for the creation of a commission on industrial relations. Mr. Dan's comment was that this "seems to cover the field . . . from which I fear I am 'knocked out' again from doing something in the direction contemplated." That more than a decade later he found in aviation the sort of charitable project he was seeking was largely his son's doing. Harry had been a flier in the war, and his enthusiasm for the field had much to do with his father's choice.[1]

"Time Effectually Cures Us. . . ."

Born in Philadelphia in 1856, Daniel Guggenheim, second oldest of the eleven children of Meyer and Barbara, was seventeen when his father removed him from a local public high school and shipped him off to Switzerland to spend the ensuing decade acquainting himself with the embroidery business and picking up the French and German languages. Apparently the experience was a memorable one. Years later when his own son Harry left home to learn the mining business in Mexico, Mr. Dan endeavored to impress on him the importance of devoting himself with patience to acquiring the fundamentals of his job by recalling his own training days.

"I was sent into a foreign land among strangers," he was writing his son in 1908, "to take up my business career about the same time of life that you are entering upon yours, and . . . many of the conditions that obtained then with me obtain now with you. Of course there are some exceptions; I did not have . . . a special cook . . . and many luxuries of that kind, but . . . my hours of work were long like yours, from early morning until evening . . . [and] in addition from four to six months in the year, we went through what was known as the 'Shipping Season' during which all hands had to . . . return to the office after supper . . . and work until eleven or twelve." To which remarks Mr. Dan, with a gentle and parental didacticism, appended his moral. "I do not think," he told Harry, "I ever lost anything by spending ten years . . . in Switzerland. The experience in business education that I acquired has been of benefit to me all through life."

His life was something of a classic as the lives of American businessmen go. Not, of course, a rags-to-riches classic. The riches, a comfortable proportion of them, were already there when in the 1870's Mr. Dan set forth upon his long and eventful career. What he did—he and his brothers—was increase them manyfold, a process in which Mr. Dan played a consistently dominant and often creative role.

When in the 1880's the family turned from embroidery to mining and smelting, he became his father's chief lieutenant in the initial development of these projects. During the 1890's he took the lead in obtaining the governmental concessions that enabled the Guggenheims to build up their mining empire in Mexico. Later he was to play a key part in the development of other foreign ventures, and when the Guggenheims took control of ASARCO, he became its leader and chief planner, serving first as chairman of the board and then as president, holding

Harry Guggenheim in training as a pilot, one week before U.S. entry into World War I. Glenn Curtiss on the left.

the latter position until his retirement from business in 1919.
Baruch is not the only person to speak admiringly of his qualities. William, in his autobiography, calls him the brother who led the family firm "out of the simple but profitable operating field into the more hazardous terrain of promotion and exploitation." Harold Loeb describes his uncle as "one of those men who wherever they are make themselves felt. To be with him was to be keenly aware that you were in the vicinity of a 'presence.' " Mrs. Roger W. Straus recalls how one day, while out for a walk, her father ran into his friend Adolph Ochs, publisher of the *New York Times*. Ochs looked gloomy and when Mr. Dan asked why, the publisher revealed that he was "extremely worried," that he needed $250,000 for his newspaper. Without a second of hesitation, "Well, that's all right," said Mr. Dan. "You can have it. I will give it to you." The matter was arranged on the spot: a straight friendly loan with no interest or other conditions attached. And son Harry passes on with feeling his earliest impressions of his father as a business man.

"Right after my return from Cambridge in 1913," he says, "I was permitted for the first time to sit in on the daily conferences of the brothers in my father's office. Having spent the previous three years at an English school, where courtesy was standard procedure, I was struck at once by the good manners which prevailed at the conference table. My father and his brothers treated one another with an old-world deference that was rare even in those days and, I suppose, practically non-existent in the business world of today.

"One of the rules of the firm was that no important step could be taken without the unanimous consent of the partners. Frequently it was my father's task to introduce these new steps and to bring the others along with him. It wasn't always easy. I vividly remember his explaining some proposed change, and then re-explaining it, and then re-explaining it again. He never lost his temper, never lifted his voice, never ran out of patience—and never gave up! I think he was the truest example I have ever seen of what is called the 'velvet glove over the iron fist.' "

But the man himself was not made of iron. The combination of inner intensity and outer restraint took its toll. While still in his early fifties, a long-standing "stomachic trouble," as he labeled it, forced him for a time to refrain from work. Forbidden by his doctor to engage in any "violent exercise," including horseback riding which he loved, the head of the House of Guggenheim was restless. "Thirty-five years of continuous activity with such a sudden cessation," he wrote Harry, then in Mexico, "is a greater hardship than I thought possible. I frequently feel that I prefer the illness to the cure. . . . I realize now . . . how I miss not having acquired a hobby with which I might in time of need like now, occupy myself." And in another letter to Harry, dominated by the same caliginous mood, "time cures us effectually of all conceit," he philosophized, "and brings us from the much we design to the little we can accomplish." Communications of a later date bring out that the "stomachic trouble" was an ulcer and find Mr. Dan speaking of it, not too fondly, as his "little Mary."

His marriage to Florence Schloss of Philadelphia took place there in 1884, and on Thanksgiving Day thirty-three years later he was writing Harry, then in the war and overseas, "During dinner Mother wanted to drink your health, but she filled up. Poor Mother dear! She is . . . one in thousands; her thoughts are always for others." And in a slightly later letter, "Your mother is really wonderful" and "I can well understand, my dear son, where you get many of your good qualities."

The Daniel Guggenheims created about them the same warm family life that the Meyer Guggenheims had enjoyed before them. For a time they lived at 12 West 54th Street, just off Fifth Avenue. It was a plush area. Among their neighbors were the Rockefellers, Morton F. Plant, Chauncey M. Depew, and Mrs. Jacob Astor; and biographer O'Connor has it that when after a few years the Daniel Guggenheims moved into the just opened St. Regis Hotel, it was because they had "tired of the swagger" of 54h Street. Perhaps so. "Because of their prominence in the business world," Harry says, "my father, his brothers and their families were regarded as leaders in American Jewish society and took their responsibilities in that regard very seriously. As for society with a capital 'S,' however, that didn't interest them. Newspapers used to picture us youngsters as being brought up in a very pretentious manner, with private railroad cars and all that sort of thing. It wasn't so. My father and his brothers were always ready to spend money to make their families comfortable, but they never spent it for show. You don't run into any frou-frou of that sort until you get down to my generation. No one of my father's era had the slightest interest in making the society columns. Their families, their homes, their work, and their country —those were the things they valued."

To the children of his marriage—M. Robert, born in 1885; Harry, 1890; and Gladys, 1896—Mr. Dan was a conscientious father. Such is certainly the impression left by his letters to his second son, a correspondence that began in 1908, when Harry left home for the first time, and that was to continue intermittently until within a few months of the older man's death twenty-two years later. They are the letters of a warm and thoughtful man; and it is a toss-up as to whom they picture the more clearly, the father who wrote them or the son who received them. Harry speaks of them as Chesterfieldian. His reference, of course, is to that prime example of a father-son epistolary adventure, the letters of Philip Dormer Stanhope, fourth Earl of Chesterfield, to his lone offspring. It is possible that Mr. Dan took the eighteenth-century English statesman as his model. At any rate he frequently quotes him, as in 1911 when Harry, then a student at Cambridge, was temporarily considering politics as a life work and writing home to get his father's opinion of this plan. By way of answer Mr. Dan reproduced Lord Chesterfield's recital of the overwhelming body of knowledge a man needed to succeed in politics. "If you agree with me," he wrote, "that the quotation from Chesterfield's letters covers the duties of a politician, you will also probably agree . . . that it is wise for you to consider more particularly the career of a businessman."

As one by one his children embarked on their own independent lives, Mr. Dan gave expression to an age-old lament. "[I]t does not seem just right," he wrote Harry, "to raise a family and just when they reach an age when they can be companionable to their parents, it is to their best interests . . . that they should leave the nest. However . . . it is a debt that is only paid from one generation to another . . . my parents made the sacrifice for me that

I am compelled to make for you. I do so cheerfully under the circumstances, but at the moment it does seem hard."

In 1912 Mr. Dan's letters evidenced perturbation following the news from England that Harry and his wife were expecting their first child. What if the child were a boy? Would its birth on foreign soil, Mr. Dan wanted to know, rule out the possibility of its becoming President of the United States? A few months later this problem had been twice resolved: First, by a long letter to Mr. Dan from his brother Simon, then a United States Senator, citing authorities and snatches of history to the effect that the child of American parents, born abroad, was not necessarily barred from the highest office in the land; and second, by the announcement early in 1913 that the child was a girl, and had been named Joan Florence.

Many of the earlier letters, especially those written while Harry was in Mexico learning the smelting business from the ground up (which is to say, from the sampling mill), were rife with parental admonition. "From time to time as they occur to me," Mr. Dan informed his son on January 19, 1908, "I will call to your attention matters that I believe you will understand are meant for your present and future welfare."

The older man was true to his word. The burden of letter after letter was that Harry must not waste the precious energies of youth. First of all, he must cultivate his mind. "I have received your first letter from Aguascalientes," Mr. Dan wrote. "I scrutinized it carefully for misspelled words, but failed to find any . . . I hope you have commenced your lessons in Spanish. Do not overlook having a tutor competent to teach you the language as it should be spoken. . . ." He urged Harry to devote his spare time to reading. "Nights wasted," he warned, "are a poor recompense for you in after years." Frequently he listed the titles of books he himself had found worthwhile, and on one occasion he thanked Harry for sending him a copy of a current novel called *The Man from Wall Street,* commenting, however, that "I appreciate the gift, but not . . . the book. Life is too short . . . and it is an absolute waste of time to read something that has no merit."

Living in an age when free will was still regarded as playing a substantial role in the development of character, the writer of the letters expatiated at length on the old-fashioned virtues. "The present number of failures in life, as I see it," he lectured his son, "are due to lack of tenacity." And in a subsequent communication, "I am expecting you to relieve me" in the family business "in the not too distant future. You have the brains, I am confident; I hope you will not fail in the tenacity."

Over and over he reminded Harry that the *mens sana* needs a *corpore sano*. "Costiveness," he cautioned, "is a malady easily acquired in Mexico, due to the kind of food you are compelled to eat." Mr. Dan recommended "green vegetables, fruits and salads and plenty of oil," adding that many "ailments to which flesh is heir are traceable to costiveness; a word to the wise should be sufficient."

Letters written during a tour of Europe in 1908 with Mrs. Guggenheim and twelve-year-old daughter Gladys found him in a variety of moods. A letter from Paris was playful: "I have some important letters to High Catholic prelates in Rome. I shall probably ask for and get a private audience with the Pope. I can see no special benefit unless I should take up politics. . . . Mother will write you in a few days. She is quite busy now with dressmakers. They get her time and my money."

One from Rome (where the audience was granted) was laced with *Weltschmerz:* "It is nearly one-third of a century since I was here. The impression was rather depressing. I do not know how to account for it, unless it is in the realization that so much of my life has been spent. I will not dwell longer on this. However, I simply wished you to have the knowledge of such feelings from one who is having them. . . . Your dear mother . . . bubbles with enthusiasm. . . . She is not only younger in years than I, but much younger in spirit. It has been to me a great sacrifice to come abroad because . . . I feel continually that keen desire to be home, in harness, and doing my share of the work."

One from Florence emanated contentment: "I am really leading a life of simply looking on, making no plans—living as if it were from hand to mouth and letting tomorrow, in fact the day after, take care of itself. This may be due to real fatigue or overwork in the past, or I may have merely grown lazy. We are enjoying the life and ourselves immensely. Touring pleases me; sightseeing pleases your mother; and there is a ban on shopping."

And from Venice: "Man proposes, but his wife disposes. I came abroad with the firm conviction that I would do little or no shopping or sightseeing . . . I am doing both with a vengeance."

Down through the years that followed the letters continued to fluctuate both as to mood and content. "I would very much like to be with you in Caux [a resort]," Mr. Dan was writing during Harry's Cambridge days. "One gets into a rut here in New York; no matter what varieties of pleasures there are, they are still always the same—opera, concerts, theater, dinners. . . . A run and a romp in the snow in the country would be very much pleasanter." A wartime communication bristled with parental indignation. "Mother is not particularly pleased with your short letters. Put on your thinking cap, Harry, and see if you cannot give us more news. . . ." And in another wartime letter, written in 1918, he dilated for the first time on the possibilities of aviation: "I wonder whether you think as much of the aeroplane in bringing the war to a final end as I do?"[2]

The Universal Highway

Eight years later Mr. Dan would have a great deal more to say on the subject of aviation in a letter of January 16, 1926, to Secretary of Commerce Herbert Hoover—the letter which formally launched the Daniel Guggenheim Fund for the Promotion of Aeronautics by tendering it to the American people via their government. "You yourself," Mr. Dan reminded Hoover

have pointed out that a Government public service must be provided to cooperate with aviation. . . . There is undoubtedly a function in this situation which the Government alone can perform.

I have also been much impressed by . . . the report of the President's Aircraft Board, which . . . said:

"How can the civilian use of aircraft be promoted? . . . A great opportunity lies before the United States. We have natural resources, industrial organizations, and long distances free from customs barriers. . . ."

Such considerations . . . have convinced me that there is a function

> which can only be performed by private enterprise aside from the proper function of the Government. So much remains to be done before civil aviation can realize the possibilities before it, that everyone must recognize that there intervenes a period of necessary study and experimentation.
>
> In these circumstances I have decided to establish the Daniel Guggenheim Fund for the Promotion of Aeronautics and to place at its disposal the sum of $2,500,000 [subsequently increased by slightly more than $500,000]. . . .
>
> The trustees will have unrestricted power to do anything which, in their judgment, may develop aeronautics, the only condition being that the Fund shall not be a profit-making enterprise. . . .
>
> The trustees are to have power to spend the principal sum . . . and there is no purpose to establish a permanent foundation. The thought is, rather, that, the whole art and science of aeronautics and aviation being now in its infancy, it will be possible with the sums thus contributed, to bring about such an advance in the art that private enterprise will find it practicable and profitable to "carry on" and thus render a continuous and permanent endowment for this purpose unnecessary.

Plainly, Mr. Dan conceived of the Fund as a seed-money operation. So it was to function, becoming an example of the ability of privately given money to take risks that private-enterprise money cannot take and that in a free country government money is legally or morally enjoined from taking. Following an organizing meeting of the trustees on January 26, 1926, the Fund buckled down to work with Harry Guggenheim as president and retired Rear Admiral Hutchinson I. Cone as vice-president and executive officer. To the end, the younger Guggenheim remained a prime mover in the organization's affairs. Harry's personal view, as he once put it, was that the sky was a "universal highway," that this country should take the lead in its development as such. Throughout the four years of the Fund's life his ideas and personality permeated its work to an extent that makes an account of the man a fitting prelude to that of the organization.

Mountains of His Own

During the melancholy 1930's Harry Frank Guggenheim, then in his early forties—a tall, blue-eyed man of athletic build—was beseeched by friends to abandon his custom of traveling from his country place on Long Island to his offices in the Wall Street district, in a custom-built automobile driven by a uniformed chauffeur. The friends' argument was that in a country stricken by depression, any display of wealth was dangerous. Mr. Guggenheim argued that it would not help the unemployment situation for him to fire his chauffeur, and that as long as he could afford to pay the man it would be "silly" not to use him. "Besides," he predicted, "nothing will happen."

In this he was wrong. One morning as the long car pulled to the curb in front of the Equitable Building in lower Manhattan, two men, idling along Broadway, spotted the expensive car and watched with disapproval as the chauffeur left the driver's seat to open the rear door. Approaching, they poked their heads through the windows and stuck out their tongues at the car's well-dressed occupant. "Capitalist! Capitalist!" they jeered. Mr. Guggenheim returned the compliment and the gesture. "Flatterers! Flatterers" he jeered back, leaving the car and shouldering his way past the two men to disappear into the coruscating lobby of 120 Broadway.

The incident offers some clues to seventy-four-year-old Harry Guggenheim's variegated makeup. It suggests spunk along with refusal to pretend to be anything other than what circumstances have made him, the possessor of a large inherited fortune. In the words of G. Edward Pendray, consultant on rocketry to the Daniel and Florence Guggenheim Foundation, "Harry has always shown great tenacity about accepting the responsibilities of a wealthy man."

In his sixty-fifth year, "I have reached the time of life," Harry stated in a letter to his daughter, Nancy

> when it is wise that I prepare for the future, either with or without the help of my children. I have always hoped that my children and grandchildren would carry on the best traditions of the Family to the best of their abilities. . . . I believe there is a responsibility to use inherited wealth for the progress of man and not for mere self-gratification, which I am sure does not lead to a happy life.

Harry himself has practiced the doctrines preached in his 1955 letter. Since the death of his father in 1930, he has been the principal executive officer of the Daniel and Florence Guggenheim Foundation, its president since the death of his mother in 1944; and since the death of his Uncle Sol in 1949 the moving spirit of the Solomon R. Guggenheim Foundation.

He is not especially fond of business, or more exactly, he enjoys the planning aspects of it but becomes impatient with the details of execution. "There is nothing more 'soporific,' " he has remarked, "than the 'whereat's' and 'whereas's' of a commercial document." Nonetheless he has labored in many vineyards in an effort to reserve to the name of Guggenheim the commercial luster imparted to it by Meyer and his seven sons. In 1949, at which point Harry had been absent from the family business for a quarter of a century, he responded promptly to the request of his Uncle Sol, then the only survivor among Meyer's sons, for help in reorganizing Guggenheim Brothers to keep the family banner aloft in the business world. In 1951 he became senior partner of the firm, a position he still holds. Also in 1951, again for similar reasons and after an absence of many years from the enterprise at hand, he oversaw the merger of two smaller Guggenheim-controlled organizations into the present Anglo-Lautaro Nitrate Company, whose plants in the Chilean Andes produce approximately 65 per cent of the world's natural nitrate and iodine, and over whose destinies Harry presided as board chairman and chief executive officer until his retirement in 1962. In 1959, once again with the idea of resurrecting past familial glories, he engineered the revival of the old mine-hunting firm of Guggenex. The time had come, he said in a letter to the partners of Guggenheim Brothers, to "return to the first principles of the founders and seek new projects in the field of exploitation of the products of nature useful to man," a field, he added, "in which we have a rich tradition. . . ."

While an undergraduate at Cambridge University, he was enthralled by several of his professors, notably G. Lowes Dickinson in political science, J. Maynard Keynes in economics and Oppenheim in international law. He was seriously considering some combination of their fields as a profession when in 1912 he dispatched a characteristically tactful letter to his father. "You," he wrote Mr. Dan, "have reached the summit of your industrial mountain, and I ought now to climb my own." In his reply the elder Guggenheim denied having reached any "summit" and added that there was still room for Harry on the old Guggenheim mountainside. Harry went along with this, returning to the States after taking his first degree at Cambridge, to devote the following decade—with time out for service in World War I—to the family business. When he retired from the original firm of Guggenheim Brothers in 1923, he had been a partner since its formation in 1916, and for the next six years he was to retain his directorships in the Braden Copper Company, the Kennecott Copper Corporation, and the Utah Copper Company.

As the years wore on he found other mountains more to his liking. Diplomacy was an early enthusiasm. In 1928 influential friends sought to inject him into the Coolidge administration as Assistant Secretary of the Navy for Aeronautics. He discouraged their efforts. Hoover, then Secretary of Commerce, offered him a similar post in that department. He turned it down. He regarded aeronautics, he said, as primarily a means to an end, an adjunct to international relations, a method of improving communications among peoples. What he would like was a diplomatic post, preferably in Latin America, which was "terra cognita" because of his long years there tending to family business interests. When Hoover succeeded Coolidge in the White House, he heeded Harry's wishes and sent him to Cuba.

Cuba's troubles during the period of Harry Guggenheim's ambassadorship make timely reading in the light of recent developments. Following its inception as a republic in 1902, the Pearl of the Antilles had known many difficulties and these had reached a new height after the collapse of the sugar boom in 1920. The island to which Harry came in November of 1929 was, in his own words, a land "of closed mansions, mortgaged farms, uncultivated cane fields . . . unemployment, misery, and undernourishment." Naturally there was political unrest, aggravated by the tendency of educated Cubans of the professional class to regard politics as first of all a means of livelihood, "to live on the budget," as an island philosopher once wrote, "not on the soil."

Commenting on the new ambassador's official reception, the Toledo (Ohio) *News* headlined its editorial, "Guggenheim Meets

Harry Guggenheim making a speech at the Maine Monument, Havana, in 1931 during his ambassadorship in Cuba.

the Terror." The reference was to square-faced, bespectacled General Gerardo Machado y Morales, president of the republic since 1925. Earlier in his administration Machado had introduced social and agrarian reforms, had adhered to constitutional procedures. Later, he had contrived to increase the presidential term from four to six years. Following his re-election in 1928, he had embarked on a dictatorial regime marked by illegal imprisonment and murder of his political opponents.

Over this tempest floated the Platt Amendment, under which the United States was empowered to intervene in island affairs to preserve orderly government. In theory, American interpretation of the amendment—an interpretation originated by Elihu Root as McKinley's Secretary of War—was that intervention would be justified only in the event of governmental breakdown. In actual practice American policy had been inconsistent, with frequent departures from the narrow Root interpretation. Guggenheim's first official act was to ask clarification. His instructions were to follow a policy of strict nonintervention, of neutrality as between Machado and his opposition. It was a policy which put him in the position of a soldier armed with a gun he was forbidden to shoot. Conceivably he would not have fired even if he had been free to do so, for wherever he turned, his gaze took in a dead end. On the one hand Machado was a tyrant, ruthless and corrupt. On the other hand the numerous leaders of the opposition were united only in their hatred of the man in power. On other issues they were divided, a situation that indicated the overthrow of the dictator would only dump the country into the damaging turmoil of a scrabble for position among the victors.

Harry adhered to his instructions through thick and thin. There was a good deal of thick. In the summer of 1931 the opposition mounted a short and unsuccessful armed rebellion. Even under the narrowest interpretation of the Platt Amendment, to say nothing of international usage, Harry would have been within his rights in calling for American intervention on the side of the prevailing government, at least to the extent of an embargo on the shipment of arms to the rebels in Cuba. No such action was requested or even considered.

Throughout 1930 and 1931 his neutral course was widely

condemned in the American press. "Guggenheim's Support Is All That Holds Machado in Power," the Washington *Evening Star* declared in a headline characteristic of many. The charge, as the *Christian Science Monitor* pointed out, was "shallow," a misinterpretation of what was happening. In the spring of 1930 the American government informed the Cuban ambassador of its desire to send two warships to Cuba on a friendly visit. Machado was delighted with the prospect. He perceived in the exchange of courtesies between himself and the commander of the visiting fleet an opportunity to show the world that his government had the support of powerful U.S.A. Harry, determined to avoid any such impression, saw to it that the warships did not come.

From the American left came the accusation, in the words of Carleton Beals, that Harry was the real tyrant of Cuba, that Machado was only a "minor . . . executioner carrying out the mandates, transmitted by Ambassador Guggenheim, of an unholy trinity of American bank and utility magnates." Less melodramatic versions of this charge were repeated in many segments of the press, buttressed by information from "reliable" sources—meaning Cuban rebel leaders stationed in the United States—that Ambassador Guggenheim had urged his government to endorse a $350 million loan to Machado. The facts: At the time of Harry's assumption of his post in Havana, negotiations were under way between the Cuban government and American bankers for refunding $40 million of Special Public Works certificates and for borrowing an additional $20 million to complete Cuba's central highway and other projects. Harry advised his government to put no obstacles in the way of these negotiations. He argued that termination of work on the highway would only increase Cuban unemployment. Furthermore, the highway had been built in sections. Failure to obtain the requested loan would leave incomplete and useless a road into which millions had already been poured. After the financing was consummated, Harry consistently advised his government against further monetary aid for the Machado administration.

At intervals, unofficially, he persuaded the Cuban strong man to release political prisoners. On several occasions his behind-the-scenes intercession saved the lives of rioting students and other adherents of the rebel junta. He conferred repeatedly with the leaders of both sides in an effort to find a peaceful resolution. His own memoranda of conversations with Machado trace his efforts to bring about long overdue adjustments in the island economy; to persuade the dictator to revoke his suspension of constitutional guarantees, to lift his censorship on the opposition press, and to open the University of Havana, closed after its students assumed a dominant role in the rebellion. In 1930 Machado gave Harry his promise to effect these reforms, going so far as to introduce a bill in the Cuban Congress. The bill never became law. In a quiet doublecross, Machado, acting on advice from his ambassador to Washington, secretly informed the members of his rubber-stamp Congress that the reforms had been suggested by Guggenheim, acting as an individual, and that the latter's government would hold to its hands-off policy whether they were passed or not. Knowing that approval of the reforms would pave the way to their political ouster, the Cuban congressmen happily voted them down. Following the unsuccessful revolt of 1931, Machado intensified his terroristic practices and remained in power until 1933 when, during the ambassadorship of Harry's successor, Sumner Welles, he was forced to flee by a general strike and a defecting army.

In short, Harry appears to have done his best under circumstances where in the absence of a realistic American policy no one's best was good enough. During the outbreaks of terrorism he protected American lives and property in Cuba without violating his government's nonintervention policy, although personally dubious as to its wisdom. "The continuance of the policy," he reported to the State Department in January of 1933, "does not commend itself as a thorough, progressive or final solution of the Cuban problem. It does not itself remedy existing conditions in Cuba, and because of its misinterpretation the Cubans do not feel wholly free to demonstrate their capacity to do so." His struggle to persuade the opposing parties to settle their differences by bloodless means was much criticized at the time. Today it looks anything but reprehensible in view of the subsequent overthrow of another Machado-like Cuban dictator, friendly to the United States, and his replacement by Fidel

Castro, subservient to the Soviet Union. An interesting aftermath of Harry's experience in the island republic were the changes wrought by the Roosevelt administration in U.S.-Cuban relations: abrogation of the Platt Amendment, conclusion of new commercial and political treaties, and a cut in the sugar tariff—all moves previously recommended by Guggenheim.

Officially, Harry Guggenheim's diplomatic career ended in April of 1933 when he resigned his Cuban post. Unofficially he has made a number of subsequent forays into the international arena. In 1934 he published his *The United States and Cuba,* a review of the relations of this country with its Caribbean neighbor. It received a large and universally favorable press, the Springfield (Mass.) *Republican* asserting that "for an understanding of the new Roosevelt policy toward Cuba, no book is of more pertinence or value." On December 8, 1950, at the University of Florida, he delivered before the Conference on the Caribbean at Mid-Century his *Hemisphere Integration Now,* a speech that is still frequently quoted. It was a call for changes in American foreign policy, which he criticized on several grounds, one of them being that it was Europe-oriented whereas it should be Western Hemisphere-oriented. To forestall Communist intervention in Latin America, his argument ran, this country's efforts "should be directed toward the most complete . . . integration among all the states in this Hemisphere that can be effected by diplomacy. We should make this our cornerstone of foreign policy, because this Hemisphere is our last line of defense. . . ."

Throughout the Eisenhower administration, Harry was a frequent visitor in Washington. At luncheon conferences with the President and Secretary of State Dulles, he spelled out his conviction that in its relations with Latin America the United States should go beyond Roosevelt's policy of good-neighborliness to one of "good-partnership." His concrete suggestion was that "overall charge of our Latin American diplomacy" be placed in the hands of "a man of international reputation and outstanding ability, to whom the Assistant Secretary of State for Latin America would report." Eisenhower was favorable to this proposal, but Dulles was cool, objecting principally on the grounds that it would create organization troubles within the State Department.

In the fall of 1957, with the Castro-led rebellion against Batista gaining ground, Harry was host to some worried visitors at his Long Island home—a Cuban delegation, accompanied by attorney Mario Lazo and sent north by Batista to take counsel with the former ambassador. Via the delegation, Harry relayed to Batista the same advice he had given years before to Machado—that the only way the Cuban president could head off his enemies was to abandon his dictatorial stance and institute free elections. Two years later, with Batista out and Castro in, attorney Lazo recalled the conference at Harry's home in a letter to an American friend. "In September 1957," he wrote, "Harry . . . in my presence predicted with absolute accuracy the events which have in fact occurred. It was the second time in his lifetime that he had warned a Cuban President of what was in store for him. . . . In both cases the [Cuban] President seemed to be impressed at first with the logic of Harry's advice, but also in both cases he was eventually steered away from the only course that could save him by some of his intimate political advisors."

Of recent years Harry has been known to mutter regrets at having abandoned his professional status as a diplomat. "Who knows," he has said, "if I'd stayed in the field, I might be of some use to it now, instead of becoming a jack of all trades and a master of none." He doesn't luxuriate often in these doleful might-have-been's. When he does, old friends smile. "Harry," they say, "would never be content plucking away at one string. He was born to pluck many. He's happiest that way."

The years 1936 to 1940 found him plucking a string for his home town as president of the Citizens Committee on the Control of Crime in New York, established to supplement the campaign against industrial rackets then being waged by Special Prosecutor Thomas E. Dewey. Working out of committee headquarters on Lafayette Street, a staff of trained observers maintained an hour-by-hour check on the progress of criminal cases from arrest to conviction or acquittal. By the end of the committee's last year, its files contained records of 22,000 cases and the dossiers of 43,000 offenders, all arranged and classified to present a picture of crime in the metropolis and of how it was being handled. The study brought a reform in the law enforcement and judicial proceedings of King's County along with what the New York *Herald-Tribune* described as "a marked improvement" in crime conditions in Brooklyn.

Newspaper reporters dubbed the committee members "vigilantes" and feature writers had a good time contrasting urbane Harry Guggenheim with the "ferocious, black-bearded" vigilante chieftains of the early-American West. In a syndicated column Lemuel E. Parton described Chieftain Guggenheim as "a dual personality." He said Harry was both a man of action—witness his "tearing through the sky" as a World War I aviator "like a rampageous thunderbolt"—and a man of thought who spent much of his time lying on his back in the sun piecing "cause and effect as Spinoza used to do—although Spinoza, in this mood, used to hang head downward over a cliff, to disjoint the universe." According to Parton, Guggenheim had found "the universe already disjointed" and was only interested in putting it to rights.

The committee was hampered by financial problems. A campaign to raise funds fell short of its $200,000 goal, and during the committee's final months the budget was underwritten by Harry at the rate of $800 a week. Its liquidation in December of 1940 was followed by a scrappy exchange of correspondence between its president and its official progenitor, Mayor Fiorello H. La Guardia. In a January letter Harry reminded the Mayor of the latter's request for Harry to draft for the "Little Flower's" signature a letter of appeal for funds to put the committee back in business. The Mayor had decided instead to write the appeal himself, and "Frankly," Harry wrote, "I do not think this letter [the appeal drafted by La Guardia] is any better and maybe not as good as the last letter we used, copy of which is enclosed." The Mayor's reaction to Harry's January letter was to return it, scrawling his own reply in pen at the bottom of it.

"Dear Harry," he wrote. "As usual you are wrong—my [appeal] letter is better—but have it your way—Send along the letter & I'll sign it. Fiorello." The appeal failed to raise the necessary funds and the committee took its place among things past.[3]

Fun's Fun, But . . . .

Leo Gottlieb, Harry Guggenheim's attorney and a man of notable perception, has stated that he finds "revealing" what he calls Harry's practice of turning his hobbies into paying businesses or into civic services or both. "Harry," he says, "just can't play. Apparently he feels honor-bound, perhaps out of deference to his hard-working father and uncles, to convert even what other men consider play into work."

His racing career is an example. He "came on the track" in 1934 with the purchase of a thoroughbred yearling called Nebraska City for $400. Nebraska City didn't amount to much. Undiscouraged, Harry bought more horses and established a stable, which he subsequently named after Cain Hoy, his plantation on the Wando River some twenty miles north of Charleston, South Carolina, Cain Hoy being a Gullah Negro corruption of "cane hay," a native plant whose palmlike leaf is eaten by cattle and whose stalk is used in rattan chairs. By 1951 he had made a sufficient impact on the racing world to become a member of the New York Jockey Club, the first Jew to be admitted to its socially rarefied roster. In 1953 his Dark Star gave the immortal Native Dancer its only defeat to win the Kentucky Derby. Ragusa earned Harry the title Breeder of the Year for 1963. He also bred Bald Eagle, the only horse to win the Washington, D. C. International twice. Cain Hoy's *Turn-to is one of the most desirable studs in Kentucky, and Never Bend—two-year-old champion in 1962 and among the three best in the country the following year—was put to stud in 1964. In 1959 Cain Hoy, with $757,000 winnings, led the country in purses won; and in 1960, with $715,000, it came in second. Today the Cain Hoy stable is a highly successful operation. In 1954 Harry was a ringleader in the establishment of the New York Racing Association, the nonprofit organization which now owns and operates most of New York State's thoroughbred race tracks under a unique plan which permits all profits to go to the state in taxes or back into the tracks in improvements. John W. Hanes, former president of the organization, credits Harry with being the prime mover.

Another example of Guggenheim's aversion to fun for fun's

sake is the manner in which he went about acquiring the land he now owns in South Carolina. His instructions to the agent who negotiated the purchases in 1934 were that "I am not looking for a game preserve. I want property that can be made productive enough to contribute to the security of my children and grandchildren." Eventually, for an expenditure averaging six dollars an acre, he acquired the 11,000-acre Cain Hoy plantation and 4,000-acre Daniel's Island (geographically a peninsula since only a creek separates it from the mainland) in Charleston Harbor. Today Cain Hoy supports a thriving timber-cutting enterprise, the island a growing cattle-running operation.

It was Harry's conviction that "people who make a business out of pleasure seldom are happy" that prompted him to help found the Long Island newspaper *Newsday*. A venture that was to become one of the legends of American journalism, its development goes back to the early months of Harry's marriage to the late Alicia Patterson, second oldest of the three daughters of the late Joseph Medill Patterson, founder of the New York *Daily News*. Trim, petite and appealing with her stabbing Celtic smile and temperament to match, her ready wit and throaty, halting way of speaking, Alicia Patterson, at the time of her marriage to Harry, was a refugee from two previous marriages, both childless, both terminated by divorce. Restless and energetic, she had spent the last few years fighting a losing battle with boredom as a roving sportswoman and nightclub habitué. In 1940 Harry diagnosed her discontent as that of a lively mind not having enough to occupy it. In his opinion "everybody ought to have a job," so he purchased for $70,000 the facilities of a little Long Island newspaper that had gone out of business after nine issues.

From these beginnings grew *Newsday*. It was not an easy growth. It took about seven years of brilliant editing on Alicia's part, and a total investment of some three-quarters of a million dollars on Harry's part to bring *Newsday* from a struggling tabloid with average first-year circulation of 15,000 to its present status. Now the eighth-largest evening newspaper in the country, it has a circulation in excess of 385,000, occupies its own new plant in Garden City, employs over eleven hundred people (not counting six thousand delivery boys), carries more advertising

Alicia Patterson Guggenheim.

Harry Guggenheim at his desk at *Newsday*. (Below) The *Newsday* plant, Garden City, Long Island.

linage than any New York newspaper—more than any United States newspaper except the Los Angeles *Times*—and is possessor of the 1954 Pulitzer prize for an exposé of a union shakedown in the suburban counties it serves. During her lifetime Alicia owned 49 per cent of what is now Newsday, Incorporated, against Harry's 51; and when moved by a great national issue, he put in his "two per cent worth," to utilize a bon mot struck off by *Time* magazine, *Newsday* readers were sometimes regaled by opposing editorials on facing pages, signed respectively by Harry (moderate Republican) and Alicia (progressive Democrat). From the beginning Harry has supervised all of the newspaper's business and financial matters, concerning himself with its expansion and construction policies and with the direction of all labor relations and negotiations. During the last twenty-three years of her life Alicia ran—or rather "drove," as one of her editors once said—the editorial department. Alicia drove herself, too. She was still very young, only fifty-six, at the time of her death on July 2, 1963. Almost a thousand people packed the Garden City church in which her funeral services were held and few women of modern times have been the recipient of more tributes in the American press.

She was the third Mrs. Harry F. Guggenheim. Harry's first marriage, in 1910, was to Helen Rosenberg, member of a New York industrial family; his second, in 1923, to the former Caroline Morton, daughter of Paul Morton, Theodore Roosevelt's Secretary of Navy. Two daughters were born to the first marriage, one to the second. Joan Florence, born in 1913, is now Mrs. Albert Van de Maele of New York and an interior decorator. Nancy, born in 1915, is Mrs. Thomas Williams of San Francisco and the mother of two sons, Dana and George, Jr., Draper, by a previous marriage. Diane, born to Harry's second marriage in 1923, is Mrs. William Meek and the mother of a grown daughter, Carol Langstaff, the child of the first of two prior marriages, both terminated by divorce.

For two years Harry and his second wife spent much of their time in Europe, gathering art objects for their Sands Point home on Long Island Sound. A thirty-room Norman-style manor, built of rough bricks, and perched on a promontory overlooking the

Sound, with walled-in court and numerous towers, the house was completed in 1923 and called Falaise, French for "cliff."

From the Sound side Falaise presents a fortress-like façade, but its interior, with its rich woodwork and subdued decor, has an air of intimacy despite the spaciousness of some of the first-floor rooms, notably the living room with its walk-in fireplace overhung by an imported flamboyant Gothic mantel of rough-hewn stone under a Norwegian Gothic tapestry. Also on the main floor are two libraries, two dining rooms, a small card room, and a central hall boxed by an open stair to a gallery dominated by full-length portraits of Mr. and Mrs. Dan. Off the living room, on the Sound side, an open terrace overlooks the water. On the other side, a broad door-window gives access to a swimming pool, cornered with white dolphins and shaded by honey locusts above plantings of orange trees and massed lilies. Most of the furnishings are in keeping with the architecture, but not all. On the tile floor of the central hall stand some little cast-iron cows of abstract design, the work of a modern sculptor; and the figure of a South Seas island girl on a nearby table is one of the few sculptures by the French impressionist painter Paul Gauguin. Harry keeps his racing trophies in two basement rooms, gentles and stables his yearlings in a far corner of the 89-acre estate whose alternating parks, woodlands and orchards provide a scenic approach to the house itself.

Carol, as the second Mrs. Guggenheim was known to her familiars, was with Harry during the Cuban days. Newspaper pictures of the period show a slender, fine-boned woman with a piquant face and dreamy, half-moon eyes. She was the mistress of Falaise in 1927 when Lindbergh, soon after his New York-to-Paris solo flight, came here to write *We,* a handwritten page of which still hangs in the windswept "Sound Room" on the second floor where most of the book was written.

The Lindbergh who now sits on the terrace of his Connecticut home, reminiscing on those bygone days, is physically little unlike the "wonderful boy" who became America's hero in the late 1920's. Graying somewhat, a little heavier than in youth but still slender, he moves quickly when some errand takes him from his

The entrance to Falaise (above) and the lodge at Cain Hoy, the Guggenheim plantation in South Carolina.

chair, with a tendency to lean forward as if eager to reach his destination.

Of his quiet, brown-haired hostess at Falaise, "Anne [Mrs. Lindbergh]," the flier remarks, "often says that Carol belonged to the Long Island society world, but she was never of it. She had little interest in the social whirl. She was happiest at home, knitting on rugs and tapestries, or painting and drawing in a studio in one of the tower rooms. One of her hobbies was making silhouettes of her guests. She'd throw a light on you so that the outlines of your profile were transferred to drawing paper on the wall. Then she'd black in the outlines. There used to be dozens of profiles in one of the libraries. Many were of well-known people. You could recognize them right away."

Of Harry Guggenheim: "He has great faith in the future and the vision that goes with it. He has ideas and ideals and he implements them with action. In addition he is always good company and a gentleman."

In 1939 Harry's second marriage ended as had his first, in the divorce courts. What happened? "Me," is his answer. "My first two wives were both wonderful women. The failure of both marriages was entirely my fault."

Always the gentleman![4]

Patient, Impatient, Perfect and Otherwise

Gentleman Harry has one trait that more of his friends speak of than any other. Lindbergh's way of saying it is that he is "a man of informed intuitiveness. Insight with stability," the famous flier adds. "I'd say those were among the qualities that have made him an influence in the aerospace world. I remember a conference at Falaise—it was about 1928. Doolittle was there, and I was there, and there was an executive of one of the big manufacturing companies who was both an engineer and a highly experienced pilot. We got to talking about specifications for passenger-transport planes of the future. The executive-engineer said that the future airliner should be a biplane because of the structural advantages, that it should be of wood, wire, and fabric construction to obtain lightness, and that it should carry a lot of passengers rather than have a fast cruising speed. Harry didn't agree with this at all. He didn't argue about materials or types of construction. He passed right over those details and said the success of aviation depended on building planes that would fly very much faster in addition to carrying a lot of passengers. Of all the aviation pioneers I knew, I think the two who had the clearest vision into the future, and of the steps that had to be taken to get there, were Juan Trippe* and Harry Guggenheim."

John R. Dunning, Dean of Engineering at Columbia University, expresses it differently: "Intuitive, yes, but Harry's no guesser. He knows how to listen. He listens to the scientists around him and that way he senses the future direction of their line of interest. Call it justified brain-picking, brain-picking on the benevolent level."

To English-born Walter Moulton, his valet for forty years, Mr. Guggenheim is a hero. "I know it's an odd way to put it," Walter says, "since I'm only two years his junior, but the Boss has been a father to me. I've learned, oh, such a lot just from watching his mode of life. There's that insight of his, you know; that way he has of really seeing what he's looking at. When the Boss looks at you he isn't just gazing at you over his whiskers. He's sizing you up. Then there's the way he takes care of himself. Never more than a finger of hard liquor at a time, and not many times in a day, I can tell you. Never overeats. Great on the exercise, especially in the old days before the doctor made him give up his tennis. And then there's his patience—ah, that's his great quality."

There are others whose positions entitle them to call Harry Guggenheim "Boss" who say his patience has its limits. They describe him as a perfectionist. They say that when he's displeased with the way work is done he can be sharp to the point of drawing blood, so sharp that some employees become immobilized, preferring to do as little as possible rather than incur the Boss' wrath by doing the wrong thing.

No one can be long in Harry Guggenheim's company without noting the ease with which he becomes bored. An interesting

* President, Pan American World Airways, Inc.

problem, a new idea, so long as the conversation revolves around these things, his attention rarely flags. Let the problem be solved, the idea lose its freshness, and he begins to blow air through his teeth, venting a breathy, tuneless whistle, sure sign that Mr. Guggenheim has temporarily deserted the conversation to browse among his own thoughts.

On the whole he is an attentive listener, genial, frank (but never indiscreet), engaging, sensitive to and respectful of others' concerns. No matter how warmly he expresses these qualities, however, there is always a margin of impersonality—the self-protectiveness of a highly self-aware and self-controlled man who has taught himself to be at ease with his own company and whose patience, whatever its limits, is largely the result of having learned not to expect too much of others. "You know," he was once heard to remark with a tremulous smile, "in this life you have to deal with a good many sons-of-bitches!"

From Cambridge Upward

The occupations already mentioned by no means comprehend the range of Harry's activities. He saw overseas duty in both World Wars, returning from the first with the rank of lieutenant commander in the Navy, from the second with that of captain. He was over age at the time of Pearl Harbor. Even so, "I'm going back in the service," he told Alicia a short time later. "You stay home and keep store"—store being the then struggling *Newsday*. Volunteering in the Navy, he served first as assistant executive officer at Floyd Bennett Field, later as commandant at Mercer Field, New Jersey, and still later from a carrier as machine gunner on air raids against Japanese positions in the Pacific.

Born on August 23, 1890, Harry, like his sister Gladys, who came along six years later, was a "vacation baby." He began life in the town of West End on the Jersey coast where in those days all of the Guggenheim families took the sea breezes during the warmer months. He grew up partly in West End, partly in Elberon, another Jersey coastal resort, partly in New York City. There were also weeks nearly every summer at Saranac Lake in upstate New York, where Mr. Dan joined the Knollwood Lake

Club so that he could fish, hunt, and go boating with his two sons.

When Harry was ten, Mr. Dan decided that the time had come for him to learn that life is not all fishing, hunting and "naphtha launches." Accordingly, he put Harry and his cousin Edmond into the chicken business. The Elberon summer place was the locus of this enterprise; an accountant and a professional chicken raiser were hired, and Mr. Dan's friend, Louis Marshall of the law firm of Guggenheimer, Untermeyer and Marshall, launched the venture by composing a poem entitled "To Henry and His Hennery." For months the youthful partners tended incubators, mixed rations, repaired the ravages to their "hennery" left by an autumn cyclone, and delivered eggs to the manager of the St. Regis Hotel, their principal customer. After two years Mr. Dan liquidated the business on the assumption that its entrepreneurs had got the idea. "Father's objective," Harry explains, "was to give us experience in business and to teach us how easy it is to lose money. He was eminently successful. We got the experience and father lost the money."

In nostalgic moments Harry produces other vignettes from his youth: His excitement on the day of the sinking of the *Maine* on the eve of the Spanish-American War—he was eight at the time and unaware of the ways of Hearstian propaganda . . . the day he was arrested for speeding in the family car, the officer insisting that he was going 40 miles an hour—he was fifteen then and full of beans. A year later, having been graduated from Columbia Grammar School in New York, he enrolled in The Sheffield Scientific School at Yale to study mining and metallurgy. At the close of the term, he informed his father that he had fallen in love with the pretty brunette who was to be his first wife. He wanted to leave school and get married. Mr. Dan was heartbroken—not about Helen Rosenberg, whom he admired—but that his son had no wish to complete his education. However, "All right," he said, "since you insist on going to work and getting married, down to Mexico with you." Down Harry went to labor in the ore-sorting bins of the family smeltery at Aquascalientes for a dollar a day, Mexican money.

By the time Harry's marriage took place on November 9, 1910,

Harry Guggenheim ready to take off for a strike from the U.S.S. *Nehenta Bay,* near Okinawa, June, 1945.

Mr. Dan had persuaded his younger son that higher education had its advantages, and through the offices of an English friend, whose own son was studying at Pembroke, third oldest of the Cambridge colleges, he arranged for Harry to seek entrance there. Harry proposed to study economics, political philosophy and government. The examinations assumed a knowledge of Latin and Greek. He had no Greek, but with the aid of a "pony" he got by, and in. From Cambridge he was to obtain two degrees, a B.A. in 1913 and an M.A. in 1923, and during his three undergraduate years he became a Cambridge tennis blue and president of the Pembroke College Lawn Tennis Club. Today one of his valued possessions is an album of that period. There are reviews of tennis matches in the spring and summer of 1913. "Guggenheim," says one, "is weak on his service, but has a pretty style, volleys well and uses his head. He is a hardened offender at foot-faulting, which must be remedied. . . ." There are pictures of Harry, looking outrageously handsome in his playing togs; pictures of his powerfully built partner, H. C. (Carly) Webb of Christ's College, whose fate was to have a curious effect on his own.

The Cambridge years were to exert a pronounced influence on his future attitudes. He returned from England a confirmed Anglophile, convinced of the rightness of the English reliance on tradition, of the belief, as expressed by an English essayist of American descent, that "the most truly and deeply democratic doctrine is that which . . . does not disdain to poll the franchise of the dead." During the intervening years he has received several honorary degrees from American universities, accepting them gracefully but with the reservation that "I think honorary degrees should be given only to those who have distinguished themselves in literature or science." An invitation in 1962 to become an Honorary Fellow of Pembroke, however, was accepted with gratitude and enthusiasm.

Indirectly the tennis courts of Cambridge were to be the matrix of the Daniel Guggenheim Fund for the Promotion of Aeronautics, or at any rate of Harry's share in its conception. The annals on this go back to the onset of the First World War. Carly Webb, Harry's Cambridge tennis partner, was one of the so-called "first hundred thousand" Britishers to volunteer, one of the first to be killed. It was the news of Carly's death in battle that prompted Harry to consider learning to fly, looking forward to the day when he might be called on to take his friend's place in the fighting line. Early in 1917, while vacationing in Florida, he decided that American entrance in the war was imminent and took his first ten days of instruction at Lake Worth in Palm Beach. Returning North, he purchased a flying boat of his own—a triplane. It now lies at the bottom of Lake George, New York, where it found its resting place when a friend who had borrowed it made a crash landing.

Back North, young Guggenheim and four or five other men organized a private flying unit at Manhasset Bay, Long Island. In the fall he and other members of his unit applied for commissions in the United States Naval Reserve and Harry was sent to Bay Shore to begin taking his naval aviator's tests. Ordered overseas shortly thereafter, he won his wings at the American bombing and gunnery school at Arcachon near Bordeaux. Later, at Lake Bolsini outside Rome, he qualified also as an Italian naval aviator.

One of his missions, the one that took him to Rome, was to obtain some Caproni bombers that had been promised to the United States Navy. The United States Army also had its eye on the bombers and Harry soon found himself matching wits with the Army's agent, an Italian-speaking captain named Fiorello La Guardia. The Little Flower spread the tale that Harry was really seeking the bombers for the copper interests—"a neat stratagem," Harry would comment later, "but it didn't work." The Navy got the bombers, although the bombers never got to the Navy. All of them crashed while crossing the Alps. Years later Harry decided to back La Guardia, then running for mayor of New York on a fusion ticket. When the two met at a campaign dinner, "So," said His Honor-to-be, "you're the guy who put it over on me in Italy."

After the war Harry watched with concern the failure of civil aviation to develop in this country as anticipated. In the spring of 1925 he accepted an invitation to attend a meeting called by Chancellor Elmer Ellsworth Brown of New York University to consider ways of creating a school of aeronautics in the University's College of Engineering. Present at the conference, in addition to the university head and Harry, were a couple of aviators, a battery of public relations experts, and Prof. Alexander Klemin, who was teaching the few aeronautics courses then offered by the university and who had suggested the school.

The public relations men proposed a campaign, to be launched by a luncheon, to raise half a million dollars. Harry dissented. "A campaign," he contended, "would be futile. At present the American people aren't that interested in aviation. They're likely to fear their money would be wasted." Asked for a counterproposal, he suggested seeking out a single individual with vision and money enough to endow a school. Asked to draft a letter for submission to a few such persons, Harry agreed on condition that no members of his own family be solicited.

He outlined the letter that night. It so happened that he was spending it at Hempstead House, the Long Island mansion Mr. Dan had purchased some years earlier. Before going to bed, Harry asked his father to criticize what he had written. When the letter had been read, Mr. Dan slipped it into the pocket of his dressing gown, saying, "Let me think about this overnight." At breakfast next morning, "Well, Harry," he said, "I've thought about your letter and I've decided to endow the school myself." On June 15 Mr. Dan's gift of half a million to the university was announced, and on the morning of Thursday, October 23—standing on a knoll of the university's uptown campus at University Heights in the Bronx—he turned up a spadeful of earth on the site of the building that was to house the first School of Aeronautics in an American institution of higher learning.

"As I am an old man whose active days are past," Mr. Dan said to the some four hundred faculty members, students and aviation pioneers present, "I shall dedicate the rest of my life, with the active aid of my son, Harry F. Guggenheim, to the study and promotion of the science of aeronautics. I shall do this as a part of my duty to my country whose ample opportunities have ever been at my hand and whose bountiful blessings I have had the good fortune to enjoy."

With one School of Aeronautics under way, Mr. Dan was all

for establishing others. His son put a quietus on that. For the time being, the younger man reasoned, the proliferation of schools of aeronautics would be putting the cart before the horse. First, ways must be found of building an industry capable of supplying jobs to the schools' graduates. "My father is on my tail about this business," he informed the late Ivy Lee, father of modern public relations, "but I don't think we're ready for a lot of schools. There must be something else we can do."

There was. "Why not set up a fund for promotion?" was the suggestion of tall, impressive, world-traveling Ivy Lee.

No sooner said than begun; only now it was Mr. Dan's turn to caution against haste. Headlines were being made by aviation, or rather, by an outspoken army general known as Billy Mitchell. Brigadier General William Lendrum Mitchell, who had commanded U.S. Air Forces in France during the war, was demanding an independent air arm and buttressing his proposal with attacks on Army and Navy leaders for what he called their "neglect of air power." Soon he was to be demoted and court-martialed for his pains. Meanwhile President Coolidge had appointed a special Air Board to inquire into the matter.

"To be of any value," Mr. Dan pointed out, "our Fund must be tendered to the government. With all the hue and cry that's going on, we'd better make certain that the government will accept it." Harry got the point. Late in December of 1925 he headed for Washington to spend what he would later describe as one of the most picaresque days of his life.[5]

"Show Mr. Guggenheim to the Elevator"

It began in the morning in the Washington office of Dwight W. Morrow, New York financier and philanthropist, whom Coolidge had appointed chairman of the special Air Board. An old friend of the Guggenheim family, Morrow had arranged an appointment for Harry with the President. He listened with interest to Harry's outline of the proposed fund. "For the life of me," he said, "I can't imagine Cal Coolidge turning down what amounts to an offer to the government of almost three million dollars in private money." He then wished Harry well as the latter took off for the White House where he found Mr. Coolidge in the executive office.

As Morrow had predicted, the President showed interest in the projected fund, and, when Harry had finished his recital, picked up a phone and called the Secretary of Commerce. "Hoover, be at the White House for lunch at twelve-thirty," he said, and hung up. Gentleman Harry was somewhat shocked at the brevity of the President's invitation, of his failure to so much as ask if Mr. Hoover might have other plans for the next hour.

Hoover arrived shortly. Meanwhile the men in the executive office had been joined by Mrs. Coolidge and a presidential adviser, and the party moved to the family dining room. During lunch the projected fund was further discussed. Coolidge nodded approval of everything except Harry's statement that the airplane would satisfy the need for more speed in travel. "What's the use of getting there quicker," he asked, "if you haven't got something better to say when you arrive?" After lunch the discussion was continued in the executive office until Coolidge terminated it with the words, "Hoover, show Mr. Guggenheim to the elevator" —and Gentleman Harry hastened back to New York to inform Mr. Dan that his Fund had governmental blessing and that the Chief Magistrate of the United States was "pretty high-handed with his office help."

A few weeks later, in January of 1926, a staff was assembled for the Daniel Guggenheim Fund for the Promotion of Aeronautics, the patriotic gift of the grateful son and grandson of hard-working Jewish immigrants, who himself had never been up in an airplane and, because of a serious heart ailment, never would be.

VI

Mr. Dan's Fund

In a 1928 press release the Daniel Guggenheim Fund for the Promotion of Aeronautics complained that newspaper reports had "mistakenly connected the name of the . . . Fund . . . with a reported invention of an electromagnetic [airplane] motor." Troubled by rumors that people were investing money in the "reported invention," the Fund directors wished it understood that their organization had "no connection whatsoever with this enterprise."[1] An unusual document, since throughout the four years of the Fund's existence the aeronautical developments with which it had "no connection" were few and far between. During this period the organization's headquarters in New York City—six rooms on the tenth floor of 598 Madison Avenue—were the starting point of forty-nine distinct programs, all designed, in Mr. Dan's words, to provide aviation with "immediate, practical and substantial assistance."

Fourteen programs were addressed to the commercial development of the field, thirteen to scientific research, two to the distribution of information, and twenty to education. In addition Harry, as president of the organization, delivered a score of public addresses on aviation in all parts of the country; and the Fund prepared and distributed a stream of publications, ranging from treatises on abstruse aspects of aerodynamics to a popular study of the causes and cure of airsickness.

Many of the publications were pure promotion, pamphlets and press releases designed to awaken the public to the potentialities of aviation. Much of this literature still makes pertinent and in some cases amusing reading. For example, Bulletin 3 divided

Daniel Guggenheim with some of the trustees of his Fund for the Promotion of Aeronautics, 1927. Left to right, seated: John D. Ryan, Daniel Guggenheim, Orville Wright, W. F. Durand. Standing: J. W. Miller (Secretary), F. Trubee Davison, Elihu Root, Jr., H. I. Cone, Charles A. Lindbergh, Harry F. Guggenheim, Robert A. Millikan.

commercial aviation into two classifications: aerial transport, in which planes operate over regular routes on regular schedules; and aerial service, in which they are put to myriad uses, such as aerial photography, crop dusting, exploration, special transportation of the taxicab variety and map-making. To emphasize the values of aerial photography, the bulletin described a survey of real estate in five Connecticut towns for tax purposes. "In Middletown alone," the publication revealed, "the aerial survey discovered 1,896 buildings upon which taxes had not previously been paid." The building owners' loss was Middletown's gain, for the survey made it possible to lower the tax rate from 30 to 24 mills and to erect new schools and other improvements. Forty-two-square-mile Middletown was the first of the communities to be so appraised. Indeed, it was the first ever to be appraised by means of an aerial map, the production and delivery of which took only sixty days and cost the city fathers a trifling $4,000.

Naturally the programs sponsored by the Fund varied in size, that is, in the amounts of money appropriated. In this respect several were small, although not necessarily small in consequences: $250, for example, to the Department of Commerce toward the expenses of an international civil aeronautics conference; $945.61 for a report on the practices of European aircraft makers; $196.15 to help defray the expenses of a South American delegation interested in the practices of American aircraft makers; $2,000 to Prof. E. A. Stalker of the University of Michigan to test the possible application of two-stroke-cycle aircraft engines; $1,981.20 to the Dutch scientist, E. Kaupa and $3,750 to Prof. W. L. Everitt of Ohio State University for research looking to the creation of improved altimeters; $4,231.98 for fellowships for aviation study in Europe; and $1,000 for a survey of aviation insurance by Captain (now Brigadier General) Ray A. Dunn, whose recommendations to the industry, according to James E. Hoskins—consultant on life insurance actuarial problems to Federal aviation agencies—were to have "some useful indirect effects" on the solution of problems connected with the coverage of aviation risks.

One relatively small program produced large results—a campaign, launched in 1928, to persuade eight thousand American communities with populations of 10,000 or less to identify themselves by roof markings as a guide to aviators. Within the next two years, 4,074 towns and cities, previously unidentified, had put up such markings, and when the project came to an end, its records were placed with the Department of Commerce so that that agency could continue the campaign. Most of the work was done on a voluntary basis by local postmasters. The Fund's contribution, $16,000, went to the preparation and distribution of 51,700 letters, 68,000 bulletins on roof marking, 38,000 questionnaires, and 8,000 copies of a memo on landing facilities.

Ideas for the Fund's projects came from many sources. Some were the outgrowth of research undertaken before the organization was established, including a survey of the needs and plans of the few American universities then offering courses in aeronautics.

Some simply rolled in. No sooner was the Fund set up than it became a mecca for "all manner of people with all manner of schemes"—to quote Vice Admiral (then Captain) Emory S. Land who, when Admiral Hutchison I. Cone was named to the Federal Shipping Board in 1928, temporarily left his post as assistant chief of the Navy's Bureau of Aeronautics, to replace Cone as Fund vice-president and executive. There are some who may best remember wiry, straight-speaking, pipe-smoking "Jerry" Land as one of the country's most colorful football linesmen for twenty-five years; others, no doubt, as chief of the two agencies, which during World War II spearheaded the construction of America's 56-million-ton Navy, the largest in history. Still active at eighty-three, Land is now a director and consultant with General Dynamics Corporation. Chatting in his Washington office, he said that the memories of his eighteen months with the Fund leave him with but one regret.

"I wish now," he said, "I had kept a log of all the crazy notions that were presented to us. Scores were mailed in, others brought in by their inventors: Précis for projects that would have cost a billion dollars to consummate, blueprints of everything from perforated ailerons to aircraft propelled by blowing air out of the sides.

"Don't get me wrong. A lot of prize ideas came in, including some that we were fools enough to pass up. Personally, I made some real impressive mistakes. For instance, there was a lot of talk in those days about a bloke by the name of Goddard, Robert H. Goddard, who was shooting off firecrackers up in Massachusetts. The talk was that one of these days Goddard was going to put some of his rockets on the moon. It was all a hashish-smoker's dream to me. Fortunately, Harry Guggenheim and his father were smart enough to see what Goddard was up to and to get behind him."

According to Land, one of the most interesting things about the Fund was the streamlined manner in which it was run. Strictly administrative costs, including $110.11 for ice for the office water cooler, came to only about three per cent of all monies expended. "We were juggling a mess of projects there for a while," Land recalls. "I reckon most people were under the impression that we had a mammoth staff. Truth is, you could have drowned the lot of us in a washtub. Harry worked hard. J. W. Miller—he was our secretary—worked hard. We had a part-time treasurer and myself. For the rest we depended on the intermittent services of paid consultants, volunteers in the case of specific projects, five representatives of the Fund in as many European countries, and a handful of stenographers."

Many ideas were the product of a European junket, early in 1926, by Harry Guggenheim, Admiral Cone and Jerome C. Hunsaker, then a naval attaché with the rank of commander at the American embassy in London, now Professor Emeritus at Massachusetts Institute of Technology, whose aeronautical department he headed for many years. In England, France, Germany, Holland and Spain, Harry and the Admiral inspected educational, scientific, manufacturing and operating aviation establishments; talked with such greats among the early theoreticians in the field as Prof. Ludwig Prandtl of Goettingen, Germany; obtained in each country a report on the status of its governmental controls over aviation; and looked into the work being done by its aeronautical societies, clubs and publications. In Italy Hunsaker covered the same ground. Returning to the United States in late April, Harry and Admiral Cone laid before their trustees thirty-five suggestions, practically all of which were to take shape as Fund-supported undertakings.

During the lifetime of the Guggenheim endowment, aviation made dramatic advances. The extent of the Fund's contribution to these is impossible to pinpoint. Old-timers in the field, while assuming that American aviation would eventually have come into its own without Mr. Dan's gift, invariably assert that the Fund's coming along just when it did put the entire process ahead by at least a quarter of a century.

The fairness of this appraisal should become apparent as we examine some of the organization's larger efforts.[2]

The Model Airline

Harry Guggenheim and Admiral Cone brought back from Europe not only a list of proposed projects for the fund, but also a report containing the general observations that were to govern its selection of projects in the years ahead.

A portion of the report dealt with the status of passenger service abroad. In this field European countries were far ahead of the United States, but there were ironies. For one thing a large percentage of Europe's air passengers were American tourists, a discovery that fortified the belief of Mr. Dan that passenger service could be made profitable in this country. For another, all of Europe's passenger transport lines were dependent on subsidies. While government aid had given Europe its head start, it was Mr. Dan's conviction that in the long run it would prove detrimental and that an effort should be made to put American passenger service on a self-supporting basis.

"In the early days of the Fund," Harry Guggenheim recalls, "I was inclined to drag my feet where the passenger-business problem was concerned. My father kept after me about it, however, so finally I had the Fund arrange a meeting to which the executives of all of the country's larger air transport companies were invited."

The meeting, as Harry remembers it, was a hammer-and-tongs affair. With two exceptions, the executives took issue with Mr. Dan's free-enterprise approach. They argued that the risks involved were too great, that to install passenger service routes without government subsidy was to invite financial disaster.

Determined to prove Mr. Dan's point, the Fund on October 4, 1927, authorized an equipment trust loan to Western Air Express of Los Angeles (now Western Airlines). Conditions were attached. One was that the transport company must apply its borrowed capital to the purchase of three tri-motored planes, each capable of continuing flight even after one of its power units had become disabled. Another was that the new planes were to be used on a model airline, a 365-mile route between Los Angeles and San Francisco, and that the line must be serviced with every available safety precaution.

The events that followed were a vindication of Mr. Dan's stand. So successful was the model airline that less than two months after it began service the Fund announced that it would issue no more equipment loans since "the investment public is now ready to supply the capital for enterprises of this kind." Within two years several other companies, among them Transcontinental Air Transport, in cooperation with the Pennsylvania Railroad and the Santa Fe, had installed passenger service, and all of the money loaned by the Fund to Western Air Express had been repaid with interest. In 1928, when the model line began operation, only 48,312 passengers were carried on scheduled flights in the United States. Two years later this figure had increased to 384,506 and was to double within the next five years. Since in 1926 and 1927, the first two years of the Fund's existence, only 5,782 and 8,679 passengers, respectively, were carried on scheduled flights, it can be said that large-scale passenger service in America dates from the Fund's $150,000 loan to Western Air Express.[3]

Lindbergh and the Fund

When on May 21, 1927, a 46-foot monoplane called *The Spirit of St. Louis* circled the Eiffel Tower and came to rest at Le Bourget on the outskirts of Paris, ending the first nonstop solo flight across the Atlantic, no group of men were more overjoyed than the officers of the Fund and no individual more enormously relieved than Harry Guggenheim.

Harry's long association with Lindbergh goes back to a spring afternoon at Curtiss Field on Long Island a few days before the flier took off on his famous trip. This is the way Harry remembers the incident:

"That spring I was at Roosevelt Field making some test flights with Commander Byrd [the late Admiral Richard E. Byrd] and his pilot [the late Floyd Bennett] in preparation for their flight to Europe. One day I heard that Lindbergh was over at Curtiss, preparing for his solo attempt, so I hurried over to have a look at his plane. There were several men on the spot when I arrived, among them the designer of the Wright motor, Charlie Lawrence. I don't recall what I said to them. I do remember that when I looked inside that plane, my heart sank. Economy of weight was essential, with the result that very little room had been left in the cockpit for the pilot.* I remember looking in there and saying to myself, 'This fellow will never make it. He's doomed!'

"After a while Slim showed up. We were introduced and some pictures were taken. And as I was leaving, I said to him, with far more optimism in my words than in my heart, 'Well, when you get back to the United States, come up to the Fund and see me.' I never thought he'd make it, but of course he did. He was over there about ten days and then Coolidge sent the cruiser *Memphis* to bring him home, and the minute the *Memphis* docked at Washington, he was rushed to the White House. And on that same day I received a phone call from Washington. It was Dwight Morrow speaking. I can't give you Mr. Morrow's exact words, but they went something like this: 'Harry,' he said, 'almost everyone in the country is after this young fellow, trying to exploit him. Isn't there something you and the Fund can give him to do, to save him from the wolves—something that will give him a chance to catch his breath before he commits himself to some proposition he might regret?' "

It was at this point that Harry and the Fund took Lindbergh over for the time being. First of all, Harry saw to it that the young flier had a quiet place in which to write the book he had

* Lindbergh notes that "the cockpit probably looked cramped, since it was designed to fit me closely. Actually there was plenty of room for the pilot, more than in most planes of the time—an essential for long-distance flying."

Harry Guggenheim and Charles A. Lindbergh, July, 1927.

contracted for—a phase of the story on which Lindbergh's own recollections are graphic. Returning from Europe in June of 1927, the flier recalls, he found himself grappling with one of the problems of sudden fame. He had raised $15,000 to finance his great adventure. By the time he reached the States he had only $1,500 left. "With a lot of public appearances coming up," he says, "I foresaw that I must find some way of meeting expenses." The question was how. In Paris and again aboard ship en route home, he had received numerous business propositions, but "I pushed them all aside," he says—all but two. He had accepted an offer from the *New York Times* and he had agreed to write a book to be published by G. P. Putnam's Sons.

Since Lindbergh had had little writing experience then, arrangements had been made for the book to be written by a *Times* reporter, and two weeks after his return to the States, the manuscript was delivered. He didn't like it. "For one thing," he says, "it was inaccurate. For another, it was written in the first person and I didn't want a ghost-written book to come out over my name." His initial impulse was to throw up the job; then, learning that Putnam's had already spent money on advertising, "Okay," he told them, "I'll write it myself."

"I didn't know what I was letting myself in for," he confesses. "The next clear picture I have of this aspect of things is of going out to Falaise and of Harry and Carol [Harry's second wife] inviting me to write the book there. Frankly, I don't think I ever would have gotten it done if they hadn't offered me that retreat. For the next three weeks, it was sometimes as much as fourteen hours of work a day. There wasn't much time before I had to start on the Guggenheim Fund tour of the forty-eight states, so often I didn't re-read the sentences."

Commercial propositions continued to pour in during Lindbergh's stay at Falaise. One evening an invitation took him to the lavish New York apartment of publisher William Randolph Hearst, then in the midst of making his protégé, Marion Davies, the darling of American movie-goers. Hearst offered Lindbergh $500,000 plus a percentage of the profits to make an aviation film in which Lindbergh would star. Harry Guggenheim's remembrance of this incident differs from contemporary newspaper accounts. These have the flier promptly turning down the offer with the statement, "You know, I said I did not intend to go into moving pictures." As a matter of fact, Lindbergh was tempted by the amount of money offered and by Hearst's argument that the proposed movie would have promotional value for aviation.

Seeing that his guest was weakening, Hearst thrust the contract and a pen at him. "Sign it," he urged, "and I'll put it in my safe here. It'll stay there till you have a chance to talk things over with your friends. Then, if you change your mind, come back and we'll destroy the contract."

When the interview ended, the signed contract was in Hearst's safe, and Lindy went back to Falaise to engage in a conversation that lasted until three in the morning. Among those present was the attorney, Henry Breckenridge, who joined Harry in pointing out that much as Hearst loved aviation, he loved Marion Davies more; that his real motive was to use America's newest hero as a background for her; that he would certainly use Miss Davies in the proposed film, and that in the end it would do more for Miss Davies than for aviation.

"My guess," says Harry, "is that Hearst thought Lindbergh would never bring himself to take advantage of his offer to tear up that signed contract; but he did."

While Lindbergh was finishing his manuscript of *We,* the final touches were placed on the arrangements for him to tour the country for the Fund in *The Spirit of St. Louis,* a tour designed to convince the American public of the coming safety and convenience of air travel. The Fund underwrote the project with $68,721.27, the bulk of which, $50,000, went to Lindbergh. The tour started from Mitchel Field, New York, at noon on July 19, ended there three months later at 2 P.M., October 23. In all, 22,350 miles were flown with a flying time of 260 hours. All forty-eight states were covered and eighty-two cities were visited. In every city Lindberg arrived at 2 P.M.; and in all but thirteen, where he made only a "touch stop," the ensuing hours were given over to festivities, usually including an open-air rally at which the aviator spoke, a parade from airport to hotel, a press conference in the late afternoon and a dinner in the early evening. Throughout the trip there was only one brief delay. This occurred at Portland, Maine, in July, when a dense fog prevented Lindbergh from arriving on time.

So wearying was the schedule that, three weeks after the start of the project, the Fund sent a letter to the mayors of cities still on the itinerary, imploring them to make their plans so as to permit Lindbergh to get to bed at nine in the evening. "I hope you will pardon me for being explicit . . . ," Harry Guggenheim wrote, "but I am sure you understand that Colonel Lindbergh is making a very difficult trip. Furthermore, he is making the trip with a view to promoting interest in aviation rather than with a view to receiving personal plaudits, and he, therefore, feels that he can best accomplish the aims of the tour by limiting his activities. . . . I am sure you understand there is no commercial aspect connected with this tour and that Colonel Lindbergh is not attending any meetings where admission is charged, nor is he . . . accepting any personal invitations." In mid-August a rumor arose that The Lone Eagle was ill, a rumor the Fund promptly scotched by releasing a wire from Mrs. Evangeline Lindbergh, who had visited with her son a few days before, stating that he seemed "to be in excellent health."

Thousands of air mail letters addressed to the young hero were routed to a central depository set up by the Chamber of Commerce in St. Louis. Every letter containing ten cents in stamps for return air mail postage was acknowledged with a photo of the aviator and his plane.

Lindbergh's was the second tour to be staged by the Fund. The first, during the previous autumn, was a 7,000-mile swing by Floyd Bennett in the airplane which he had piloted for Admiral (then Commander) Byrd during the celebrated Navy explorer's flight over the North Pole in May, 1926.

One of the immediate results of the Byrd airplane tour was an increase in the establishment of properly organized airports. The Lindbergh tour gave this program further impetus. In 1927 there were in the United States 1,036 airports and landing fields, of which only a few were lighted. By the end of 1930 there were 1,782, of which 640 were lighted.

Another advance was attributed to the Lindbergh tour by Postmaster General Harry S. New, who reported that in September of 1926 American contract and government air lines had carried only 79,841 pounds of air mail, whereas in September of the following year, American contract lines (all government routes having meanwhile been placed under private operation) carried 146,088 pounds.

A further indication of the impact of Lindbergh's tour on the progress of aviation was a letter, released by the president of the Fund in September, cautioning investors clamoring to get in on the ground floor of a new industry to look before they leaped. "The greatest danger at the moment," Harry pointed out, "may arise from the promotion of ill-advised, economically unsound aviation enterprises which are unwarranted in the present state of development . . . and the conservative investing public should be extremely wary of investing its money with unknown promoters for plans of this kind until the science, art and operation as a whole have been more thoroughly perfected." Commenting on this letter years later, Brigadier General Lindbergh, to give him his present title, said, "It is easy, in recalling the career of the Aeronautical Fund, to over-emphasize some of its more spectacular projects and to overlook such mundane things as Harry Guggenheim's repeated efforts, both by public letter and by private conversation, to persuade the builders of the new industry to put it on a sound financial basis. Personally I think that quiet aspect of the Fund's work should be placed high on the list of its worthwhile endeavors."[4]

Doolittle and the Full Flight Laboratory

"To give the airman eyes in the fog, to enable him to orient himself both as to the altitude of his aircraft and its position with relation to its goal in swirling mists, in blinding snow, in the heart of the cloud blanket, when all the landmarks by day and the lights of great cities and airports by night should be blotted out, this was a task at once of underlying scientific importance and of high romance."

With these words Cleveland, in his *America Fledges Wings,* opens his account of one of the Fund's most spectacular experiments, its establishment at Mitchel Field, after months of planning and research, of the Full Flight Laboratory to tackle the problem of blind flying.

One of Jerry Land's first jobs, following his assumption of the Fund vice-presidency on August 17, 1928, was to pick an aviator to direct the Laboratory. "If ever my crummy character was put to the test," Land says, "it was right then." As a Navy officer his first hope was to find the right man in his own service; but from the start, he realized that by far the best man for the job was the Army's Lieutenant (now Lieutenant General) James Harold Doolittle.

Harry Guggenheim persuaded Major General James E. Fetchet, chief of the Air Corps, as the Army's flying branch was then known, to give Doolittle a leave of absence, and on September 24, the flier, his auburn-haired wife, Jo, and their two small sons moved into quarters near the hangar assigned by the Army to the Fund at Mitchel Field.

Doolittle was then thirty-two, five feet six inches tall, with gray eyes and steel nerves. Many of the high points of his career still lay in the future: his command in the Second World War of the bombers that raided Tokyo and other Japanese cities from the aircraft carrier *Hornet,* of our North African Strategic Air Forces and the 8th Air Force. Even as early as 1928, however, his was a name to conjure with in flying circles. He was a daring pilot. In the preceding year he had won a Chilean contract for an American plane maker in a demonstration, during which he was compelled to fly with his feet tied to the rudder bars because of broken ankles suffered while doing acrobatics on a window ledge. Earlier he had become "the Army's only Admiral" by winning the Schneider Trophy Race for Seaplanes at Baltimore. He was also an engineer, with a doctorate in aeronautical science from M.I.T. and a mature understanding, quite at odds with his somewhat exaggerated reputation as a daredevil, of the theoretical needs of his profession.

In the late summer and early fall, the Fund released two brief announcements. One was that Doolittle had been obtained to direct the Full Flight Laboratory, the other was that he had started work assisted by Army Air Corps Lieutenant Ben Kelsey and mechanic Jack Dalton. In January the Fund issued another short report, stating that one of Doolittle's former professors at M.I.T., Army Air Corps Captain William Brown, had joined him as a technical assistant. After that all was silence until September of 1928, when the Fund issued a long release, one copy of which its president stuffed into an envelope addressed to Mr. Dan, having first written across the top of it in red ink, "Dear Father & Mother, This is the story. Love, Harry."

It was quite a story, for during the one-year life of the Full Flight Laboratory, Mitchel Field and its adjoining airways were the scene of an unusually swift and concentrated attack on what was then the most crucial problem in aviation. When it began, a pilot whose plane was equipped with all the navigational aids then available, could fly in fog but he could not land safely. When it ended, a procedure had been developed whereby he could go aloft, fly and land his plane in fog of any density.

Doolittle's initial step was to requisition two aircraft. One was a Consolidated N.Y. 2, equipped with all known instruments for blind flying, which he used for daily test flights in the vicinity of Mitchel Field. The other was a Corsair O-2U-1, a lighter and a higher-speed ship which he utilized for point-to-point trips whenever it became necessary to make a fast pickup of needed equipment. He and his assistants devoted most of their efforts to a search for instruments that could be relied on to take the place of the pilot's eyes in bad weather. Half a dozen organizations were pressed into service, including the Bell Telephone Laboratories and the Radio Frequency Laboratory at Boonton, New Jersey.

All sorts of new ideas, old ideas warmed over, new instruments and improved old instruments were tried out. The United States Bureau of Standards worked with the Fund in an effort to develop blind-landing radios, work that was not completed during the time of the Full Flight Laboratory but that led eventually to the perfection of the so-called "inclined beams" now successfully in use. In Cleveland, Harry Raeder noticed that men breaking rock in quarries near Lake Erie were using blowtorches to expand the rock and that when a fog descended, the flames punched great gaps in it. Raeder passed on his discovery to the Full Flight Laboratory, and the Fund promptly brought him to Mitchel Field where he set up a system of giant blowtorches.

Two months elapsed before the field was visited by a "real thick fog," and the torches were lighted. Their blue flames cleared the area, but only for a minute or so, after which more fog rolled in. Doolittle and company concluded that the system was workable only in the absence of wind. Raeder was paid off and sent back to Cleveland where he continued work on his idea, versions of which were subsequently employed with success at airports in America and in England.

Ultimately Doolittle's efforts narrowed to a search for three things: A reliable altimeter, the device which tells a pilot how high above sea level his plane is; an instrument to indicate the "attitude" of the plane; and a reliable directional guide, an instrument capable of showing the exact direction of flight during a bank and under turbulent conditions. The theory was that, supplemented by proper radio signals from the ground, these three instruments together would allow a pilot to land his ship in any weather. That is, they would allow him to do so if they were accurate enough. There was the catch!

In 1928 there was no such thing as an accurate altimeter. The best in use gave only approximate height above sea level. One solution came from a mild-mannered young genius named Paul Kollsman, who now heads his own organization, the Kollsman Instrument Company, and whom Doolittle fondly refers to as "Mr. Altimeter."

Shortly before Kollsman became known to the Fund, he had been fired from his position at the Pioneer Instrument Company for making nasty remarks about their altimeter. To show Pioneer that he knew what he was talking about, he built a barometric altimeter of his own in a garage behind his house in the Greenpoint section of Brooklyn. A graduate of one of Germany's leading scientific schools and a perfectionist, Kollsman, once his invention was under way, called on some Swiss watchmakers. "I want you," he told them, "to cut me a better gear for this altimeter than you ever cut for a watch. It must be more precise, more accurate. . . . We will start by first rebuilding your gear-cutting machines." The watchmakers were startled, but they went along.

When Doolittle, having learned about Kollsman's invention

from the Bureau of Standards, paid a visit to the Brooklyn garage, he found the young scientist putting the final touches on his altimeter. It looked good to Doolittle, and back at Mitchel Field a few hours later it proved good. "Mr. Altimeter," Doolittle recalls, "held his instrument on his lap during that first trip, and it worked perfectly."

One problem solved, two to go—the creation of instruments giving aircraft attitude and constant direction of flight regardless of turbulence. The combination of a magnetic compass with a bank-and-turn indicator, in use in 1928, was far from being satisfactory for these purposes. In rough air, the magnetic compass would often swing many degrees to each side of the course being flown, making it very difficult to estimate the actual heading of the plane. Doolittle figured that the solution to this was to find a "light, compact gyroscopic compass," and another gyroscopic instrument to show the exact position of the wings and fuselage of the plane in relation to the earth's surface. To obtain such devices he went to see Dr. Elmer Ambrose Sperry.

"I called on him," says Doolittle, "cap in hand," for the late Dr. Sperry, then approaching seventy, was a towering figure among inventors, and the Sperry gyroscope was famous. Doolittle drew a sketch to show the elderly scientist what he needed, and Dr. Sperry put his son Elmer on the job. For weeks genial young Elmer and Doolittle worked together, Doolittle himself making some contributions to the finished products: A directional guide and an artificial horizon, each based on a gyroscope. They are still standard equipment on commercial and military aircraft.

When the guide and horizon were ready, Doolittle tried them out in conjunction with Kollsman's sensitive altimeter. The test flights were made in clear weather. Fog conditions were simulated, however, by placing a hood over the pilot's cockpit; and it wasn't long before Doolittle could report to the Fund that he was making more uniform landings under the hood than without it.

Now Doolittle had a sensitive altimeter and a dependable directional guide. Mission accomplished, except that an official test remained to be flown, and this must be done in real fog. Kollsman and Sperry could make instruments, but they couldn't make a fog—not a big one, anyhow. For that Doolittle had to wait.

On the morning of September 24, 1929, he awakened early, looked out his window and yelled to his wife, "At last, Jo. Perfect weather . . . !"—meaning, of course, that a mass of thick fog off Long Island Sound, a real "pea-souper," had enshrouded Mitchel Field. Doolittle assembled his gang, put in some phone calls and hurried off to the hangar.

The early morning hours were given over to testing Mr. Raeder's blowtorches, which were found wanting—wanting, that is, for the time being. By about eleven o'clock some fifty people had arrived to serve as official witnesses of the blind flight, among them Harry Guggenheim, Land and Ben Kelsey.

Harry was nervous. "One suggestion," he said to Doolittle. "I want Ben to be in that second cockpit—just in case."

"In case of what?" he was asked.

"In case anything goes wrong. If it does, Ben may get enough visual aids to land the plane."

"But nothing can go wrong, Harry. We've got this thing all taped. It's a simple matter of trusting our instruments."

"I'll feel better, Jim, if Ben is along—just for insurance. You might meet another plane in the air."

No further argument. Ben climbed into the front cockpit, making up his mind even as he did so that, unless ordered by Doolittle, he wouldn't put his feet near the rudder bars or touch the stick.

Meanwhile Doolittle had settled himself in the rear cockpit and Harry, clambering onto the wing, pulled the canvas over him, muttered "Good luck, Jim," and hopped off.

Inside, under the hood, Doolittle switched on his lights. His illuminated panel board displayed all of the standard navigation and engine instruments including tachometer, voltmeter, compass, bank-and-turn indicator, air-speed indicator, altimeter, rate-of-climb indicator—*plus* the Kollsman sensitive altimeter, the Sperry artificial horizon, and the Sperry directional gyroscope. Doolittle put his ship in motion. It joggled over the turf—there were no concrete runways at Mitchel Field in those days. He revved his engine, set the Kollsman altimeter and the directional gyro, opened his throttle and released his brakes. Seconds later he was in the air. Five miles due west he executed a 180-degree turn to retrace the course.

The fog was thinning rapidly. As the plane passed over the field at a few hundred feet, those below could see Ben Kelsey's hands resting outside the cowling of the front cockpit. He kept them there throughout the flight, mute evidence that the man under the hood behind him—and he alone—was guiding the craft. Four miles to the east Doolittle banked his plane, turned and streaked back. A mile short of the field he switched from the long-range beacon to pick up the runway localizer beam. His plane was 30 feet up as it cleared the edge of the field. Nosing smoothly down, it touched its wheels to the earth only a few yards from where they had left it. As it rolled to a stop, Ben Kelsey grinned, lifted his hands and clasped them behind his neck. Once more Harry climbed onto the wing, this time to unfasten the canvas hood and pull it back. Doolittle blinked and looked around. "What happened to the fog?" he asked. "Sort of rolled away while you were up there, Jim," was Harry's smiling reply.

For thousands of future aviators fog had to a large extent been rolled away. A significant step had been taken toward its elimination as an aviational hazard. The Aeronautical Fund, having planted $66,518.85 in seed money—the cost of the project—in fertile soil, closed up its Full Flight Laboratory, gave its test plane to the Army Air Corps and turned to other matters.[5]

Helping Make the Airways Safe

Doolittle's attack on fog was part of the Aeronautical Fund's many-pronged attack on the problems of safety in flying. While on their exploratory junket in 1926, Harry, Cone and Hunsaker were impressed by the attention these problems were receiving in Europe. They found this especially true in England where Harry witnessed demonstrations of Handley Page's slotted wing, G. T. R. Hill's Pterodactyl, a tailless airplane, and Juan de la Cierva's Autogiro—all developments aimed at making it possible to control and stabilize heavier-than-air craft at low speeds. On his return home he had no trouble convincing his associates that the Fund should seek ways of encouraging (1) the perfection of flying instruments and accessories, with particular emphasis on radio and other aids to navigation; (2) research in aerology, the name given to aviational meteorology; (3) development of means to prevent collision in air; (4) development of aircraft with motors accessible, and therefore capable of being repaired, in flight; and (5) development of fire- and splinterproof fusilages.

Soon about a score of programs directed to these ends were under way. On October 4 and 5, 1928, members of the National Safety Council, previously concerned only with persuading motorists to desist from maiming and killing one another on the highways, gave their attention for the first time to the traffic dangers of the airways above. The occasion was a meeting in New York at the Hotel Pennsylvania (now the Statler-Hilton) of the Council's seventeenth annual congress in conjunction with the first National Aeronautical Safety Conference, which the Fund had made possible with an appropriation of $10,000. Delegates to the joint convention listened to a program, organized by Jerry Land, headed by Jerry Hunsaker, and consisting of papers covering all aspects of aviation safety, prepared and delivered by thirty-seven American and European aeronautical experts.

Already in progress at this time were preparations for what was to be one of the Fund's most ambitious undertakings, the Safe Aircraft Competition of 1929. In its initial announcement on June 18, 1926, the Fund merely revealed its intention of organizing a contest in which airplanes, submitted by manufacturers the world over, would compete for prize money, the bulk of which would go to the plane exhibiting the best safety features in both structure and performance.

The Fund issued its announcement well in advance of the projected contest for considered reasons. It was believed that the manufacturers should have plenty of time to study the objectives and qualifying rules, to carry on their research and development, and to build, test and revise as necessary the planes they intended to enter. The Fund, therefore, announced in 1926 a competition that was to take place three years later.

During the months following the initial announcement, a body of experts assembled by the Fund hammered out the tests every plane entered in the competition must pass in order to participate in the final runoff. In his *America Fledges Wings,* Cleveland offers a lively picture of the conferences at which these tests were devised, and of the conferees themselves. They were not, he tells us, "yes men." They often disagreed with Fund president Guggenheim. They also often disagreed among themselves.

One of the more forceful conferees was Major R. H. Mayo, the Fund's representative in England, whom Cleveland describes as belying the characterization of the English as a strong, silent people. "Strong he certainly was," we are informed, "but by no means silent. Long, exceedingly thin, sharp-featured . . . he could talk longer, more clearly, more logically and with more determination than most other members of the conference."

To quote Cleveland further: "Another forceful personality in the debates was the late airplane designer Anthony H. G. Fokker. During the discussions there was much argument about what could or could not be done through the use of slots, flaps and other high-lift devices. 'I do it all without slots or flaps,' said Tony Fokker. '. . . I can give you a flight in which I stall one of my ships right into the ground and she will be in perfect control all the way. You are wasting time drafting these rules. My ships already have done all that is required.' . . . Rosy and tubby . . . the typical Dutchman, Fokker looked the very embodiment of good humor, but was adamant in sustaining his views. . . .

"Among the practical men who attended the discussions was Major R. W. Shroeder, holder of the then altitude record. . . . Six feet three inches in height and weighing not over 140 pounds, he was . . . the Yankee personified. Before designing and flying a plane, 'Shorty' Shroeder had a habit of sitting in the cockpit and taking . . . imaginary flights. During the drafting of the rules for the competition he would adopt a similar attitude, imagine himself in the cockpit and illustrate his points by movement of imaginary controls."

Other men frequently present at these conferences were J. D. Hill, a veteran of the air-mail routes; G. M. Bellanca, American designer of Italian origin who made his views known "in a suave, soft tone which, nevertheless, carried conviction"; Edward P.

Warner, then assistant secretary for air in the Department of Commerce; Professor Klemin, head of the Guggenheim School of Aeronautics at N.Y.U.; and Doolittle.

Two schools of thought emerged from the discussions. One "held that the Competition should be run on purely scientific lines which would incorporate to the greatest possible degree exact and quantitative tests; the other . . . that scientific tests would not reveal the true qualities of the aircraft and . . . the test should be of a wholly practical nature to determine whether the craft was in fact safe for ordinary flying."

In the end the rules reflected both approaches, with a slight leaning toward the scientific. Briefly summarized, they called for three speed tests, one of which allowed a plane two points for every mile per hour less than 35 at which it was able to maintain level and controlled flight; a test of landing run which allowed two points for every three feet less than 100 feet at which the plane came to rest after first touching ground; a test of landing in confined space that allowed a point for every two feet less than 300 from the base of an obstruction 35 feet high at which the plane came to rest after gliding in over the obstruction; and two tests of take-off, one of which allowed a point for every 15 feet less than 300 required by the plane to take off from a standing start.

On the evening of Friday, April 29, 1927, the New York Yale Club was the scene of a banquet sponsored by the Fund and attended by 101 prominent Americans, among them practically all of the aviation leaders of the era. In the main after-dinner speech Harry Guggenheim formally invited airplane makers to enter the contest and revealed that the Fund had authorized $100,000 for the winning plane and $10,000 for each of the first five competitors (including the winner if it were among this group) to satisfy all of the safety requirements set forth in the rules. September 1, 1927, was designated as the beginning date for entries; September 1, 1929, as closing date.

One of the hopes of the Fund was that Europe would be well represented, but this was not to be. Of the twenty-seven planes on the list when entries closed, only six (five British and one Italian) were from outside the United States. Only two foreign planes remained in when the competition got under way at Mitchel Field in June of 1929. There were other shrinkages. Of the original twenty-seven entries, only fifteen actually appeared at the field—and this figure was further whittled down when three planes withdrew without taking tests, eight were deemed unprepared to enter the qualifying rounds, and two suffered damages in preliminary flying.

Ten planes—one British, the others American—took part in the qualifying tests. Two survived for the big try: the British entry, a product of Handley Page, Ltd., and the Curtiss Tanager of the Curtiss Aeroplane and Motor Company. The winner: Curtiss Tanager, whose items of structural superiority were described by the judges as "manually-controlled flaps, floating ailerons, design of tail surfaces to eliminate blanketing, long stroke, rugged landing gear with latch, independently-operated brakes, and adequate accommodation for occupants."

On January 6, 1930, in a ceremony at Mitchel Field, the prize money was presented to C. M. Keys, president of the Curtiss company. Jerry Land spoke. Characterizing as "exaggerated" some of the predictions about the outcome of the contest, he pointed out that no one in the Fund expected to obtain a " 'foolproof' plane—there isn't any such animal. Moving masses cannot be made 'foolproof' but they can be made safe. Old man 'Kinetic Energy' can always do damage to a fool. The Fund's idea was to see a plane developed that the lay pilot could fly with satisfaction, security, efficiency and safety.

"Officials of the Fund have always felt that the intangible results of the Safe Aircraft Competition would be far greater than the tangible results. We still feel that way. . . . The seed planted by this competition will bear fruit for the next decade."

Earlier in his talk, "The best plane won," Land had declared, "all hands agreed to that." In truth, some were dubious. During the ensuing months complaints appeared in the London trade magazine, *The Aeroplane,* to the effect that the judges of the Safe Aircraft Competition had been overlenient in applying the rules. Edward P. Warner, in the American magazine, *Aviation,* came to the defense of the Fund. He pointed out that it was not the practice of American judges to interpret contest rules too

Daniel Guggenheim breaking ground in October, 1925, for the School of Aeronautics at New York University.

rigidly and that whatever leniency had been shown had been as beneficial to the English entry as to the American.

Some of the Fund's prize money went begging. All that was awarded, $100,000 for first prize and $10,000 for being one of the first five competitors to satisfy all safety requirements, went to the Curtiss Tanager. No other plane qualified for any of the five subsidiary awards. This was a disappointment to the Fund officials, who had hoped that enough planes would meet its requirements to use up all of its $150,000 of prize money. During the early rules-making conferences, some of the experts had said that the requirements under consideration were too high. Most, however, supported the position of Harry Guggenheim that the standards should be kept up.

Today, old-time aviation men say this was the best decision the Fund could have made. By easing the requirements it could have benefited the plane makers by making it possible for more of them to win prizes, but by sticking to its guns it benefited the traveling public by giving future plane makers a higher safety standard.

At the time of the Safe Aircraft Competition, Curtiss' chief engineer was Theodore Paul Wright, later vice-president in charge of research at Cornell University. A slender, gray-eyed scientist, genial and unassuming, Dr. Wright enlivens his recollection of the competition with a chuckle. Says he, "It cost us [the Curtiss company] $105,000 to develop the Tanager, so since the prizes came to $110,000 we didn't make an exorbitant profit. That's not a complaint, you understand. The competition was a great thing. Ultimately it had the effect of shooting aviation upward, and naturally our company shot up with it."

That the competition helped to shoot "aviation upward," so far as safety is concerned, is borne out by the record. In 1927 when the contest was officially opened, there was a fatal accident on American domestic scheduled air carriers every 1,464,047 passenger miles. By 1930 this ratio had considerably bettered with one such accident every 3,627,189 passenger miles. In 1930 the passenger fatalities per hundred million passenger miles flown in this country stood at 28.2. The percentage was down to 23.4 in

1931, and since then the decline has been almost constant, reaching in 1957 the heartening low of 0.1.[6]

The Model Weather Service

One afternoon in the mid-1920's Francis W. Reichelderfer—subsequently chief of the United States Weather Bureau for many years, then a meteorologist with the rank of lieutenant in the Navy Department—stepped into what was known as the "forecast room" of the Bureau in Washington, D.C., in time to overhear a telephone conversation that made him "wince." To whoever was at the other end of the line, one of the men in the room was saying, "The Weather Bureau does not attempt to forecast fog."

In the mid-1920's modern meteorology was an infant (some said an "infantile") science, scarcely a hundred years old. Few attempts were being made to collect, collate and broadcast the sort of weather data a pilot needs. It was not only the aviator caught in fog who had to fly blind. So, in a sense, did the man who took his ship up from a smooth and sunlit runway. His weather forecast, if he had one at all, gave him a picture of the general pattern of the area over which he was about to travel and of conditions momentarily prevailing at the field toward which he was headed. Seldom did it give him any idea of the variations from the pattern he might encounter, or of the conditions at off points along his way, or of whatever changes were taking place at his terminal field. Nor did it tell him what to expect on the airways above. As he made ready to take off, the wind coursing the field at ground level might be from the east at ten miles per hour; but at flight level, for all he knew, it might be coming from another direction at a different rate of speed.

Before the end of the decade all of these deficiencies were being remedied, thanks largely to the emphasis placed by the Guggenheim Fund on projects aimed at providing pilots with exact, comprehensive and up-to-the-minute information concerning weather conditions along, in the vicinity, and at the end of their routes of flight.

Since the advancement of the science raised multiple problems, the Fund tackled it in multiple ways. Among other things, it gave $6,000 to Prof. Edgar W. Woolard of George Washington University to prepare a treatise, "more comprehensive . . . than anything" then available, on an advanced form of meteorology important to pilots; $10,000 to the University of Michigan to help underwrite a meteorological research expedition to Greenland; and $34,000 to M.I.T. to organize a three-year course in aeronautical meteorology. And in 1928, in cooperation with the Weather Bureau, other government agencies and the Pacific Telephone and Telegraph Company, a Bell System subsidiary, it set up and administered in California a one-year experiment in aeronautical weather reporting, commonly spoken of as the Model Weather Service.

Actually, work on the Weather Service got under way in 1927 with the establishment of the Daniel Guggenheim Committee on Aeronautical Meteorology, composed of representatives of the Fund and several Federal agencies. Chairman of the committee and the Fund's representative was a likable, high-spirited, round-faced Swede named Carl-Gustaf Arvid Rossby, whose death at age sixty-one in 1957, according to Dr. Reichelderfer, deprived meteorology of one of its most constructive scientists.

In 1918 Rossby, the son of a construction engineer, was a nineteen-year-old student at the University of Stockholm, restlessly looking about for some profession sufficiently challenging to hold the interests of a vigorous and inventive mind. For a period he considered astronomy, admitting at a later date that this interest was generated by romantic novels picturing astronomers as bearded fellows working on mountaintops and waited on by lightly tripping young girls in lacy and revealing nightgowns.

After a year at Stockholm, Rossby moved on to the Geophysical Institute in Bergen, where he came under the influence of Prof. V. Wilhelm Bjerkness, whose theories concerning the movement of air masses as the basis of weather forecasting had put European meteorology far ahead of American. After further wanderings and stops at other schools, Rossby returned to Stockholm, picked up his licentiate (graduate degree) and joined the Swedish Weather Bureau.

It was dull work there. Rossby was delighted when, in 1926,

he was given a fellowship to the United States as an observer at the Bureau in Washington. His mission was to "sell" the Bjerkness air-mass theories—a mission that went slowly because, under its then chief, conservative C. F. Marvin, the U.S. Weather Bureau resisted new ideas. Toward the end of his first year Rossby was asked to leave after issuing a forecast covering Lindbergh's flight to Mexico. The forecast was correct but Rossby had released it without consulting his superiors. The Bureau's loss was aviation's gain, for when the young Swede parted from his duties in Washington, the Guggenheim Fund, acting on advice from Reichelderfer and others, snatched him up, first to direct its meteorological committee and then to help in the organization and supervision of its Model Weather Service.

By 1928, when the plans for the Weather Service were being completed, Jerry Hunsaker was no longer a naval attaché in London. He was with the Bell Telephone Laboratories where one of his tasks was to keep a close eye on the development of the California experiment, since the system being set up made considerable use of telephonic equipment. To his reports he brought a passion for clarity that makes them one of the best descriptions of the Model Weather Service available.

To paraphrase the Hunsaker memos: Rossby and his fellow planners did not have to begin from scratch. Already in existence was a smaller aeronautical weather reporting experiment under the aegis of the Weather Bureau. For use on the Guggenheim model line, however, its methods were greatly expanded and refined.

As finally installed, the Model Weather Service consisted essentially of thirty observation stations, so located as to constitute a network from the Pacific to the Sierra Mountains, all along the air routes from Los Angeles to San Francisco. Thrice daily each of the thirty observers made a report, based on local weather conditions, relaying this information by telephone and radio to trained meteorologists at the two terminal cities and at two intervening airports. So effective was this communications system that only twenty minutes were required for the information from the observation points to be received at the terminals, collated and released as forecasts.

A feature of the system was the installation of an alternate flying route so that a pilot, having advance notice of gummy weather along his route, could change course. At take-off every pilot was supplied with the latest forecast. If his plane had radio-telephone, he received further reports en route. For planes not so equipped, ground signals indicating the weather ahead were displayed at designated points about midway of the route.

A significant element of the Model Weather Service was a complete system for measuring wind speeds and direction in the upper air. This was done by sending up pilot balloons. Thus was laid the base for the later development at the Guggenheim-endowed aeronautical laboratory at Massachusetts Institute of Technology of the now widely used radio-meteorograph, or radiosonde, an instrument which, on being elevated by balloon, simultaneously transmits to earth and records wind velocities, barometric pressure, temperature and other data.

The Fund's pilot balloon experiments were to redound to the benefit of both meteorology and aviation: To meteorology because, in the words of Dr. Reichelderfer, "It is impossible to predict weather near the earth without detailed knowledge of temperature, humidity, pressure, direction and velocity of winds above." To aviation, for reasons demonstrated by the experience of a pilot on the Model Air Line who, by climbing to 9,200 feet, found a tail wind with a velocity of 96 miles an hour while at ground level the wind velocity was only 18. The advantage to a pilot of knowing the location of a favorable wind stratum is obvious, as shown by this instance in which cruising speed of the plane was greatly increased. One of the long-range benefits of the Guggenheim experiment is that today pilots can make use of the best flying levels as a matter of routine.

Throughout the life of the weather service, Harry Guggenheim kept close tabs on it, headquartering most of the time at Santa Barbara. Rossby, shifting his headquarters from place to place along the route as circumstances warranted, became a popular figure among West Coast pilots, joining them when time permitted in drinking bouts and winning their admiration—and envy—for his way with the ladies. "Every girl in California," one of his colleagues joked, "is in love with Rossby." To which Rossby, then a bachelor, added, "And vice versa." Another scientist closely associated with the planning and administration of the service was Edward H. Bowie, meteorologist with the Weather Bureau in San Francisco. Considerable cooperation was received from the Bell Telephone system and from interested government agencies, generously in the case of most of the latter, somewhat reluctantly in the case of the Weather Bureau whose chief, Dr. Marvin, saw little future in aviation and was at first inclined to resent the Fund's plans as an "implied criticism" of the Bureau's forecasting methods.

The experimental service began in June of 1928 and ended a year later. During this period the crowded California airway was flown without a single accident attributable to weather. Several months before the end of the experiment, the Federal government announced its intention of taking it over—an action that occurred officially on July 1, 1929, when the government also made arrangements to begin extension of the service to all parts of the country. Once again the Fund had planted seed money—this time $27,562.22 worth—in fertile soil.[7]

In January of 1930 the Daniel Guggenheim Fund for the Promotion of Aeronautics closed its offices and wound up its affairs; and on the following September 28, a Sunday, its benefactor, Mr. Dan, died at the age of seventy-four in his big country home on the shores of Long Island Sound.

During the last years of his life, the old man had been a frequent visitor at the Fund's headquarters, a constant observer of its activities and a critical reader of its literature. From first to last he preached his favorite aeronautical doctrine: that the progress of the field was certain to be in direct proportion to the extent to which its theoretical aspects were furthered by the creation of centers of research and study at the university level. His strictures were not ignored. When the Fund ended its work, it could point to grants of $2,093,372.31 for educational purposes; to the installation at the Library of Congress of a Chair of Aeronautics and of an aeronautical collection; to the founding of new schools of aeronautics at five American universities, plus a number of other university research-and-study centers; to the establishment in Akron, Ohio, of the Daniel Guggenheim Airship Institute for the development of lighter-than-air craft; and to the achievement of having transplanted from Europe to America Dr. Theodore von Kármán, one of the world's foremost authorities on aerodynamics, whose activities, along with those of some of the Guggenheim centers, will concern us next.

VII

Millions for Science

Scientists in the aerospace field—using the term that includes man's efforts to conquer not only the atmosphere but also the galactic areas beyond it—are fond of a story of one afternoon in the late 1950's when an American businessman and a Hungarian writer working in Hollywood found themselves sitting side by side on a transcontinental plane winging westward across the United States.

Introductions were made, backgrounds exchanged. "So," said the American to his seat mate, "you were born in Hungary. Well now, are you Hungarian like Zsa-Zsa Gabor?"

"Not exactly," the scriptwriter said. "I would say rather that I was Hungarian like Theodore von Kármán."

"Theodore von Kármán? And who is he?"

"Who is *he*!" exclaimed the writer with indignation. "Why, sir, he is the man who made it possible for this plane to fly the way it does—so smoothly that you can sit here, talking comfortably to me, or eat a meal, or read a book, or. . . ."

Just then the plane encountered some turbulence, so that the American was thrown from his seat onto the floor, from which humble position he aimed a scowl of disgust at his companion and demanded: "Now what did you say the name of that guy was?"

Among those acquainted with his accomplishments, "that guy," during much of his long life, was variously referred to as "the elder statesman of aviation," the "father of the supersonic age," the "dean of world scientists." When in the summer of 1961 two world-famous scientists visited Moscow for a conference, they paid their respects to von Kármán in a letter that read, "On any occasion when specialists in applied mechanics gather together, they warmly remember and send their greetings to Professor von Kármán, who is our father and the classic of our time."

Von Kármán, who was eighty-one at the time of his death on May 7, 1963, specialized in aerodynamics and astronautics. In both fields, as inspired teacher and creative investigator, his contributions were seminal. While still a young man he built one of the first practical helicopters; subsequently he brought about improvements in the structure of gliders, airships, windmills, airplane hangars, commercial and military planes. No manufacturer today would dream of putting up a new plane without first testing it in a wind tunnel to determine its probable behavior in the air and especially under the stress of turbulence. Most modern wind tunnels are von Kármán's "children." Scientific colleagues are fond of mystifying the layman by writing down mechanical formulas bearing his name or by describing a discovery concerning the behavior of liquid or air in the wake of a moving body known as the "Kármán Vortex Street."

His name had been a household word among scientists for decades when, in 1940, it became familiar to the general public because of his role in the dispute over "Galloping Gertie," a $6 million suspension bridge over the Tacoma Narrows in Washington State. Galloping Gertie was so nicknamed because of her tendency to sway in the fierce winds of the Narrows. One night the winds, slashing along at 42 miles an hour, got the upper hand and down went Galloping Gertie. At his home in Pasadena, von Kármán read newspaper stories of plans to reconstruct the bridge, shook his head and dispatched a letter on the stationery of the Guggenheim Aeronautical Laboratory of the California Institute of Technology, of which he was then director. "Dear Sir," he wrote to the governor of Washington, "maybe you will find that if you build the bridge in the same way, it will fall in the same way."

A few weeks later the Federal government asked von Kármán to join a committee to investigate the bridge disaster and he traveled to Spokane. His arrival at the Washington governor's chambers gave a secretary the giggles. "Oh, but of course," she sputtered, having finally attuned her ears to von Kármán's accent. "You're the man who wrote the governor that funny letter."

The governor saw nothing funny in the situation. He wanted to know why von Kármán was so certain that if Galloping Gertie were rebuilt as before, she would collapse again. Before the governor and the experts of the investigating committee, von Kármán demonstrated by setting up a model of the fallen span in the path of a ventilator.

"I explain all about wind eddies forty-six years ago," he lectured, "but bridge builders, they do not think such eddies can cause trouble to something as big as a bridge." Apparently the demonstration was convincing, for the governor's next request was that von Kármán recommend structural changes to make the bridge aerodynamically safe. Von Kármán's suggestion was a scientific version of the saying that "if you can't beat them, join them." He would design the new bridge so that the "wind eddies" went through it, instead of banging against it. He would use an open grille in the deck instead of a solid piece, a truss underneath instead of solid side plates. His specifications were incorporated in the new Tacoma bridge, and ever since, bridge designers have been testing their models in wind tunnels. "The solution of the problem was simply a matter of cutting down on the resonance frequency of vibrations," von Kármán said with the shrug of a man laboring the obvious.

A first meeting with von Kármán in the latter years of his life was an unforgettable visual experience. He was short and stocky, with striking features: firm mouth, high-bridged nose and flared nostrils, bushy eyebrows and a broad forehead. His head, covered with thick white hair, was leonine, and when he sat he rolled it slightly forward so that it rested, or appeared to rest, on his chest. His dark eyes stared out piercingly on a world toward which, in the words of a magazine writer, he was inclined to adopt an attitude "of fatalism dipped in humor." If the conversation interested him, he sometimes placed the receiver of his hearing aid on a convenient table; if not, he sometimes surreptitiously turned it off. A gentle wit pervaded his own conversation. A favorite among his stories was of the time he was hired by the U. S. Army to do a job, during which he and his co-workers discovered some new principles of airplane design. Since von Kármán's contract did not call for these discoveries, the Army refused to pay his salary. "However," he said later, "I reminded them of Columbus, who was commissioned by Queen Isabella to find a new seaway to the Indies. Instead he discovered America, and he was put in jail. The Army thought this over and decided to pay me."

He was forgetful and absent-minded. In Moscow, during World War II, he attended a Soviet military parade wearing an American army uniform and a civilian hat. His former students, many of whom hold key positions in the aero-space world, will tell you that "it was par for the course for von Kármán to be late in arriving at an important conference, either because he opened his invitation and forgot about it or never got around to opening it at all." He spoke six languages; and at Cal Tech there is a legend that he once lectured in German to a class for half an hour before realizing that he was doing so. Like most creative people, he insisted on being left alone to do his work. When in 1946 he was requested by General H. D. (Hap) Arnold to make a study of what would be needed by the United States Air Force by 1960, he agreed to undertake the survey on two conditions: "That no one gives orders to me and I don't have to give orders to anyone else."

Born in Budapest, where his father, Maurice von Kármán, was a professor of philosophy and founder of a famous secondary school, he received the major part of his higher education at the German University of Goettingen. One morning in 1908, as he sat in a Paris café pondering his career, an attractive newspaper woman approached and begged him to drive her to the aerdrome at Issy-les-Moulineaux, outside of the city. Von Kármán protested that it was only five in the morning. Never mind, the young woman told him; a historic event was about to take place at Issy-les-Moulineaux. As a reporter she had to be there. At the airfield they witnessed the first circular flight of one kilometer ever made by a heavier-than-air craft in Europe. Later von Kármán recalled being fascinated by "that odd box kite bobbing along the horizon," and said, "At that moment my future was plain. I would study the wind."

Study it he did, rapidly becoming a pre-eminent authority on its behavior and on the structure of wind tunnels. In 1912 he joined the faculty of the University of Aachen in Germany, first as Professor of Mechanics, later as Director of the Institute of Aerodynamics. He was still at Aachen when, in the fall of 1926, the Daniel Guggenheim Fund for the Promotion of Aeronautics initiated the arrangements that were to bring him to the United States, a development closely associated with the establishment of GALCIT (the Guggenheim Aeronautical Laboratory at the California Institute of Technology).[1]

Textbooks, Yes; Groceries, No!

One of the visitors to the headquarters of the Fund in the late summer of 1926 was tall, silver-haired, Midwest-reared Robert Andrews Millikan, chairman of the executive council of CIT (the California Institute of Technology), director of the Norman Bridge Laboratory there, and holder of the 1923 Nobel Prize in physics. Millikan had come East in the role of money-raiser. He had done so, even though his contract specifically exempted him from such errands, because of his conviction that CIT, then a relatively small institution, needed only money to become one of the country's great centers of scientific investigation.

At this point the Fund had already made possible several new schools of aeronautics in various parts of the country. What Robert Millikan wanted was a fully equipped aeronautical laboratory and graduate school. His arguments were many and persuasive. One had to do with the location of CIT in Pasadena. With both the great Huntington Library and Mount Wilson Observatory within shouting distance, obviously CIT had the making of a first-rank research center. Another had to do with the stature of its faculty, which included such contributors to the science of flight as the theoretical physicist P. S. Epstein, formerly of the Dutch University of Leiden; and Harry Bateman, Cambridge-trained mathematician. Finally Millikan pointed out that if the Fund wanted to assist commercial aviation, its best bet was to concentrate on helping develop "the run from Los Angeles to Chicago," since those were the two largest cities in the world to be "separated by a thousand or more miles of desert." To do this properly called for the creation of an aeronautical research center at the western end of the run, since, said Millikan flatly, the continued advancement of aviation now depended on the efforts of its theoreticians.

Mr. Dan was among those who listened carefully to the famous physicist. He was impressed, especially with Millikan's stress on theoretical work. "As you know," he said, "my son Harry was in Europe recently, and he tells me that they have men over there who know more about the theoretical end of the business than we do. Now, if we give you the money you want, what are the chances of your luring one of those European scientists to Cal Tech?"

Millikan pointed out that he had already lured one—Epstein —from Leiden, and he thought he could lure another.

Had he any suggestions?

He had several. He headed his list with the names of Prandtl of Goettingen and von Kármán of Aachen, a circumstance that would later give rise to von Kármán's often-voiced quip that "they wanted the great Prandtl, but he couldn't come at that time, so they had to settle for me."

Millikan, having made his pitch, asked Harry to come West to talk matters over with the CIT trustees. Harry did so, his speech to the trustees later finding its way into Millikan's warm and plain-spoken autobiography.

What Harry said, in effect, was that so far aviation had been developed by practical men of the Wright brothers type. It was now his father's belief that henceforth the advances in aviation would come mainly from the "theorists" of the field, from the highly trained aerodynamicists. For this reason Mr. Dan had decided to go along with Millikan's request for funds to build an aeronautical center at CIT.

The official grant was made by the Fund in October—$350,000 to enable CIT to erect the laboratory and set up the graduate school, now referred to as GALCIT. Meanwhile the process of luring von Kármán from his post at Aachen had been started. Von Kármán's first inkling of it came during his summer vacation with the arrival of a cable from Robert Millikan, reading, "Which is the earliest ship you can come U. S.?" There was not another word. What had happened was that Epstein of CIT had undertaken to prepare von Kármán for Millikan's cable by sending a preliminary letter. Somehow the letter was held up, reaching von Kármán seven days after Millikan's cryptic message.

In September von Kármán left for the United States, accompanied by his sister and constant companion, Josephine de Kármán, a remarkable woman whose death in 1951 would be one of the most trying moments of her bachelor-brother's life. They traveled on a French ship. "So, naturally," von Kármán said later, "you can imagine my bewilderment on our arrival here to find this country having prohibition." Handed a glass of ginger ale by Millikan with the assurance that it was "delicious," von Kármán took a sip and said to himself, "Well, I'm in a strange land." Another aspect of it was to prove equally strange. The Guggenheims suggested that he tour all of the research and study centers established thus far by the Aeronautical Fund. The third week of November found him in Boston where the agenda included a Thanksgiving dinner at Massachusetts Institute of Technology. "I am green," he later said, "so I assume this festivity is to be a dinner of thanks to me." Fortunately, on the Wednesday before the holiday, von Kármán went to a barber "to be polished up for the occasion." He learned about another American custom when the barber asked him where he was having Thanksgiving dinner. "So," he sighed to himself, "Thanksgiving isn't just for me. It's general!"

Since for Dr. von Kármán America was a stopover en route to Japan, whose government had requested his aid in setting up a wind tunnel, his first stay here was brief. He visited the Guggenheim Centers and delivered a series of lectures financed by the Fund, a tour that ended in Washington, D.C., where his talks created a stir in the scientific world. In Pasadena he helped the CIT men plan their new aeronautical laboratory and consulted at length with Millikan, Epstein, Bateman and others, including such younger members of the staff as Clark Blanchard Millikan, Robert's son, who at twenty-three was a teaching fellow already displaying the talents that were to characterize his own brilliant career as a physicist and educator. One result of these conferences was an exchange arrangement, under which, beginning in 1927,

Epstein was to spend a semester of each school year at Aachen and von Kármán a semester at CIT. Von Kármán also paid a call on Mr. Dan, an encounter which was to induce the Fund to part with $60,000 for the preparation of a six-volume encyclopedia of aerodynamic theory under the editorship of Dr. William F. Durand of Stanford University.

In 1926, as had been true for many years, Mr. Dan was spending the warmer months at Hempstead House, the forty-room Sands Point mansion that, some years after his death, was to be given by his widow to the Institute of the Aeronautical Sciences (now the American Institute of Aeronautics and Astronautics), as a research center. Hempstead House stood on some 350 acres of land, with a water frontage extending two-thirds of a mile along the Hempstead Harbor section of Long Island Sound. Modeled after what remains of Kilkenney Castle on the River Nore in Ireland and surmounted by a 60-foot tower and turret, the massive stone structure, 228 feet by 110, was originally the property of Howard Gould, who planned it in 1901 as a home for his actress-bride. Before it could be finished, Gould and his wife had separated; and in 1917, negotiating by cable, since Gould was in Europe, Mr. Dan purchased the mansion with its grounds and outbuildings, completed it, and changed its name from Castlegould to the one it now bears.

Then as now, the Hempstead House estate was a place of internal as well as external vistas. Among the components of the house itself were a second-floor glass-enclosed sunroom; a library copied after the Bromley Room on display in the South Kensington Museum; a living room hung with sixteenth-century tapestries (some of which are now in the Metropolitan Museum) and opening on one side into a sunken court lined with palms. Serpentine roads laced the lawns, whose landmarks included a nine-hole golf course, a casino with bowling alley and guest rooms, a tea house in formal gardens.

The conference attended by von Kármán and his sister took place after dinner in the living room. Later von Kármán remembered a radio tucked away in a seventeenth-century cabinet, an item that touched his cosmopolitan funnybone. He remembered Mr. and Mrs. Dan sitting in two of the large chairs, a police dog named Bismarck snoozing at the old man's feet; Harry and his wife on a nearby sofa.

"Now then, Professor," said Mr. Dan. "What do you propose we do in this country so that aeronautical theory can become as advanced here as it is in Europe?"

"Two things are needed," was von Kármán's reply. "First, we must get out a textbook or a collection of textbooks covering all that is known about the art, so that American students won't have to go over the same ground. And second, we must set up some sidewalk cafés, such as they have in Europe, so American scientists will have some place to sit down and talk things over."

Mr. Dan gave these propositions some thought; then, "All right, Professor, I will give you the money for the textbooks. But as for going into the 'grocery business,' I don't think that at my age I should attempt that, even for science."[2]

The Aerospace Centers

Mr. Dan was happy to give millions for science. The $350,000 to Cal Tech was one of ten grants made by the Fund to establish aeronautical research and study centers at the university level. The others included $230,000 to the Massachusetts Institute of Technology for the construction of an aeronautical engineering building; $195,000 to Stanford University for enlarging its aeronautical engineering facilities and staff; $60,000 to Syracuse University for an aerial photography and mapping center; $78,000 to the University of Michigan to complete its aeronautical laboratory and to endow a professorship in aeronautical engineering; $290,000 to the University of Washington to put up a building for its aeronautical school; $300,000 to the Georgia School of Technology in Atlanta to provide the South with a center of education in the flight sciences; and $250,000 to the city of Akron, Ohio, to establish the Daniel Guggenheim Airship Institute.

In 1928 the GALCIT building was completed, and two years later von Kármán was persuaded to cut his ties with Europe and settle in Pasadena as director of both GALCIT and the Airship Institute at Akron. Von Kármán's recollection of his reasons for this move furnish a sidelight on the unrest in Germany on the eve of Hitler's takeover. "It was thus," he said. "I was in the First World War—four years with the Austro-Hungarian forces, doing scientific things. That was enough war for me. I loved my work at Aachen, but after the war I soon have the feeling that everything we are doing there is really part of the preparation for another war." What attracted him to GALCIT, he said, was "this feeling I have that the work there is primarily for developing the commercial, the peaceful, side of aviation. This, I reason, is good. This is healthful." Beloved "Pipo," his nickname for his sister, had much to do with the decision. "She was for the change. She was always a little anti-German."

As director of GALCIT from 1930 until his retirement from full-time academic work in 1949, the Hungarian-born scientist brought to his teaching and investigation not only an outstandingly original mind and a facility for communication with students and colleagues, but also a flair for dealing with hard-headed American businessmen. Plane manufacturers were quick to avail themselves of the testing facilities at GALCIT. Occasionally one of them complained about the costs, and when this happened von Kármán seized the opportunity, as he once said, "to educate these near-sighted gentlemen."

"What do you do in your own plant," he would ask, "when one of your planes turns out to be ailing? You turn it over to your technical men and they investigate until they find the 'bug'—and then stop. At GALCIT we don't stop when we find the bug. We keep right on until we know everything there is to know about that plane. As a result, we not only remove the bug, we improve the plane. In addition, we make discoveries you can use in designing future planes. In short, your research is partial and, if you'll excuse the expression, second-rate. Ours is complete and first-rate. Naturally, ours is more expensive."

The importance of "complete and first-rate" testing was demonstrated by GALCIT's first industrial job, a development recorded by Robert Millikan in the memoirs he wrote shortly before his death in 1953. "The first plane," he wrote, "that went through tests for nine months in our Guggenheim Laboratory was Douglas' DC-3, built to have the same power as a Boeing plane which had a cruising speed of 150 miles per hour. When the Douglas DC-3 came out of its tests and the corrections made in our new wind tunnel, it had a cruising speed of 185 miles per hour and Mr. [Donald] Douglas [president of Douglas Aircraft Company] publicly gave credit to CIT aerodynamicists for the extra 35 miles of speed without increase in power.

"In no small degree," Millikan added, "because of the spectacular success of the DC-3, Southern California captured the larger share of the airplane business of the country and has held it to date [1950], at least half of the country's planes being still produced in Southern California."

During its first twenty-five years GALCIT ran 790 separate wind-tunnel test programs and issued over 700 formal reports on 550 distinct aircraft types for some 35 United States and foreign plane-making companies and six government agencies. Since World War II, as is also true of some of the other Guggenheim Centers, it has been doing a large amount of research for the Federal government—about $547,000 worth in the fiscal year 1962, according to Clark Millikan, von Kármán's successor as director of the Southern California center. In 1933 the Armed Forces began sending officers to GALCIT for training, and as of June 1962, 310 of them had received postgraduate degrees. In 1928 when GALCIT opened its doors, its academic staff consisted of seven professors of all ranks and one research fellow with faculty standing; it now stands at twenty-eight professors and research fellows.[3]

Just as Mr. Dan's gift to CIT assisted that school in becoming a leading center of aeronautical research in the West, so his gift of $230,000 to MIT (Massachusetts Institute of Technology) was helpful in giving that school its present pre-eminence in the field. As of January 17, 1927, when the money was appropriated by the Fund, MIT had long since acquired a reputation for its work in aerodynamics. In 1909 it had become possessor of what appears to have been the first wind tunnel in this country, an apparatus patterned after existing European models and built by

Prof. Gaetano Lanza, then head of the Department of Mechanical Engineering. In 1914 it began offering aeronautical courses under the instructorship of Jerry Hunsaker, then a young MIT graduate. Hunsaker supervised the building of a second wind tunnel, which was housed in a paper-covered shack that for some years was the only MIT building on the Cambridge side of the Charles, the Institute having started life in Boston across the river.

Today practically all of MIT is in Cambridge. The court of its main building, a gigantic pile, looks south to the Esplanade and the river. Around the corner, on Massachusetts Avenue, the highway leading to an older American institution called Harvard, a string of new buildings presents a dignified façade. One of these, a buff brick, limestone-trimmed structure, three stories high, 150 feet across the front and 60 back, is the Daniel Guggenheim Aeronautical Laboratory, completed in June of 1928 and made possible by Mr. Dan's gift.

The Guggenheim laboratory provided ample cellar space for the Aeronautical Department's two wind tunnels, in addition to a working museum, library, drafting room, offices, locker rooms, rigging laboratory, and four other laboratories. The Fund's gift turned out to be true seed money, stimulating a series of other gifts and appropriations that within ten years had given the Aeronautical Engineering Department $630,000 worth of plant and facilities—including a new $250,000 wind tunnel named in honor of the Wright brothers—and had increased its operating budget from $35,000 to more than $100,000 a year.

From 1928 to 1941 Professor Rossby, formerly associated with the Model Weather Service, worked in the new laboratory, organizing and conducting the graduate course in meteorology installed with the aid of a second grant of $34,000 from the Fund. From 1933 to 1951 Hunsaker administered the laboratory as chairman of the joint aeronautical and mechanical engineering departments of MIT. Now retired with the rank of professor emeritus, he still spends many hours in his first-floor office, working at huge, leather-inlaid desk that was once the editorial desk of the weekly newspaper published for many years by his father in Creston, Iowa, where Hunsaker was born in 1886. Small, spare, bald, with sandy-colored mustache and bright, moist, nut-brown eyes, Jerry Hunsaker can look back on an unusually distinguished career. It was he who in the period between 1916 and 1923 designed the airship *Shenandoah* for the Navy along with the first airplane, the flying boat NC-4, to cross the Atlantic. Among the honors he has received is the Daniel Guggenheim Medal; and in 1954 the Daniel and Florence Guggenheim Foundation appropriated $25,000 to help set up a chair in his name at MIT.

The Daniel Guggenheim Aeronautical Laboratory at MIT has made innumerable additions to the theory of the flight sciences. Among the practical developments originating with its personnel have been the dynamic damper and vibration-free mount for Wright engines; detonation indicator and vibration-recording apparatus, marketed by the Sperry corporation; and blind-landing instruments for the Civil Aeronautics Administration.

During the Second World War, work on gyro instruments by C. S. Draper, one of the laboratory professors, led to a demand that something be done about the inability of our anti-aircraft guns to hit Japanese dive bombers. As a result, a lead computing gun sight was designed at the Guggenheim center, tested and turned over to Sperry for large-scale manufacture. Because of this spectacular success, what is known as the Instrumentation Laboratory was set up at MIT. The art known as "inertial navigation" was invented in this laboratory, which, under present cold war pressure, has grown rapidly, to become the principal source of instrumentation and control ideas for guided missiles.

When the Guggenheim Laboratory began operations in 1927, there were eight members of all ranks on its staff. By the fall of 1962, this number had increased to 135. During the same period the aerodynamic tests on aircraft carried out under the general direction of the staff resulted in some 600 reports, and in 1963 the value of research projects carried out under the staff was in the neighborhood of a million dollars. Guggenheim Laboratory graduates—2,357 in all, as of June 1962—are now found in key positions throughout the aerospace world.

When the Daniel Guggenheim Fund for the Promotion of Aeronautics was discontinued in 1930, its efforts on behalf of education and research in the flight sciences did not end with it. Shortly afterward, these phases of its work were taken over and expanded by the oldest of the Guggenheim foundations, whose varied activities, including its support of the Father of Modern Rocketry, are the subject of the next chapter.

VIII

The Daniel and Florence: Sponsor of Goddard

The way of the philanthropist is not always attended by hosannas. Occasionally there are raspberries, as in the early 1920's when two of the Guggenheim families, Mr. and Mrs. Dan and Mr. and Mrs. Murry, came to the aid of one of New York City's best-loved institutions, the free concerts in Central Park by the band then conducted by the late Edwin Franko Goldman, now by his son Richard. As of 1923 the Goldman concerts had been a feature of New York summer life for six years. Although designated as "municipal," they received their support from voluntary contributors, the most generous of whom were the two Guggenheim families.

In 1923 there were 2,000 donors. Even so, the season ended with a deficit. Then the Guggenheims stepped in, picking up the unpaid portion of the tab and announcing that in 1924 they would defray all of the expenses for what was to be a sixty-concert season—an action, as would be learned later, that the two families regarded as preliminary to endowing the concerts.[1] This generous action loosed the hosannas, in the press and even from the lips of people who only yesterday had been denigrating the Guggenheims as the despoilers of Alaska, Mexico, and other countries into which their mining ventures had taken them. Midway in the 1924 season came the raspberry, with the discovery that the Guggenheim gift horse was being looked in the teeth by Hearst-sponsored John Francis ("Red Mike") Hylan, mayor of New York, a burly, red-haired politician whom the

New York Times once described as a man of "marvelous mental density."

It appeared that Mayor Hylan had decided it would be politically expedient to let some of the glory of the Guggenheim-Goldman concerts rub off on himself. On a Wednesday night in June the City Park Department confiscated the regular concert program and substituted one headed, "City of New York. The Mayor Hylan's People's Concerts." Red Mike followed up this sally in the summer of 1925 by banning the Goldman band from Central Park Mall and supplanting it with concerts by police, fire, military and biscuit-company bands. Meanwhile the Guggenheims, their offer to support the concerts turned down by the city, routed the Goldman organization uptown to New York University, which had placed its Washington Heights campus at their disposal.

Never mind what music does to the savage breast; the denial of it to frequenters of Central Park aroused the citizens of New York. At the Municipal Building in downtown Manhattan, pickets assembled, consisting largely of school children who, egged on by their elders, carried posters uncomplimentary to Red Mike and chanted in unison, "The Goldman Band we kiddies all/Want next summer on the Mall." Contemporary rumor has it that His Honor was about to retreat from his position as New York's patron of the arts when the voters saved him the trouble by ejecting him from City Hall and replacing him with lyric-writer Jimmy Walker, who assured the Guggenheims that henceforth the Central Park band shell belonged to them and to Conductor Goldman.

No one was more pleased by this victory than Mr. Dan's wife. Born in Philadelphia in 1863, the daughter of Lazarus and Barbara Kahnweiler Shloss, and married there in 1884, Mrs. Florence Guggenheim was an attractive and gracious woman of aristocratic bearing. Gladys Straus says her most vivid memory of her mother is connected with opera night. "My parents were fond of music," Mrs. Straus says, "and during the season going to the opera with Uncle Murry and Aunt Leonie was a weekly ritual. I used to wait in the hall while mother was dressing in her room. In those days women wore a tremendous lot of clothes for formal occasions, and when Mother emerged ready for the opera, she was the sort of vision a little girl likes to see and remember."

Throughout much of her life, Mrs. Dan devoted herself to a number of philanthropies as a contributor to hospitals, art centers, and Jewish religious and welfare bodies. When in 1942 she transferred title to the Hempstead House estate to the Institute of the Aeronautical Sciences, she added to the gift a typically modest note. "Obviously," she wrote, "I am no specialist in the art or science of aeronautics, but for a score of years aviation has been a familiar subject of discussion in my family life. No cause challenged more keenly the interest of my husband or my son, Harry. . . . Their enthusiasm was contagious and I caught it, though not having their thorough knowledge."

Earlier, in 1940, she had lent Hempstead House to the United States Committee for the Care of European Children as a home for English war refugees. During the First World War she had worked long hours for the four Liberty Loan campaigns, selling $8,000,000 worth of bonds to set what the *New York Times* said appeared to be a record for a single individual. For twenty years she was treasurer and trustee of the Temple Emanu-El Sisterhood of Personal Service. She was a member of the Board of Governors of the American Woman's Association, its treasurer during 1928-1937; and from its creation in 1921 until the end of her life, she was an officer of the Women's National Republican Club, of which she was a co-founder.

Mrs. Dan survived her husband by fourteen years, during which she made her home at Mille Fleurs, a fine house overlooking the Sound, a short walk along the beach from Falaise. Death came on May 13, 1944, and on the following June 14, for the first time in twenty years, she was not in the first-night audience at the opening of the Goldman Band's outdoor season. New York, that evening, was "cool with occasional showers," but by the starting hour 2,000 people had gathered in the Central Park Mall. They stood while Edwin Franko Goldman led his sixty musicians in the Chopin *Funeral March* and listened to brief speeches by Goldman and Mayor LaGuardia. "We all have the sweetest memory of this great public-spirited gentlewoman," the

Daniel and Florence Guggenheim, establishers of the foundation bearing their names and of other philanthropic enterprises.

Mayor said, "and I know she would want us to continue these concerts. . . . As Maestro Goldman said, no better tribute could be paid to Mrs. Guggenheim than through this great music."

Year in and year out, the great music has continued. Now officially known as the "Guggenheim Memorial Concerts," the free Goldman Band summer seasons have long since been placed on the list of projects underwritten by the Daniel and Florence Guggenheim Foundation, established by Mr. and Mrs. Dan in 1924.

Although the Daniel and Florence is the smallest of the permanent Guggenheim endowments, it conducts the most diversified program. During its first thirty-seven years it has made approximately three hundred grants to sixty-two different organizations. Its funds have added to the plants, facilities and staffs of hospitals, and helped underwrite the work of medical units in this country, Chile, the Congo, and Palestine. They have made possible museum exhibits in New York, Illinois, California, New Mexico, and Washington, D.C. They have aided educational institutions and associations on two continents, and contributed to civic, welfare, philanthropic and cultural endeavors all over the world. When this useful organization was set up, nobody seems to have been aware of it. One scans the 1924 newspapers in vain for any mention of its activities; this held true for the next six years, during which the founders contented themselves with using the endowment's resources to support philanthropies in which they had long been interested. Then in the early 1930's the oldest of the Guggenheim foundations shook itself loose from its run-of-the-mill beginnings to become a partner in one of the great adventures of the twentieth century—those experiments with rockets by the late Robert Hutchings Goddard that were to lay the scientific basis for the Age of Space.[2]

The Goddard Story

As supplemented by the recollections of his widow and friends, the story of Robert H. Goddard, inventor, physicist and for many years professor and head of the Physics Department at Clark University in Worcester, Massachusetts, is one of the most appealing to tumble out of the files of any Guggenheim foundation.

It is a success story on the grand scale. It is also a love story, for when in 1924, after a long and persistent courtship, Robert Goddard finally persuaded Worcester-born-and-reared Esther Christine Kisk—tall, stately, blond and eighteen years his junior—to give up her job as secretary to Clark University President Wallace W. Atwood, he found the right wife. Herself no scientist, Esther had a bump of curiosity that made her the perfect partner for one. She once initiated an investigation into the significance of "Kisk," her maiden name, discovering that it was Swedish for the French word casque (helmet). Presumably her ancestors were warriors of such stature in Sweden that they were not only known by the helmets they wore but were also permitted by their chieftains to hand the name down to their descendants.

Although Mrs. Goddard was lacking in science, there would come a moment years after her husband's death when a brilliant patent attorney would fix her with an admiring gaze and say, "Esther, I believe you are the only woman in the country who can look at a rocket and say what is inside of it." Esther would be the last to deny it, since throughout the twenty-one years of a happy marriage, her unspoken slogan was that if "Bob" made it, sooner or later, she, Esther, was going to find out what was in it.

To list only some of the things that Goddard made is to highlight that sensational development between 1912 and 1934 which saw one of the older weapons and playthings of man—the Fourth-of-July skyrocket—converted into the multi-gadgeted steed that would soon carry him into space.

In 1912 Goddard proved that a rocket could travel in space, which is to say he disproved the arguments to the contrary, including what was thought to be the clincher, that no rocket would work in the frictionless-void of a vacuum. By actually shooting a rocket in a vacuum in 1914 he unveiled the principle of rocket thrust using liquid propellants. He also invented the multi-stage rocket, progenitor of the giant cylinders that now roar from their pads at Cape Kennedy. In 1925 he developed the first rocket motor to use liquid propellants. In 1926 he was the first man to launch a rocket of this type, and in 1935 the first to send up one that attained supersonic speed.

As early as 1929 Goddard, in a letter to the famous astrophysicist, Charles Greeley Abbot, then secretary of the Smithsonian Institution in Washington, D.C., was expressing his conviction "that the high efficiency rocket is the only complete answer to an attack by airplanes" and that if "this country allows the thing to slip through its hands because of inadequate protection of the early work, and it is carried forward for military purposes by some other country, our own War Department officials may come in for some criticism."

And in 1940, to come quickly to the incredible anticlimax of all these events, Goddard offered his rocket to the Armed Services, including the Army, Navy and Air Corps, only to have it turned down by the Army, with the other services accepting it only on a limited basis. So it was that the Germans, with their devastating V-2 (hurled at London in 1944 and patterned after ideas published by Goddard twenty-one years earlier) came first into a field where this country could easily have taken the lead.

Born October 5, 1882, in the large frame house in Worcester where his widow still lives, Robert Goddard grew up in what his distinguished friend, G. Edward Pendray, co-founder of the American Rocket Society, has described as an "atmosphere of machinery and engineering accomplishment." His father, Nahum Goddard, was a manufacturer of power-driven knives, operating his own factory in Boston during a portion of his son's boyhood, later moving back to Worcester as an executive of a similar company there.

Stimulated by the high principles displayed by his elders, young Goddard rapidly developed qualities that were to stand him in good stead. One was a great precision of mind coupled with a literary imagination. "I have tried," the adult Goddard would be writing one of his students in 1934, "to train you as I was trained, namely, in the prewar German research ideal, but times have changed and a certain flashiness and lack of thoroughgoing detail is the order of the day." Another quality he picked up early in life was that capacity for passionate concentration which may not be the equivalent of genius but is obviously a *sine qua non* of it. Still another was a sense of fiscal responsibility, along with an almost total indifference to mundane matters. "I think that probably most research workers in pure science," he would one day observe in a letter to a Massachusetts author, "have no inspiration other than an intense interest in the work they are doing. If it happens that their achievements meet with very general public recognition, they are often more surprised and bewildered than elated. Their attitude of mind is, I believe, quite different from the outlook of those who struggle all their lives for the rewards most people think worthwhile."

Mrs. Goddard believes that her husband was fortunate also in that he grew up before the American home was overtaken by its present stress on conformity and "organized busyness." Like most youths of his era, young Goddard could moon around on his own without running the risk of being hauled off to the nearest child psychiatrist. In short, he was free to dream a little—and to find himself.

One summer found him dreaming over H. G. Wells's *War of the Worlds.* Thirty-four years later he would reveal what it meant to him in a letter to Wells himself. "In 1898," he informed England's master of science fiction, "I read your *War of the Worlds.* I was sixteen years old and the new viewpoints of scientific applications . . . made a deep impression. . . . I decided that what might conservatively be called 'high altitude research' was the most fascinating problem in existence. . . . What I find most inspiring is your optimism. It is the best antidote I know for the feeling of depression that comes at times when one contemplates the remarkable capacity for bungling of both man and nature. . . ."

On October 19, 1899, while pruning a cherry tree in his Worcester backyard, seventeen-year-old Goddard was visited by a dream of startling vividness. Suddenly, pausing in his work high in the tree, he let his imagination conjure up the kind of vehicle in which man might some day move from planet to planet. So clear was this vision, so persuasive was it in shaping his future course of study, that in after years he and Esther would celebrate October 19 as his "scientific birthday," and each year he labeled it "Anniversary Day" in his diary.

He began his higher education at Worcester Polytechnic Institute, where during his junior year he started submitting papers to technical publications and collecting rejection slips. *Scientific American, Popular Science Monthly, Popular Astronomy*—all turned down an article entitled "On the Possibility of Navigating Inter-Planetary Space." One editor commented that "the speculation is interesting but impossible." The reference was to Goddard's assumption that some day radioactive materials would provide power for space craft, an assumption that is now being realized. During his senior year, he made a futile effort to prove his thesis by an unauthorized test of a solid-fuel rocket in the cellar of a campus laboratory building. Although the rocket filled the building with smoke, the Worcester Polytechnic authorities were sufficiently impressed, when Goddard graduated, to offer him an instructorship. He combined it with advanced study at Clark, obtaining his master's degree there in 1910, his Ph.D. in 1911. The following year found him at Princeton where he worked by day in the college laboratories as a research fellow, by night in his room on his own rocket ideas.

If in some directions Goddard's early life was marked by advantages, in one it decidedly was not. His mother was a victim of tuberculosis, a wheelchair invalid. Toward the end of her son's year at Princeton, he was prevailed upon to consult a physician about his own fits of heavy coughing. The medical examination showed serious damage to both lungs, and the doctor pronounced sentence. Robert Goddard had two weeks to live!

It wasn't much time for a young man determined to lead his fellow men into space. Goddard took to his bed, but "I have to finish my work," he told the doctor, "and I don't intend to die." He didn't. A year in bed did not cure him, but it arrested the illness sufficiently to permit him, in the fall of 1914, to join the faculty at Clark on a part-time basis. There, his tall, spare frame cut a noticeable figure on the campus and in the lecture hall. After his marriage Esther would "fatten him up" from a skeletal 125 to a presentable 150 pounds by plying him with beefsteaks and potatoes; but when he started teaching at Clark, he was very thin and already getting bald, a boyish-appearing man with a small, straight mustache and large, warm, brown eyes in a handsome face. Years after his death a statue of him was placed on display at the Smithsonian Institution, and Dr. Abbot, commenting on it to Mrs. Goddard, said, "It shows a great and noble scientist, Esther, and that's enough for posterity. But, of course, it is not the Goddard you and I knew." The Goddard they knew, according to Esther, was "as plain as blueberry pie," a man who laughed easily and loved a good joke, who worked like a fiend and relaxed thoroughly by painting in oil, playing the piano by ear, taking long walks in all weathers, and smoking cigars. He loved cigars, but because of his illness he allowed himself only one on ordinary days, two on Sundays and holidays—"and," adds Mrs. Goddard, "he became adept at inventing holidays."

One of his first undertakings after joining the Clark faculty was to devote $800 of his own money to the erection of a complex apparatus for firing a rocket in a vacuum, thus establishing experimentally what he had already proved on paper, that a rocket could and would travel through airless space. Having gone this far, his logical next step was to develop one capable of getting there. But this required money—a great deal more than he could squeeze out of his small salary as a teacher.

In view of the astronomical sums now spent on rocket development, a certain irony attaches to Goddard's efforts, during the next few years, to raise a few thousand dollars. His only hope lay in getting a grant from a scientific institution. To this end in 1916 he prepared a summary of his findings—a 69-page monograph entitled "A Method of Reaching Extreme Altitudes" that is now a classic in the field of astronautics—and sent it to the Aero Club of America, the National Geographic Society, and the Smithsonian. One of the more prophetic passages of Goddard's 1916 paper was his description of what he called the "step-rocket," now better known as the multistage rocket, on which he had obtained the basic patent two years earlier. A step-rocket, Goddard explained, was "a multiple rocket, in which the larger part is consumed, to give high velocity to the smaller part." Anxious weeks followed Goddard's dispatch of his paper to the three scientific organizations, a long silence broken, shortly before the Christmas holidays, by a brief note from the Smithsonian, consisting essentially of a question: Could Professor Goddard estimate the cost of constructing and launching a high-altitude rocket?

The professor could and did, viewing with trepidation what appeared to be the minimum required: $10,000. Fearful that the Smithsonian would refuse this staggering sum, he sliced his estimate in two and mailed it to Washington. Another long silence followed, broken this time shortly after the holidays by a letter that caused him to make the following entry in his faithfully kept diary:

"Jan. 8, 1917—Got grant for $5,000. Got check today of $1,000 from Hodgkins Fund of Smithsonian Institution. Read letter to Ma and Pa. . . . Pa said, 'You certainly put it up to them in wonderful shape.' Ma said, 'I think it's the most wonderful thing I ever saw. Think of it! You send the government[3] some typewritten sheets and some pictures and they send you $1,000 and tell you they are going to send you more.' "

Goddard banked the money and made ready to go on with his experiments, only to be halted by World War I, during which, at the request of the military, he designed and built a modern rocket weapon that was never employed in the field until World War II, when it became a familiar object to G.I.'s, who nicknamed it the "bazooka."

In 1920* the Smithsonian published a slightly revised version of the paper that had won him his grant, his "Method of Reaching Extreme Altitudes," and Goddard got his first taste of the diligence with which the press sometimes bestirs itself to protect its readers against a new idea. One of the assertions of his monograph was that in theory the moon could be hit with a rocket so rigged that flash powder in its nose would explode on impact and make known its landing. Because of this speculation, newspapers across the country derided Goddard as "the Moon man," eminent scientists accused him of "headline-hunting" and the *New York Times* science writer dismissed his mathematics as of less than high school level.

Stung but unbowed, Goddard plunged into the time-consuming calculations and experiments that were to produce the first

* Issued in January of that year, the paper was dated as of the year before.

rocket to be propelled not by a solid fuel (powder) but by a liquid fuel, a combination of gasoline and "lox" (liquid oxygen). Dozens of problems had to be reckoned with simultaneously. One, solved in relatively short order, was the task of developing a metal construction as thin as a dime, yet capable of withstanding the intense heat the engine of a high-altitude rocket must generate. Another, solved years later, was the intricate task of creating dependable steering and stabilizing mechanisms.

A distant relative, Miss Effie Ward, lent Goddard a section of her farm on the outskirts of Auburn, a small town some six miles from Worcester. There—in the secluded hollow of what was then Effie Ward's south pasture, now a part of the rolling fairways of the Pakachoag Golf Club—Goddard set up as a launching tower a 60-foot windmill frame, ordered by mail from Sears, Roebuck and skillfully adapted to his purposes. Here, over a period of years, he tested several rockets, aided by a small crew, of which Mrs. Goddard was a regular member. On March 16, 1926, he succeeded in sending up the first liquid-propellant rocket for a 2½-second, 41-foot-high-at-zenith 184-foot ride that a popular magazine later described as "the parent of all the 9000-mile Atlases and Redstones that will ever fly, all the Sputniks that will ever circle Planet Earth, all the Project Mercury, Saturn and Jupiter capsules that will ever soar to Venus, Moon and Mars. . . ."

More calculations followed, more work at the drawing board and in the laboratory, more "shots" in Aunt Effie's pasture. Mrs. Goddard has the most graphic memories of her part in these proceedings. One of her jobs was to take moving pictures of the rocket in flight. Another was to grab a broom when the flight ended to help put out the inevitable brushfire. Still another, after the test, was to help pick up the pieces, as the rocket always smashed to some extent on landing. Money was scarce, and one of the jobs of the crew, after each shot, was to salvage every scrap of metal that might conceivably be utilized in constructing the next test rocket. It was often cold in Aunt Effie's pasture, and Mrs. Goddard remembers slipping away on occasion, to walk up the hill and across the cabbage patch to warm herself with a home-made malted milk in the farmhouse where Aunt Effie lived with her eight cats.

Over the years, improvements were achieved. In due time Goddard was ready to test a "medium-sized rocket having high center of gravity and low center of air resistance." It was 12 feet tall, 2 feet wide at the waist, weighed 32 pounds unfueled, used 14 pounds of gasoline and 11 of lox—and carried equipment unknown to its predecessors, including a parachute to reduce landing impact, vanes at the rear for guidance, camera set to photograph instruments at zenith of flight, and such data-recording devices as aneroid barometer and thermometer.

At 2 P.M. on July 17, 1929, a "still, hot day," according to Mrs. Goddard, it was fired from its tower, to become probably the first rocket, definitely the first liquid-propellant rocket, to bear recording instruments aloft. The guidance vanes did not function properly, the camera didn't work, and the parachute failed to open; but the rocket soared to a height of almost 100 feet and whistled downwind at 55 feet per second to land 171 feet beyond the tower after an 18½-second flight. Moreover, several of the instruments survived intact, including the barometer, its reading accurate.

All in all it was a spectacular success. And a loud one. Too loud. For years Goddard had been testing rockets in Aunt Effie's pasture without disturbing the neighbors. But there was something new about the shot on that July afternoon in 1929. Perhaps it was the size of the rocket, larger than those previously fired and therefore noisier. Perhaps it was the hot stillness of the day. At any rate, within minutes after the test rocket thundered to earth, the switchboards of police stations in the vicinity were jammed with calls from alarmed citizens, some certain the world had come to an end, other insisting they had seen an airplane come down in flames on the outskirts of Auburn. Before Goddard and his aides could put out the brushfire and collect the pieces, a rescue plane was hovering overhead, two ambulances had come rumbling down the slope into the launching area, and a crowd had gathered, including reporters from the local press.

Next day's Worcester *Evening Post* headlined the incident: "Terrific Explosion as Prof. Goddard of Clark Shoots His Moon

Rocket. . . . Ambulance rushed to Auburn to care for 'victims of crash.' " The *Evening Post* stuck pretty close to the facts, but over the country many newspapers dressed up their stories of "the explosion" with the same heavy humor that had greeted the publication of Goddard's monograph by the Smithsonian a few years before. "Moon Rocket," jeered one typical headline, "misses target by 238,799½ miles." But if the American press continued to treat the hard-working professor's efforts as a big joke, the Soviet Union was beginning to see the light. Two months before the "explosion" in Aunt Effie's pasture, Goddard received a letter from three Russian physics students, a letter prompted by a respectful, if not altogether accurate, report in the Soviet press.

> In the magazine *Truth* of Moscow [the students wrote] there was inserted a notice that you will send a rocket to the moon carrying an explosive. According to this article, you are not certain in advance of the safety of this flight, and this is the reason that you will send it without passengers. Then, in case the apparatus arrives safely on the moon, which will be confirmed by an explosion of flash powder, you will send out a second apparatus, with passengers.
>
> It is said that you are inviting those who wish from all countries to go to the moon (or a neutral point). We, expecting there will be a large number of applicants for the second flight, beg . . . that you give us permission to leave on the first flight. We do not know if there is a cabin for the passengers; and the apparatus—can one steer it? . . .

Contrary to newspaper reports at the time of the "explosion," Goddard and his rockets were not banned from Aunt Effie's pasture. The state fire inspector, after investigation, reported that there was no danger involved in the tests. Further work at the farm, however, was soon found to be impractical. For one thing, the Massachusetts fire marshal informed the professor that henceforth he must restrict the landing of his rockets to the half-mile-square area in which his launching tower was located. To date this had been sufficient space, but Goddard was already dreaming up missiles of a much longer range. For another, as Goddard explained in a letter to Dr. Abbot of the Smithsonian, after the explosion, Aunt Effie's farm was besieged by newspaper men and sightseers bent on photographing and measuring the tower and on gathering "souvenirs." Goddard expressed worry over possible danger to spectators, plus the chance of misinterpretation by reporters. "Thus," he wrote, "whenever we conduct a static test, with the rocket weighed down and supported on a spring balance, the idea will be to broadcast that the rocket was not able to rise from the tower." Everything considered, it seemed wise to seek another proving ground, and after almost three months of negotiations, during which all testing had to be held up, Abbot persuaded the War Department to let the professor use the artillery range of Camp (now Fort) Devens near Ayer Junction, Massachusetts, 25 miles north of Worcester.

Although the delay it caused was irksome and the Camp Devens site proved less than satisfactory,[4] the explosion in Aunt Effie's pasture turned out to be a blessing in disguise. It might be gilding the lily to liken it to "the shot heard 'round the world," but fortunately for Goddard, and for the future of rocketry, it *was* heard one autumn afternoon in the manorial living room of Falaise, Harry Guggenheim's place on the shores of Long Island Sound.[5]

Lindbergh was at Falaise that afternoon. His reconstruction of the incident and of the events leading up to it runs thus: "I had been doing a great deal of cross-country flying," he begins. "Flying cross country in good weather in those days you had plenty of time to think." What Lindbergh was thinking about in 1929 was the remote future of flight. Its immediate future was already taking shape. Obviously planes were going to get bigger, better and faster. Obviously the day was not far off when men could say they had conquered the atmosphere. Then, in Lindbergh's opinion, they were going to get restless. Then they were going to want to go higher. Human nature abhors a conquered frontier, and in the words of the late Indian poet, Rabindranath Tagore, all men are essentially "Travellers/Whose eternal journey is toward the future/ . . . Into the Unknown, into the Unseen. . . ."

The plane as it was taking form, Lindbergh reasoned, would never take men "into the Unknown, into the Unseen." But if rocket power could be added to aviation power—then perhaps!

One day in the summer of 1929 this possibility carried him

to Wilmington, Delaware, to have a talk with officials of the Du Pont Company, makers, among many things, of the black powder used in solid-propellant rockets. Lindbergh realized that to interest the Du Pont Company in supporting the advancement of rocketry he would have to suggest some immediate practical application. With this in mind, he said to the officials, "Now, couldn't we develop a rocket that could be attached to a plane for the purpose of giving it one minute of thrust in case of engine failure on take-off, thus avoiding having to land it in a city or in trees?"

The Du Pont men were dubious. They gave it as their opinion that there was no future in rockets connected with airplanes; and a month later one of them made it official with a letter asserting that the flier's idea did not look feasible, since "to equal the thrust for one minute of a Wasp engine would require about 400 pounds of black powder, and the heat would be so intense that the powder would have to be burned in a fire-brick combustion chamber."

Lindbergh was downcast, and one afternoon later that year, as he sat with Harry Guggenheim in the living room at Falaise, his discouragement was the burden of their conversation. The flier no longer recalls the exact date of this conference. To the best of his memory, however, it was "sometime in November," about three months after the "explosion" in Aunt Effie's pasture.

"Carol, Harry's second wife, was with us," he says. "Naturally she wasn't interested in our technical discussion, so she was sitting over to one side, reading a newspaper. I thought she was paying no attention to us at all but suddenly she said, 'Listen to this, you two,' and proceeded to read aloud an article from a back page of the newspaper."

The article was a wire-service story dealing in part with the noisy doings at Aunt Effie's farm during the previous July. When Carol finished, Harry was smiling. "May be the answer to our problem," he told Lindbergh. "Why don't you check up on Goddard? Go have a talk with him, if you think it's worthwhile."

Lindbergh checked. The late fall found him at MIT, making inquiries among the scientists there, and on November 22 he phoned Goddard from New Jersey, where the aviator and his family were then living in a rented farmhouse near Princeton. At that time, as had been true for years, the Goddards were at Number One Tallawanda Drive (formerly Maple Hill) in Worcester, in the frame house that had been the professor's birthplace. The professor, however, was in his office at Clark University when Lindbergh's call came through.

He had already learned that Lindbergh was looking into his work. All the same, hearing a strange voice claiming to be the famous aviator, he suspected a practical joke. It took Lindbergh a few seconds to identify himself convincingly and to arrange for a meeting with the professor at Clark the following day.

It was a fruitful session. The Du Ponts had said that to generate sufficient power for a high altitude rocket, their *solid* propellant would have to be burned in a fire-brick combustion chamber. Naturally then, Lindbergh was pleased to learn that Goddard was burning his *liquid* propellant in one lined with a metal only one thirty-second of an inch thick.

November 23, 1929, the date of Lindbergh's visit, was a Saturday. Mrs. Goddard was listening to a football game on the radio when her husband brought Lindbergh to the house after their talk at Clark. The aviator's arm was in a sling and he looked tired after his long drive by car from New Jersey. Mrs. Goddard asked what had happened and found his answer engaging. It apppeared that the first man to fly the Atlantic nonstop and alone had injured his arm while crawling under a bed to retrieve a puppy.*

Goddard kept his diary in the top drawer of his dresser and that night, as every night, his last act before retiring was to get it out and scribble his daily entry while standing at the dresser in his pajamas. "Brought Lindbergh home for coffee," he wrote, adding that the young man struck him as having "a good head on his shoulders." On the Clark campus, people had spotted the flier's tall figure and familiar face. Sunday's local papers were full of his visit and a friend of the Goddards called to inquire teasingly, "Who have you got at your house now—President Hoover?"

* In 1925, during an emergency parachute jump, Lindbergh dislocated his right shoulder. Since that incident, he writes, the "bone has slipped out of joint on a number of occasions . . . rather too easily."

Realizing that Goddard would need a great deal of money to complete his experiments, Lindbergh tried a couple of other possible financial sources before going back to Harry Guggenheim. Once again he arranged for a meeting with the Du Pont people in Wilmington, this time taking Goddard with him.

This conference, taking place on the day before Thanksgiving, was not a fruitful one. All Goddard took away from it was the conviction that the Du Pont people, far from being interested in underwriting his work, were only interested in picking his brain. Three Du Pont laboratory men interviewed him, and "I realized soon," he would shortly be writing to Abbot, "that the object of this questioning was . . . to find every last detail of the rocket I have developed during the last nine years, and after I saw this I avoided further questions as to these construction details, as much as possible."

Goddard's reaction to the Du Pont meeting is of interest in view of the assertion of several of his close associates that where his scientific work was concerned he was unusually secretive. Some friends attribute this trait to the rude treatment he received for so many years from the press. Most, however, believe that the published ridicule merely strengthened a natural tendency.

"In the 1930's," Lindbergh recalls, "after Goddard had brought his rockets to a high state of efficiency, I urged him to patch up one of the test models and send it to the Smithsonian Institution for exhibit purposes. He was most reluctant, and when he finally did so, the rocket arrived at the Smithsonian in a sealed case with instructions that, except to make sure that *Nell** had arrived intact, it was not to be opened without his consent. It was still sealed at the time of his death, and two years later I had a letter from the Smithsonian authorities, saying they were eager to open the case but that Goddard had stipulated that this was not to be done without the consent of Harry Guggenheim and myself."**

Having once more failed to interest the Du Ponts, Lindbergh

* Professor Goddard's rockets were all nicknamed "Nell."

** In 1947, with the consent of Lindbergh and Harry, this *Nell* was removed from her case and can now be seen along with other Goddard rockets in the National Air Museum at the Smithsonian Institution in Washington, D.C.

turned to the Carnegie Institution of Washington. There he met with some success. On December 10, the Carnegie authorities listened attentively to Goddard's description of his work and plans. A few days later they authorized a grant of $5,000, simultaneously taking under consideration the possibility of a far larger sum—a development that never materialized.

Finally, in the spring of 1930, Lindbergh wrote his friend Harry Guggenheim, then in Cuba as our ambassador, asking if he had any objection "to my talking to his father about the possibility of financing Goddard's work." Harry replied promptly, telling him to go ahead, and shortly thereafter Lindbergh called on Mr. Dan at Hempstead House. There Lindbergh gave the older man a resumé of his talks with Goddard and of the status of the professor's experiments. The conversation was brief and to the best of Lindbergh's memory went about like this:

Mr. Dan: "Then you believe rockets have an important future?"

Lindbergh: "Probably. Of course one is never certain."

"But you think so. And this professor, he looks like a pretty capable man?"

"As far as I can find out, Mr. Guggenheim, he knows more about rockets than anybody else in the country."

"How much money does he need?"

"He'd like to have $25,000 a year for a four-year project."

"Do you think he can accomplish enough to make it worth his time?"

"Well, it's taking a chance, but if we're ever going to get beyond the limits of airplanes and propellers, we'll probably have to go to rockets. It's a chance but, yes, I think it's worth taking."

"All right, I'll give him the money."

Within the next few weeks arrangements were made for Goddard to take a leave of absence from his teaching and for Mr. Dan's grants to be made to Clark University for transference to the Professor; and on July 15, Goddard and his wife closed up the Worcester house and piled into their car to head west—destination, Roswell, New Mexico—in search of a stretch of relatively uninhabited country suitable for the testing of high altitude rockets.[6]

All around the big living room of the Goddard house in Worcester are oil paintings made by the late Professor during his Sunday outings with brush and canvas. Six of them show scenes in what is known as the Eden Valley area of east-central New Mexico: billowing masses of flowers, lavender, pink and white, their slender stems bowing before the wind; a lone cottonwood in an expanse of caliche-whitened soil, with the El Capitan mountains in the blue distance and beyond them the snow-capped crest of the towering Sierra Blanca. Here, in July 1930, Goddard found his final proving ground, his sky-high outdoor laboratory, "relatively uninhabited" save by scorpions, gophers and rattlesnakes. Here in the fourteen-room adobe house of the eight-acre Mescalero Ranch, three miles northeast of Roswell and at the end of the power line, Esther set up housekeeping. As rapidly as he and his crew could manage it, Goddard erected a shop of 35 by 60-foot floor space at the rear of the ranch house and a 20-foot proving stand for static tests some 200 feet from the shop, and installed the 60-foot tower previously used in Massachusetts at a point some 13 miles away. And here for a period of almost eleven years, he tested and refined the modern rocket. Sooner or later, "in one form or another," to quote Dr. Pendray, he tried out "practically every one of the ideas that have since been developed successfully in large rockets and guided missiles, including gyro-controls, clustered rockets, research instrumentation, turbopumps for propellants, and gimbal-mounted tail sections capable of being moved in flight for steering. . . ." Pendray adds that the "culmination of Goddard's work in New Mexico was a rocket that made a successful altitude shot of some 9,000 feet, and that contained almost all of the features later incorporated into the German V-2 rockets."

The New Mexico record, as summarized by Mrs. Goddard, shows at least 103 static or proving-stand tests and forty-eight flight tests, of which thirty-one gave flights. There were successes —and failures. When there was a success, the professor would cry, "All right, boys, let's go see what we did right." And when there was a failure, "All right, boys, let's go see what we did wrong." The professor knew that failure is man's best teacher.

Years before, in a notebook kept as a boy, he had written, "Failure crowns enterprise!"

An occasional guest at the Roswell establishment was Harry Guggenheim, sometimes alone, sometimes with Lindbergh, once with Alicia. On every visit a flight test was attempted. "Boy, that's power!" Harry would mutter delightedly as the rocket was fired up by means of controls in the little shack behind the corrugated-iron barricade set up for the protection of personnel. And on each visit the attempt failed, with the result that Harry never witnessed one of Goddard's increasingly improved rockets roaring skyward.

In the beginning the money that kept Goddard going came not from one of the Guggenheim foundations but from Mr. Dan's personal funds. The aging philanthropist agreed to support the professor's work for two years and then, if an advisory committee set up at Clark so recommended, to do so for another two. But matters did not work out quite like that. At the conclusion of the two years the committee approved a continuance, but the money was not available, partly because the depression had set in but chiefly because the estate of Mr. Dan, who had died in 1930, was still in the process of being settled.

Back went the Goddards to Worcester and Clark University where, with the aid of another small grant from the Smithsonian, the professor continued his rocket studies on a less ambitious scale until the summer of 1934, when the Daniel and Florence Guggenheim Foundation took over where its founder had left off, making the first of the many annual grants—each of them in the neighborhood of $18,000—that would keep Goddard in New Mexico for nine more busy and fruitful years, a period that Esther often speaks of as "the golden period."

In the early spring of each of these years there was always a nervous few weeks for the Goddards while they waited to see if the trustees of the Daniel and Florence would renew the grant. Clark University also found these waiting periods trying. With Goddard in New Mexico, the university had to hire a substitute professor, an action that, in fairness to the substitute, had to be taken well in advance of the school year, at a date prior to the annual meeting of the foundation trustees. On at least two occasions Harry Guggenheim eased the situation by assuring the university that if the Goddard grant were not renewed, he would personally guarantee the salary of the substitute professor. Goddard was touched by this gesture. "Harry sure has a very wonderful thumb," he told his wife. "He can put it on the sore spot in less time than it takes to tell it."

Mention has already been made of the anticlimatic nature of the closing chapter of the Goddard story. It was Harry who, in May of 1940, arranged the Washington meeting with representatives of the three branches of the Armed Forces—the meeting at which Goddard, for the second time in his life, offered his work and services to his country, and was turned down. The Army representative said his branch still believed that "the next war will be won with the trench mortar." The Air Corps and Navy men could see no possibilities in the rocket as a missile weapon. Later the Air and Navy branches did engage Goddard, to carry on research in the development "of liquid-fuel rocket motors to assist heavily loaded aircraft take off from water on short runways and to power fast climbs in emergencies." This was not unimportant work, but in the words of Pendray, to waste a man of Goddard's caliber on it was "like trying to harness Pegasus to a plow."

For six months Goddard did his work on JATO (the jet-assisted take-off project) in his own shop at Roswell. During this period he functioned under a letter of intent issued by the Navy, without immediate funds. To keep going he and Esther mortgaged everything they had and obtained from Harry a loan of $10,000, which they later paid off. In July 1941, the professor was transferred to the Navy Engineering Experimental Station in Annapolis, where he remained for the duration of World War II.

In Annapolis Esther served as her husband's secretary until she discovered that it was "not proper" for a "Navy wife" to work. After years of working at her husband's side, she found it difficult to dedicate herself to housekeeping. Besides, it failed to fill her day, so she became a commuter to Baltimore where she obtained a degree in history with an English minor at Johns Hopkins University. Since Johns Hopkins would not give a B.A. degree to a woman, she had to content herself with a B.S. This

Harry Guggenheim, Robert H. Goddard, and Charles A. Lindbergh at Dr. Goddard's New Mexico rocket launching site, 1935.

irked her at first, but today, with people from all over the world coming to her for information about her late husband's work, she is glad to have the B.S. "since it makes it sound as if I had a degree in science."

Even before the Goddards left Roswell, the professor's health had shown signs of deterioration, and at Johns Hopkins Hospital in June 1945, as Esther says, with irony, he made "still another contribution to science." Previously doctors had had reason to believe that tuberculosis and cancer did not occur together, but in the course of two operations, both necessitated by his old enemy, TB, the professor was found to have cancer of the throat. "Our friends were wonderful while Bob was in the hospital," Mrs. Goddard says. She especially remembers Harry telephoning to say, "I want you to tell Bob that I will finance him after the war is over for whatever he wants, as much as he wants, as long as he wants." But there was to be no "after the war" for Robert Hutchings Goddard. On August 10, 1945, "this quiet, gentle, persistent and dauntless man," to quote Pendray again, was dead at the age of sixty-two.[7]

Naturally the Goddard story has its epilogues. One has to do with the professor's patents. At the time of his death Goddard held or had applied for eighty-three patents, taken out in connection with rockets and other items. But these were only the beginning. He left behind an extensive file of memoranda, plans and blueprints; and at the conclusion of a twelve-year battle that began in 1945, Mrs. Goddard and the Daniel and Florence Guggenheim Foundation found themselves joint owners of another 131 Goddard patents and joint sharers in a settlement for one million dollars made by the Federal government for infringement.

Another epilogue: In 1948 a Goddard exhibit was mounted under the auspices of the Daniel and Florence and toured around the country, beginning at the American Museum of Natural History in New York City. On the day of the opening ceremony in New York, a small crowd gathered to hear speeches by Mrs. Goddard, Harry, Doolittle and others. On the following day Mrs. Goddard rose early and hurried out to the museum, thinking that at that hour there would be no crowd and she could spend a little time alone with the main attraction of the exhibit, the rocket that had been put aside in 1942 when Goddard started working for the Navy.

When she arrived, the exhibit hall, as she had hoped, was empty, "and I was able to sit there awhile by myself, talking to *Nell* [the rocket] in my mind. Suddenly I was no longer alone. The doors exploded open and in flocked a busload of school children. There was much shouting, laughter and pointing, but after all the other children had chattered their way to far parts of the building, one nice-looking little boy remained behind. If he noticed me sitting there, he gave no sign. He just stood for a long time silently gazing at *Nell,* and I said to myself, 'There's a coming Faraday,* another Goddard.' "

More Centers

The Goddard story is a convincing demonstration of the ability of a private-giving organization, in this case the Daniel and Florence Guggenheim Foundation, to keep alive a new field of human endeavor at a time when its practical applications are not foreseeable. True, during World War II, the blasting of London by the German V-2's had given sickening proof of the ability of the rocket as a weapon of destruction. Here and there men of vision had started talking about its peacetime possibilities. Nonetheless, when in 1945, shortly after Goddard's death, the Daniel and Florence set out to find "appropriate means of giving further momentum to the work he [Goddard] had so magnificently begun," it was still in advance of its times. Seven years would elapse before the United States government would begin construction of large military rockets on a serious scale, ten before this country and Russia would publicly announce their intention of launching satellites and other space-probing de-

* The English scientist, Michael Faraday (1791-1867), was one of Goddard's idols. Once while the Goddards were visiting a museum of science and industry in London, Mrs. Goddard lagged a little behind. "Suddenly," she says, "my husband, all excited, called and beckoned to me from the far end of a long hall, and when I arrived at his side, he was pointing to some object and shouting, 'Just think! Faraday actually *touched* this.' Believe me, at my first opportunity I got hold of an encyclopedia and looked up Faraday."

vices, seventeen before the orbiting of Telstar and the multi-million-mile drifting of Mariner II to the orbit of planet Venus would bring the rocket into its own as a contributor to the arts of peace.

It was principally with those arts in mind that the Daniel and Florence, in 1947, commissioned its consultant on rocketry, G. Edward Pendray, to carry on a study aimed at uncovering the answers to such questions as: What was the situation in this country with regard to rocketry and jet propulsion; that is, precisely what was being done in the laboratories of universities and in the workshops of industry? What direction was present development taking? What sort of work was in progress or being planned with peacetime applications in view? What was the current status of availability of trained personnel? What skills were in shortest supply and in what fields should future personnel be trained? What kinds of research were not being adequately provided for by governmental expenditure? What projects, over and above those under way, should be put in train to speed development of the field? What were its most pressing and immediate needs, its long-range needs, and in what ways could a small foundation like the Daniel and Florence be of assistance in helping fulfill them?

One hundred and five letters and questionnaires were sent to representatives of government and military agencies, to individuals distinguished for their contributions to the field, and to officials of those industries and universities which, according to a previous study, were known to be engaged in rocket and jet propulsion work. Replies were received from 87 per cent of the institutions queried, from 76 per cent of the individuals. Most were highly detailed. Consequently the Pendray report, published by the Foundation in 1948 under the title, *Opinion Survey of Leading Engineers and Scientists on Future Developments in Rockets and Jet Propulsion,* remains to this day a revealing picture of the needs and possibilities of the field.

As for what the Foundation could do, the principal recommendation was that it help establish schools where research could be carried on, techniques developed and engineers trained for the space age ahead. Acting on this suggestion, the Foundation devoted several months to choosing appropriate sites. An early decision was to finance two institutions, one in the West, the other in the East, and on December 14, 1948, the necessary grants—each for $239,000 plus additional sums for travel and other matters—were announced, one for CIT, the other for Princeton University.

Originally set up on a seven-year basis, both centers are now permanent parts of the universities at which they are located. That in the West is officially known as the Daniel and Florence Guggenheim Jet Propulsion Center at California Institute of Technology, unofficially as the JPC; that in the East, now an integral unit of Princeton's new Forrestal Research Center, was originally called The Daniel and Florence Guggenheim Jet Propulsion Center at Princeton University, was recently renamed The Daniel and Florence Guggenheim Laboratories for the Aerospace Propulsion Sciences and is unofficially referred to as the Guggenheim Laboratories or (by the students) as "Danny and Flo's Place."

In 1955, which marked the end of the trial period, the Foundation made two additional grants, $215,000 to the center at CIT and $205,000 to the one at Princeton, and on July 1, 1961, the Princeton center, aided by a further grant of $225,000 from the Foundation, enlarged the scope of its operations, changed its name, and began construction of the laboratory building it now occupies in the Forrestal compound.

One of the terms under which each of the Jet Propulsion Centers was created called for the establishment of an advisory committee to be appointed by the Foundation and to be known as the Foundation Committee. As president of the Daniel and Florence, Harry Guggenheim sits on these committees, the remaining members of which are men familiar with the field and for the most part active in it. Every year the Foundation committees meet together with the officials of the centers and with Harry Guggenheim. The work of the preceding period is reviewed and future plans discussed. Of recent years the officials of the Princeton and Caltech centers and of the Guggenheim Institute of Flight Structures at Columbia, another of the centers

A few of the men connected with aerospace centers financed by the Daniel and Florence Guggenheim Foundation. Left to right: Dr. G. Edward Pendray, Dr. J. Lubliner, Dr. Martin Summerfield, Dr. Luigi Crocco, Dr. Bruno A. Boley, Dr. Clark B. Millikan, Prof. Frank E. Marble, Dr. Theodore von Kármán, Prof. Jewell M. Garrelts, Harry F. Guggenheim, Prof. Irvin Glassman, Dr. John R. Dunning, Prof. Hans Bleich, Prof. Courtland D. Perkins.

underwritten by the Foundation, have taken part together in these confabs.

This arrangement, under which the Daniel and Florence maintains liaison with its beneficiaries, is interesting for the light it sheds on Harry Guggenheim's concept of his role as a foundation executive. "I think a foundation should try to avoid becoming a kind of absentee landlord," Harry has said. "For one thing, the gift isn't worth much unless a little of the giver goes with it. For another I believe a foundation gets better results when it spends its money on things in which its leaders are genuinely interested. Perhaps this sort of informal, intuitive, personal approach would not work for a very large foundation, handling a great variety of projects, but it has worked very well for us."

According to men close to the Guggenheim centers, it has also worked well for the aerospace sciences. The yearly conferences enable the various centers to coordinate their work. Simultaneously they provide the Daniel and Florence with the information it needs to plan in an intelligent way its future donations to the field.

To help the jet propulsion centers attract competent students, portions of the foundation's grants were earmarked for fellowships, up to six of which are given annually at each school. The fellowship provides for tuition and a stipened which ranges from $1,200 to $2,400 depending on the stage of advance of the Fellow. To honor the late "Father of Modern Rocketry," the grants provided that the staff of each center be headed by a Robert H. Goddard Professor.

Occupant of the Goddard chair at Princeton is slender, fine-featured, fifty-four-year-old Dr. Luigi Crocco. Born in Palermo, Sicily, he is the son of Gaetano Arturo Crocco, a general in the Italian air force and one of Europe's outstanding astronautical scientists. One of the younger Crocco's fondest memories is of an incident at the first International Congress on High Speed Flight, a meeting organized by his father and known as the Volta Congress of 1935. Among those present was Theodore von Kármán, then well into his work as director of the Guggenheim Aeronautical Laboratory at CIT. Chancing upon the two Croccos, von Kármán grabbed the older man's hand, saying that he wished to express his admiration "for your paper on heat flow," a treatise entitled "On the Heat Transfer from a Flat Plate to a Fluid Flowing at High Speeds." Says the younger Crocco, "It was a big moment for me when my father turned von Kármán in my direction and said, 'I didn't write the paper you mention, Professor. My son here is to blame for that one.' " A pioneer in the field of supersonic aerodynamics, the younger Crocco was a member of the faculty of the University of Rome for thirteen years prior to coming to this country in 1949 to become Princeton's first Goddard Professor.

At CIT, the Goddard Professorship has been held by two men. The first, Dr. Hsue-shen Tsien, was a thirty-eight-year-old professor of aerodynamics at MIT at the time of his appointment in December of 1948. Because he came from Red China, Tsien ran into trouble in 1951 when the United States authorities withdrew his security clearance, thus denying him access to classified documents. Five years later he resigned and announced his intention of returning to his homeland, stating that he did not wish to rear his children in a country "where under the circumstances they are certain to suffer the stigma of second-classism." At the last moment there were further troubles when immigration inspectors found in his luggage what appeared to be a classified document. As a matter of fact, the document had been declassified, but since this fact did not show on the face of it, Tsien was compelled to delay his departure until the matter was cleared up. He is now director of the division of applied mechanics at the National Academy of Sciences in Peking.

The incidents surrounding Tsien's return to China are still the subject of frequent and often heated comment by his colleagues. It was the late Dr. von Kármán's recollection that Tsien was never "at ease in his mind" while at CIT. "Even before he was cited by the McCarthy Committee," von Kármán once said, "Tsien used to come to me and say, 'Don't you think it is my duty to return to China?' My answer was always the same. 'No,' I would tell him. 'It is not your duty. You're a theorist and Communist China does not need theorists. She needs only engineers.' " Dr. William Duncan Rannie, Tsien's successor as Goddard Professor at CIT, contends that Tsien was "a victim of

McCarthyism," adding that "he was guilty of nothing but being Chinese, and his departure under a cloud deprived this country of an able and useful scientist."

Rannie, assuming the Goddard professorship at CIT in 1956, brought to his post a distinguished record as an aerodynamicist. Born in Chesley, Ontario, Canada, in 1914, he moved to the States in 1938 and was naturalized in 1941. A member of the CIT faculty since 1946, he has also worked with the Northrop Aircraft (now the Northrop-Hendy) Company. Both the Guggenheim Jet Propulsion Center he directs and the one at Princeton, according to disinterested scientists, have made invaluable contributions to astronautics. Both have proved once again the validity of the seed-money principle. As such things go in this country, the grants which put them under way were not enormous. "All the same," says Prof. Martin Summerfield of the Princeton center, "they were critical sums, in that they were made available at just the right time, under just the right circumstances. You might speak of them as the risk capital that has made possible everything that has happened since, the acorn from which the oak has grown." The Princeton center is now doing approximately a million dollars' worth of research for the Federal government every year, while the two Guggenheim-sponsored institutions at CIT, the Aeronautical Laboratory and the Jet Propulsion Center, are doing in the neighborhood of $650,000 worth.[8]

In recent years the Daniel and Florence has made possible the creation of three more centers devoted to research or training, or both, in the aerospace sciences. They are:

The Daniel and Florence Guggenheim Aviation Safety Center at Cornell University, established in 1950 by an initial grant of $180,000 (subsequently increased by annual grants totaling $298,-000 as of 1962) with national headquarters in New York City. Policy for the center is set by the Foundation Committee[9] and its work is carried out under Jerome Lederer, president of the Flight Safety Foundation and formerly director of the Safety Bureau of the Civil Aeronautics Board.

The safety center is an outgrowth, to some degree, of the crash injury program conducted some years ago by Hugh De Haven of the Cornell University Medical College in New York City—studies which, having revealed that 75 per cent of all crash fatalities are the result of injuries to the head, were to prompt the increased use of safety belts in automobiles. The center's real roots, however, go further back—to the Safe Aircraft Competition and other air safety-promotion projects carried out in the late 1920's by the Daniel Guggenheim Fund for the Promotion of Aeronautics.

It will be recalled that the winning plane of the Safe Aircraft Competition was the Curtiss Tanager, the entry of the Curtiss Aeroplane and Motor Company (later the Curtiss-Wright Corporation); and that the team which developed it was headed by Theodore P. Wright. Shortly after the Second World War, Dr. Wright, who had become vice-president for research at Cornell University, drew Harry Guggenheim's attention to the growing safety problems of modern flying; and on December 12, 1949, he proposed that a body known as the Cornell Committee for Air Safety Research be re-constituted as the Guggenheim Air Safety Center at Cornell. The Cornell committee was coordinating aviation safety work being done by the various divisions of the university. One of these was the university's medical college, where De Haven was conducting his crash injury studies, and what Dr. Wright was specificially seeking was further support for De Haven's work.

Harry's response to Wright's proposal was that any aviation safety work sponsored by the Daniel and Florence should not be the province of any single university or be confined to any single project. He suggested instead a more comprehensive plan under which all major American institutions concerned with aviation safety could join hands for a massive attack on its problems. Out of this proposal grew the present center which, although directed from a single university, is national in scope, and of late years has taken on international dimensions.

In line with the center's broad interests, the membership of its foundation committee includes the executive heads of all of the principal American governmental and civilian agencies dealing with aviation safety. Direct supervision of its work rests with an executive committee, of which Dr. Wright was the first chairman and whose personnel originally consisted of technical safety experts, each appointed by one of the official agencies represented on the foundation committee, along with the heads of all of the colleges and divisions of Cornell engaged in aviation safety research. Upon the retirement of Dr. Wright as vice-president of Cornell in 1961, General E. R. Quesada, former administrator of the Federal Aviation Agency, became chairman, and in 1963 the executive committee was reorganized. It now consists of a group of outstanding national figures with broad interests and backgrounds in aviation safety. The executive committee, as formerly constituted, has been renamed the Technical Committee, and its chairman is Jerome Lederer.

The center launched its work with a survey of aviation safety activities throughout the country. Its first report, issued January 1, 1951, listed more than 1,500 such research projects, and called attention to what it regarded as "gaps" where investigation should either be initiated or investigation already under way should be intensified. Since 1951 these survey reports have been published every other year, with supplements coming out in the alternate years.

The center has conducted a variety of projects. Notable among them was its development of a publication known as *Design Notes,* some 4,000 copies of which are distributed monthly to aeronautical engineers and students. *Design Notes* has been described by Pendray, a member of the foundation committee, as "an attempt to cope with what engineers call Murphy's law, which is, if a machine can be put together wrong, someone will put it together that way." Each bulletin presents a single mistake in design which has led to an accident, shows by easy-to-grasp illustrations the dangers inherent in the design, and suggests a safe way to achieve the same desired result. *Design Notes* has proved popular with aircraft manufacturers, several of whom regularly reproduce additional copies and distribute them among their engineers. In 1955 a booklet reproducing thirty-six of the *Design Notes* and ten *Human Engineering Bulletins*—another publication developed by the center—was published by the magazine *Aviation Age.* At the moment both *Design Notes* and *Human Engineering Bulletins* are put out under the auspices of the

Flight Safety Foundation, a related organization sponsored by aircraft manufacturers and airlines.

At Mr. Guggenheim's suggestion, the safety center has taken a strong hand in encouraging the development of so-called VTOL-STOL aircraft, that is, of aircraft capable of taking off and landing vertically or almost vertically. It was one of the first organizations in the country to fasten attention on the human and sociological factors involved in safety, stressing, among other things, the need for steps to avoid accidents caused by fatigue from overwork on the part of airplane crews or by tension in the cockpit because of the presence there of men belonging to different industrial unions.

"One of its tangential functions," executive director Lederer has said of the safety center, "is its ability, occasionally, to serve as a big shoulder on which the pilots, engineers and ground crew members of the aviation industry can come and cry. Airplane manufacturers and transport companies sometimes back away from new safety practices and devices because they cost money. We don't have to worry about that. We are not connected with any industry, so we are in a position to put a bright light on whatever is wrong and keep it there until something is done about it. Moreover, since we are not connected with any government agency, we are in a key position, when a national safety problem comes up, of bringing together all of the elements—industrial, governmental, etc.—interested in its solution."

The center has instituted a number of such conferences and every year its committee members and staff meet with key people in the industry to exchange information on what has been done during the period. "We don't necessarily meet with the high executives," Lederer points out. "We meet with the engineers and such-like, whoever can most effectively bring about results, and we don't invite the press."

In efforts to improve the safety of private flying, the center has organized two major conferences of private plane manufacturers, pilots' associations, government agencies and university research organizations. These conferences, plus much subsequent work by the center, resulted in aroused interest in private flying safety. Discovering some time ago that the pilots of America's 70,000 private aircraft were doing at least twice as much flying as commercial pilots and averaging a breath-taking 4,000 accidents and 835 fatalities a year, the center played a leading role in inducing the Federal Aviation Agency to rule that a private pilot must demonstrate basic instrument-flying capability to get a license. Not long ago the center presuaded one private plane manufacturing company to cease running an advertisement carrying a line to the effect that "If you can drive a car, you can drive a plane." "That just ain't so," Lederer says. Right now the center is trying to persuade another company to change an advertisement saying in effect, "Anyone can fly a helicopter." Comments Lederer, "Anyone can't!"

Human Factors Bulletin, another publication originated by the center, is aimed at showing engineers that in designing planes they should consider the limitation of the people who are going to operate and maintain them. "They must consider, for example," says Lederer, "the question of whether the openings provided in the engine are large enough for a mechanic to get in his hands or his head, as the case may be, to change a spark plug or adjust a valve."

In 1959 the center set up in London an office for the assembling and exchanging of aviation safety information from and among the nations of Europe. Director of this work is Yugoslavian-born Bosco R. Stanojlovic, a thin, handsome, silver-haired aviator who was a flight safety officer with the Royal Air Force for sixteen years, during three of which he headed the education branch of the Directorate of Flight Safety in the British Air Ministry. Some notion of the value of Wing Commander Stanojlovic's labors is gained from his recent receipt of a letter from officials of the West German government requesting information on what was being done in aviation safety in their own country. At the present time the center is cautiously extending its international information exchange into the Near East, and hopes some day also to send Stanojlovic to Africa. "There's a lot of questions in our mind about possible aviation safety problems in those emerging nations," says Lederer. "For instance, does the color red spell danger to an African? How do you instill sensitivity to danger in a tribesman charged with driving a fuel truck around an airport?"

Also on the center agenda is an intensive campaign to persuade airplane-makers to install equipment designed to prevent a plane from catching on fire when it crashes. According to Cornell's Dr. Wright, a member and former chairman of the Executive Committee, such equipment is now available, "but it's hard to get the plane-makers interested, because it takes up space and it costs money." Coming up on the center agenda is the problem of preventing planes from injuring people by falling on them. As of January, 1962, only thirty-three persons had died in accidents of this sort, but, in the words of Dr. R. M. Woodham, Lederer's assistant, "the world is getting fuller of people, and fuller of planes."

Each year the foundation and executive committees of the center meet in Washington, to hear reports on the progress of aviation safety, the results of the center's current work, plans for future work, and discussion on various aspects of the changing safety problem resulting from the introduction of new types of military and civilian aircraft and the growth of air traffic. Through these annual meetings, that bring together top officials and technical representatives of all the major governmental, military and civilian agencies interested in flight safety, the nation's aviation safety efforts are stimulated and given coordination, the various agencies involved are kept informed of progress, and the center's own program directed and focused.[10]

The Daniel and Florence Guggenheim Institute of Flight Structures at Columbia University, established in 1953 by an initial grant of $329,000 (supplemented in 1960 by an additional $200,000) as a unit of the Columbia Engineering center, with Dr. John R. Dunning, dean of the School of Engineering, as administrator; Prof. Jewell M. Garrelts, chairman of the Columbia Department of Civil Engineering and Engineering Mechanics, as program director; and Dr. Hans Bleich, consulting engineer for aircraft companies in Europe and the United States, as technical director and principal professor. Liaison with the Foundation is maintained by a committee similar in organization to the Foundation committees for the Jet Propulsion and Safety centers and which meets annually with those bodies. Part of the endowment is earmarked for fellowships, up to six of which are given yearly, each providing tuition plus stipened up to $2,000.

The institute is the outgrowth of 1953 conferences between Harry Guggenheim and Dean Dunning and of studies conducted by the Dean and Dr. Pendray, the conclusion of which was that one of the unmet needs of the aerospace field was a center for the development of structures suitable to flight at supersonic speeds. In announcing the creation of the institute, the president of the Foundation described its purposes as fourfold: "To train exceptionally qualified students in the comparatively new field of air-flight structures, to conduct research in aircraft structure and design (especially for supersonic flight), to act as a national clearinghouse for technical information in the field, and to disseminate technical knowledge regarding flight structures."

Through 1962 the institute had granted the degrees of Master of Science or Doctor of Philosophy to sixty graduate students, twenty-four of whom had been Daniel and Florence Guggenheim Fellows and most of whom are now occupying key positions in their field in industry, government and the universities. The institute has conducted a symposium on structures, sponsored by the Office of Naval Research, and a series of seminars to provide qualified newspapermen with accurate and up-to-date information.

The Harvard-Guggenheim Center for Aviation Health and Safety at Harvard University, established in 1957 with an initial grant of $250,000 as a unit of the Harvard School of Public Health headed by Dr. John C. Snyder, with Prof. Ross McFarland as technical director. Advisory supervision is provided by the Foundation committee which meets yearly with the Foundation committee of the Guggenheim Aviation Safety Center at Cornell. Endowment includes provision for $5,000 Daniel and Florence Guggenheim Fellowships, two of which are awarded annually for graduate study in the center.

Since 1952, under a ruling of the American Medical Association, a doctor practicing flight surgery has been required to obtain certification from a public health school; and the Guggenheim aviation health center is the outgrowth of courses leading to such certification established at the Harvard public health school in 1954. For three years the Harvard courses were open only to American and Canadian military physicians. Since the founding of the Guggenheim center, they have been open also to civilians, and to date (1962) some seventy doctors from nine countries have received certification from the center. Center graduates are found in responsible aviation-medical posts all over the world. One of them devised the battery of safety tests used in selecting the seven aviators known as the Mercury Astronauts. Six were involved in the complicated operation that sent Colonel John Glenn into space for America's first manned orbit of the earth.

Current research includes studies of night vision in relation to age; anthropometric studies as related to accidents, design of equipment, and susceptibility to stresses; evaluation of transport equipment from the point of view of human engineering, safety and performance in environmental extremes, and problems of high altitude operation, loss of cabin pressure, obesity, operational fatigue and aging, transportation of patients by air, and illness among air crews. Course work ranges from a weekly seminar in Aviation Health and Safety under Dr. McFarland to Occupational Medical Clinics under Dr. J. M. Miller at Harvard's Peter Bent Brigham Hospital. All research training and publication is under the supervision of Dr. McFarland, a tall, broad-shouldered, good-looking man, brilliant and personable, whose warm spirit and enthusiasm have made him the "Mr. Chips" of aerospace education.

One stroke remains to be made to fill in the picture of the efforts of the Daniel and Florence Guggenheim Foundation to help further the sciences associated with the Age of Space. In 1949 technical societies connected with the field set up a world organization known as the International Astronautical Federation. Composed of societies from a number of countries, rather than of individuals, the organization soon found itself limited in its technical contribution because many member nations were too small to support original research. In 1960 the Daniel and Florence undertook to remedy this situation with an initial grant of $75,000 to establish an adjunct of the Federation to be known as the International Astronautical Academy and to consist not of nations but of individuals, all of them first-rank astronautical scientists or engineers. At the eleventh congress of the Federation in August 1960, Dr. von Kármán was elected director of the Academy, a post he held until his death in 1963.

Much has now been said of two oldest of the five Guggenheim foundations, the Aeronautical Fund and the Daniel and Florence. We come next to the youngest of them, the foundation that supports the Guggenheim Museum.

IX

Solomon's Collection

Solomon R. Guggenheim, a small, stalwart-looking man with deep-set eyes under a high brow, spent Saturday, February 1, 1941, shooting quail in the pinewoods of Big Survey, his plantation near Yemasee, South Carolina. "When I die," he said that evening to assembled family and friends, "let me be remembered for this, that I shot a double on my eightieth birthday."

Solomon, who lived for another eight years, has been remembered—not, however, for bringing down a right and left in his vigorous old age, but for making possible the Solomon R. Guggenheim Museum, one of the great art centers of the world and, since 1959 when it moved into the home designed for it by the late Frank Lloyd Wright, one of the landmarks of New York City.

The Fountain of Youth

The story of the Guggenheim Museum goes back to the early 1900's when Solomon and his wife, the former Irene M. Rothschild, began collecting paintings. For more than two decades they trod a path worn smooth by other wealthy Americans. They collected old masters. They stuck to the safe and sound: the Barbizon school; the Italian and American landscape painters; the Italian, Dutch, and German primitives.

Then in 1926, when Solomon was sixty-five, a thirty-six-year-old Alsatian-born artist, the Baroness Hilla Rebay von Ehrenweisen, paid her first visit to New York, bringing with her a letter of introduction to Solomon and his wife, obtained in Paris from

Madame Enrique de Paats, a sister of Mrs. Guggenheim. Between Solomon and the baroness a friendship was struck up. It matured rapidly when Solomon asked her to do a portrait of him. At first she was reluctant. She informed "the Grand Old Man," her frequent appellation for Solomon, that she no longer wished to do portraits. In her day she had worked in many styles of art. She had been an academician, an impressionist, an expressionist, a cubist. But by 1926, she had put all these modes behind her. Now she was interested only in nonobjective art, so designated because its practitioners, eschewing the use in their work of recognizable objects from nature, achieve their effects by the exclusive employment of the pure elements of their craft: line and color, form and pattern.

"But in the end," says the baroness, now a seventy-two-year-old woman, living in Greens Farms, Connecticut, "I did the portrait." The Grand Old Man knew how to get around her. He said to her, "Hilla, you are making it up. You say you won't do my portrait because you no longer want to do academic work. But that is only an excuse. Your real reason is that you don't know how to paint a portrait."

That piqued the baroness' pride and the work was put under way. The sittings were held on weekends at Trillora Court, the Solomon Guggenheims' country place at Sands Point, Long Island. When the portrait was half finished, Solomon asked his new friend how much she wanted for it. The baroness shrugged. What did he think it was worth? The Grand Old Man offered $5,000. As the portrait developed, he liked it better. When it was three-fourths finished, he offered $7,000. And when it was finished, he gave her $9,000. Later, "he insisted on investing it for me. That," the baroness adds, "was very nice of him."

Under the baroness' influence, Solomon changed his art-collecting habits. He began gathering "new masters," soon becoming the possessor of an extensive and valuable collection of canvasses by such now well-known workers in the so-called modern-classical idiom as Vasily Kandinsky, Fernand Leger, Ladislaus Moholy-Nagy, Paul Klee, and Marc Chagall.

The search for the old masters was never entirely abandoned. Irene—Mrs. Guggenheim—saw to that. But after 1926, whenever the Guggenheims went abroad in search of paintings, they usually took the baroness along. As time wore on, their pilgrimages carried them less and less often to the repositories of the safe-and-sound, more and more often to the studios of living craftsmen.

The summer of 1929 found them in the old central-Germany city of Dessau, then home of the Bauhaus, one of the most important art schools in Europe between the world wars. Teaching at Bauhaus in 1929 was Vasily Kandinsky, the Russian-born artist who, long before his death in 1944, was to become one of the giants of his field. Originally a social scientist and lawyer, Kandinsky had turned to painting in his thirties, earning the title of "father of abstract art" in 1910 with the production of a small watercolor in this manner.

His widow, Russian-born Madame Nina Kandinsky, retains pleasant memories of the Guggenheims' first call on her husband. Taking the artist's hand, Solomon made a little speech that touched Madame's heart. "Mr. Kandinsky," he said, "you and I have something in common. You have made a revolution in art, and I and my brothers, by sponsoring the development of new methods of mining, have made a revolution in that industry." Then, with the baroness' assistance, he purchased Kandinsky's *Composition 8* and two other paintings, thus adding to an accumulation, already begun, that was to become one of the most prized possessions of the Guggenheim Museum, which now owns over a hundred Kandinskys, the largest single collection of them in the world.

The baroness was an apostle of nonobjectivism, but there is no evidence that Solomon shared her monomania, her doctrinaire insistence that this approach to painting is the only true art, that all others are but stepping stones to it. There is ample evidence that he caught fire from her enthusiasm. He enjoyed the latter-day masterpieces, many of them *not* nonobjective, she helped him to obtain. In 1932, pointing to one of his recent acquisitions, he would say as much to Daniel Catton Rich, then assistant to the director of the Chicago Art Institute, now director of the Worcester (Massachusetts) Museum of Art and a trustee of the Guggenheim. "All day as a businessman," Solomon would

(Left to right) Mrs. Solomon R. Guggenheim, Vasily Kandinsky, the Baroness Hilla Rebay, and Solomon R. Guggenheim at the Bauhaus, Germany, 1929.

say, "I look at graphs and figures. It's good to come home at night and look at these paintings. They rest my eyes."

The joy with which he sought out the treasures of modern painting is still a source of bewilderment to friends who knew him only as a hard-headed businessman. "Last person in the world you would expect to be associated with art," says attorney Leo Gottlieb. "A strange quirk, that," says industrialist J. Albert Woods.

Strange, no doubt, but explicable. Solomon's proud nature rebelled at the disabilities of age. His oldest daughter, Eleanor May, Countess Castle Stewart of England, remembers his efforts for weeks to read the menus in the dining room of the New Hampshire Inn where he often spent his summers during his later years. One day, after a futile squint, he gave up and tossed the menu to his daughter. "What's in it?" he demanded gruffly. Eleanor reached a hand across the table, squeezed his arm, and said, "It's awful, getting old, isn't it, darling?"

Awful it might have been but for the baroness, who brought to Solomon a new interest that took the sting out of it. Wandering Europe with her, he found in the ateliers of its avant-garde artists not only many magnificent pictures but also the fountain of youth.

In 1937 he gave his collection, both new masters and old ones, to the public, setting up for this purpose the Solomon R. Guggenheim Foundation "for the encouragement and promotion of art and art education," and subsequently establishing in rented quarters in uptown New York a temporary museum with the baroness as its curator and, later, director. In the early 1940's he expressed an interest in a permanent museum, and in 1943, apparently at his wife's suggestion, he commissioned Frank Lloyd Wright to design and build it. Within a year Wright's plans had been completed and approved, so that by the end of 1944 newspapers were predicting that the permanent Guggenheim Museum would see the light of day in the near future. But this was not to be. When on Wednesday, October 21, 1959, the long-awaited building opened its doors at 1071 Fifth Avenue, its architect had been dead for five months, its benefactor for ten years.

Meanwhile the history of art had been extended by an eventful and turbulent chapter, two of the main contributors to which—Solomon and the baroness—must now have our closer attention.[1]

The Grand Old Man

Many old-timers in the business world, where Solomon Guggenheim spent much of his life, remember him with special warmth. They do not all remember him in the same way, for like his brother Murry, he was not all of a piece. Financial expert Medley G. B. Whelpley speaks of him as "a gentle man," Gottlieb as "methodical, plugging and hard-bitten," and J. Albert Woods' "rough and ready" has been quoted. Woods adds that "everybody liked Sol. He had friends in all walks of life. The Guggenheim firm was known through him. He was the man the Street [New York's financial district] knew."

Similarly varied are the recollections of members of the family. Harold Loeb pictures his uncle as "the elegant one" among the Guggenheim brothers. "I recall him," Loeb says, "as a very old man. In his dressing gown he looked like a Renaissance cardinal. He had more chic than the others." Alicia Patterson Guggenheim's word for him was "tough," and her husband remembers his uncle as "a charming and delightful host" and "a stubborn man" at business conferences. "Very often," he says, "when my father wished the firm to move in some new direction, it was Sol who held out the longest." Etched on Harry's mind is the memory of his father spending long hours quietly and patiently seeking to bring Sol around. A standing joke in the family was that Mr. Dan's ulcer, his "little Mary," was "Sol-caused."

Other facets emerge from the reminiscences of his daughter, Eleanor, whose late husband, Arthur Stuart (Earl Castle Stewart) of Ulster and Sussex, England, served for several years as president of his father-in-law's foundation. Now in her sixties, the countess is a tall, handsome woman with pale blue eyes and a crisp, matter-of-fact manner. Talking in a London restaurant, she offered me glimpses of her father at various ages.

As a parent he was stern and demanding when she and her sisters were young, mellow and companionable after they grew up. "He didn't frighten easily," she said. "I remember once we were driving west to spend the summer at his ranch in Idaho. There was a fierce strike on in the mining country, and as we approached one of those little mining communities, some people stopped the car. They urged us to detour around the town. They said if father went through it in an open car, his life wouldn't be worth a nickel. Father thanked them, told them not to worry, and instructed the chauffeur to drive on—through the town."

Even for a Guggenheim, Sol was unusually fastidious. There was only one thing he didn't like about Crawford House, the inn at Crawford Notch (New Hampshire) where he so often spent his summers. "In the dining room," said Eleanor, "the guests were given napkin rings. At first Father was appalled at the idea of using the same napkin for two meals running, but eventually he found a way around it. At the end of each meal, he'd twist his napkin and wring it between his hands, leaving it so wrinkled that the waitress was discouraged from giving it to him again."

Fourth oldest of the eleven children of Meyer and Barbara Guggenheim, he was born in one of the family's Philadelphia homes in 1861. Seeing to it that he was educated beyond the grade-school level proved difficult. He had a genius for getting into fights and out of schools. On one occasion the family tried a Swiss school noted for its disciplinary effectiveness. On Sol's second or third day, he was accosted by a group of the older boys bent on testing the newcomer.

"What's your name?" asked their spokesman.

"Solomon Guggenheim."

"You an American?"

"That's right."

"You a Jew?"

"That's right."

"We don't like Jews around here."

"Why not?"

"Because they killed our Savior."

"I don't know about that," said Sol, "but I do know I'm going to kill you."

He nearly did, thus ending his career in that school. In time, apparently, a suitable place was found, for brother William, in his autobiography, speaks of Solomon as eventually "being tamed" in a Swiss boarding-school directed by a well-named "Doctor Birch."

Like the other older brothers, Sol began his business life in embroidery, later shifting to mining and actively involved in M. Guggenheim's Sons. When in 1919 he retired from full-time work, he was president of several subsidiary companies and chairman of the financial committee of ASARCO. Subsequently he was active for a time in the family's nitrate interests, and shortly before his death, he helped organized the second of the three partnerships known as Guggenheim Brothers.

Irene Rothschild, whom he married in 1895, was the daughter of a New York merchant. She was unusually beautiful. "Everyone," Harold Loeb says, "called Aunt Irene cold, but this was only because her beauty was classic and her face didn't break too readily into a smile. Actually she was a very sweet woman." There were three children, all daughters. Eleanor, the oldest, is the mother of four sons, two of whom were killed in action during the Second World War. Barbara Josephine, the youngest, is Mrs. Henry Obre of Monkton, Maryland, and the mother of two sons, each by one of her two previous marriages. The other daughter, Gertrude, is unmarried and lives near Eleanor in England.

It was Irene who first introduced her husband to the old masters, her own interest in art predating their marriage. After 1926 she often accompanied Sol and the baroness on their European junkets, but her heart was not in them. Poignant evidence of this is found in Daniel Catton Rich's recollection of a visit, in the summer of 1932, to Trillora Court.

"The man who was my boss then, the director of the Chicago museum," Rich says, "was with me, and when we arrived at Trillora, we spied Mrs. Guggenheim walking in the gardens. She hailed us before we could get into the house and insisted that we come at once to look at what she called *her* collection. 'Solomon and the baroness like all that new stuff,' she told us as we toured past the old masters, 'but I like these.' "

Later the Guggenheims and their two guests gathered on one of the porches of the house. "For a while," says Rich, "there were only the four of us and the conversation was desultory. All that changed when the baroness exploded onto the scene and promptly began talking in that effervescent way of hers. I felt a little sad for Mrs. Guggenheim, as the younger woman took over and proceeded to dominate the conversation from then on. As for Mr. Guggenehim, he just sat there, drinking it all in, calm, silent, and content."

When decades later the Guggenheim Museum sold a block of its old masters for $341,600, the youngest of Sol's daughters expressed regrets, although as a trustee she had agreed to the sale. "My mother liked *only* those pictures," Barbara reminded Cousin Harry, "though she was too loyal to let it be known."

Irene loved to talk, but after Solomon's death she suffered a stroke that deprived her of the power of speech. One day, while she was staying with Countess Castle Stewart in England, she observed that her daughter was struggling to remember the name of a sculptor who had recently paid them a visit. Eager to be of help, Irene somehow managed to provide the information. "Epstein," she said. According to the Baroness Rebay, it was her last spoken word. Irene died on November 25, 1954, surviving her husband by five years.[2]

Portrait of "An Original"

The Baroness Rebay remembers Irene with what are called "mixed emotions." In the beginning, she says, both of the Guggenheim were "as parents to me, the Grand Old Man as a father, Irene as a mother." But later on, she adds, Irene grew "cold." For this she blames "evil-minded gossips" who, she says, "whispered terrible things," including "lies" about the relationship of the baroness and Solomon.

"Rubbish!" she explodes. "Why, when I knew him first, he was an old man; old enough to be my father, and this he was exactly to the end." According to the baroness, her own late father, a German army general, never approved of her art career. "In 1913, when I am only twenty-three," she says, "my painting was accepted in the Secession [a Munich art gallery]. At once I send my receipt [the document of acceptance] to my father. Now, I say hopefully to myself, perhaps he will be proud of me. But no. How little he still respects my work I soon see when his return letter comes, written on the back of my receipt!" In the Grand Old Man, the baroness winds up this bittersweet reminiscence: "I find the father who gives me the encouragement and the respect I never received at home."

An American citizen since shortly after the Second World War, the baroness lives in a large white colonial house on a 16-acre Connecticut estate to which she has given the name of Franton Court in honor of her parents, whose Christian names were Franz Joseph and Antonia. Back in the days when she was much in the news as director of what is now the Guggenheim Museum, reporters came away from their interviews with diverse summations. One found her a "buxom hausfrau type," another "Wagnerian" in manner and proportions. Today then it is a little startling when the baroness slips into the living room of Franton Court, gently closing one of the glass hall doors behind her, to see a plump, soft-looking little bunny of a woman with reddish hair and intensely blue eyes.

This first impression is rapidly superseded by others, for the baroness is subject to infinite changes of mood. It is not uncommon, in the space of minutes, for her personality to undergo not one but a series of abrupt metamorphoses. It is easy to relish this protean quality, even, in its presence, to experience a somewhat guarded enjoyment. It is not easy to "catch up" its owner in words. She is at once fascinating and exasperating, engaging and frightening. In short, to quote the brilliant young director of the Guggenheim Museum, Thomas M. Messer, "the baroness is an original."

In conversation she is often charming and restrained. At intervals, however, the charm flees, the restraint gives way. Let the memory of some past injury, real or fancied, cross her mind. Let the visitor mention a subject on which her feelings run strong: The effect is that of a sudden and passing squall on a summer's day as the baroness offers her point of view in a stream of violent rhetoric.

One sensitive subject is the Guggenheim Museum, which, in her opinion, has been improperly run since her resignation as director. In long and curious letters to Harry Guggenheim she has likened the museum, as conducted by its recent directors, to "a Broadway show to attract riffraff . . . a downfall for the Sol R. Guggenheim collection . . . to the shudder of all people of high culture." It is her contention, a groundless one, that prior to his death the Grand Old Man stipulated that no additions were to be made to its holdings without her consent, and she stigmatizes such additions as have been made—among them a priceless painting by Paul Cézanne and an equally priceless one by Leger—as the work of inferior artists.

When individuals she dislikes are brought up, her conversation becomes a shotgun. The pellets of hate rain on her victims. Not the least of them is that talented and highly reputable citizen of the art world, James Johnson Sweeney, formerly director of the Guggenheim Museum, now of the Houston Museum of Art. One gathers from the baroness' strongly phrased criticisms that she does not approve of Mr. Sweeney's museum administration policies. "It was I," she says, "who recommended him to head the Guggenheim. My reason was because he had left the Museum of Modern Art. Since that is a very bad museum I assumed that Sweeney must be a very good director."

A large L-shaped apartment, the baroness' living room has a European feel: Crowded, comfortable, intimate, in good taste, with no touch of the decorator discernible either in the selection or arrangement of its multi-style furnishings. Piles of art books and framed photographs, including several of the Grand Old Man, cover desks and tables. On one of the smaller tables is a copy of *Big Birds of the World,* by Oliver L. Austin, Jr., with illustrations by Arthur Singer, a pair of binoculars resting on top of it. The baroness is a bird-watcher. It pleases her to tell you that this winter her garden has been favored by a thrush ordinarily seen only in California. Numberless potted geraniums and cyclamens are ranged along the heating duct of the outer wall, and the high windows across the southeast corner give a view of the terrace and the formal garden with its mammoth linden trees and tall English boxwoods, gunnysacked against the cold.

With a flip of a stubby hand the baroness indicates the gardener at work. "Every month now," she says, "he puts down between a hundred and four hundred pounds of grain for the birds." She exhales dramatically. "The responsibilities of wealth," she adds, "are very heavy." She suffers from a long-standing respiratory ailment. The heat is turned low in the living room, and at intervals she throws open one of the windows and takes a few deep breaths, leaving her guest to grin and bear it. Nor is the guest allowed cigarettes. No one smokes in the baroness' house, and since she is a vegetarian, no one eats meat.

In the living room, as throughout the house, the walls are crowded with paintings, many of considerable value. A letter concerning these works of art reposes in the files of the Solomon R. Guggenheim Foundation. Written and signed by the founder and addressed to his executors and to the trustees of the foundation, it records an agreement under which the baroness assured Solomon that after his death she would turn over to the museum all the paintings then at Franton Court. To date the baroness has not done so, and in 1961 the Foundation sent her two lists of the works believed to be in her possession, Harry Guggenheim pointing out in a covering letter that "some of these paintings were bought and paid for by the Foundation. Others were given to the Foundation by my uncle."

> It is to be assumed [his letter goes on] these lists are incomplete since, together, they include only 112 items, whereas I am advised that in 1949 you estimated there were between 300 and 400 items involved.
>
> The Foundation has been advised you are legally obligated to deliver to it all of the paintings on both lists. Realizing the pleasure you get from them, it has been our desire to treat the matter of your custody with consideration, even though it may involve some risk . . . You may recall occasions, when art collections have been entirely lost by fire, or other hazards . . . if it should happen in your case, your liability to the Foundation would be so large it would be an extremely serious situation for you.

Regularly the museum authorities remind the baroness of her agreement. Regularly she refuses to act on it, once writing to Harry that "Whatever I . . . may have promised was no obligation, only enthusiasm and devotion." Asked if she ever intends to deliver the paintings as requested, she shrugs and twinkles the fingers of an uplifted hand. "When I die perhaps then," she replies. "Perhaps not. Perhaps I will leave everything to America. Meanwhile why should I help a museum that is not even the jewel the Grand Old Man intended it to be? Why should I strip the walls of my home for that pigsty?"

Born and reared in Strasbourg, the baroness, who comes of an old German family, says her maternal grandfather, Herman Wilhelm von Eichen, was a leader in the industrial development of the Ruhr. Because of his interest in mining, she says, several of his descendants were known to the Guggenheims long before she became acquainted with Solomon. As a child she exhibited talent in both music and art. When at fourteen she announced her intention of studying at the Academy of Art in Düsseldorf, her father agreed only after sending some of her drawings anonymously to a faculty member, who informed him that his daughter had what the baroness describes as "a Holbein talent."

From Düsseldorf she moved on to the great art centers of Europe. There were more periods of study, exhibits of her work at galleries in Cologne, Munich, and Paris. Conceivably the baroness would have centered the whole of her career on the Continent had it not been for a chance meeting in Berlin, in 1917 or thereabouts, with a Polish-born nonobjective painter named Rudolf Bauer.[3]

The Course of Great Love

The significance of the baroness' encounter with Bauer, which took place while both were members of the art movement known as *Der Sturm,* is revealed by Madame Nina Kandinsky, whose acquaintanceship with the baroness dates from the early 1920's when she and her late husband left Russia to spend eleven years in Germany. As Madame puts it, "Hilla fell crazily in love with Bauer, and perhaps he responded."

Madame Kandinsky is a shapely and graceful little woman, with faintly freckled features, lovely eyes, expressive hands, and musical voice. She makes no pretense of being a disinterested source, saying that "Hilla always detested me," and implying that the feeling was mutual. Madame can remember, at the time of her husband's death, receiving "an insupportable letter from Hilla." The gist of it was that Kandinsky had never done enough for Bauer. Later, when Madame published a book on art, the baroness wrote another letter. Same subject: The book did not contain enough about Bauer.

Madame also remembers a letter of her own, written some years before the Second World War, in which she volunteered in no uncertain terms her sentiments concerning the political mentality of the German baroness. Since then, they have been together only once. "It was after my husband's death," says Madame. "Henri-Piere Roche [an important figure in the European art world] told me Hilla wanted to see me, and somehow I could not refuse." The meeting took place in the bright and comfortable flat on the banks of the river in the Parisian suburb of Neuilly-sur-Seine, where Kandinsky had maintained his last studio and where his widow still resides. Madame was "cool." As for the baroness, she was "utterly charming for a while; she can be, when she wants to be, you know." Wandering around the studio, she pointed at the many Kandinskys. "It was in front of those paintings," she told Madame, "I made the acquaintance of Bauer at *Der Sturm*." She then offered to buy all of them for the Guggenheim Museum. When Madame refused, the baroness stamped her foot. "Oh, you do nothing for Kandinsky!" she stormed, tossing charm to the winds.

"Always Bauer," comments Madame with a smile, and the eternal feminine is in her next statement. "I admire Hilla's great love for that man," she says. "He was in financial straits when they met, and she let it be known that she was going to dedicate her life to ameliorating his condition. That she did."

It is Madame's belief that when the baroness urged Solomon Guggenheim to start a museum, she was thinking of it primarily as a showplace for Bauer's work. If it was her determination to make Bauer rich and famous, she was not altogether successful. Fame, as it is measured in art circles, eluded him. For many years after the establishment of the Guggenheim Museum, his paintings were frequently exhibited, but on the whole their reception by American critics ranged from lukewarm to cool.

Thanks to the Grand Old Man, she was more successful in

making him rich, although it would appear from Madame's recollections that in this direction Bauer had talents of his own. Having learned that Solomon was interested in Kandinskys, Bauer bought several of them himself, getting them cheap on the plea that he was "only a poor artist." He then resold them, at a substantial profit, to Solomon. At the baroness' urging, the Grand Old Man also purchased numerous Bauers. A résumé of holdings for insurance purposes shows that in 1938 the Museum of Non-Objective Art owned fifty-eight paintings by the Polish-born artist. According to Madame, Solomon paid "exorbitant prices" for them. It is Madame's supposition, however, that the Grand Old Man was fully aware of this. "He did it," she said, "to humor Hilla."

Enriched by Solomon, Bauer purchased a house in Berlin's expensive West End, inscribed over the entrance the words, "The Home of the Spiritual in Art"—without apologies to Kandinsky's 1912 book, *Ueber das Gestige in der Kunst* (Concerning the Spiritual in Art)—filled the interior with magnificent furniture, including two huge clocks, neither of which ran; put two mammoth beds in his bedroom because, although a bachelor, "he thought that gave the place a better composition"; acquired a butler, a chauffeur, a maid, a cook and a huge black dog, which Madame is convinced he kept around to frighten people "because he was a sadist"; covered his walls with his own canvasses, all of them in velvet frames, and announced to Kandinsky, "Henceforth you must exhibit all of your paintings in my house." When Kandinsky said he preferred museums where everyone could see his work "and especially the young," Bauer snorted. "Bother the young," he said. "They can't afford to buy paintings!"

During Solomon's first call on the Kandinskys at Dessau, Mrs. Guggenheim brought up Bauer's name in a manner that the baroness, according to Madame, found vexing. "Why is it," Irene asked Kandinsky, "that everywhere I go in Europe, I see your work in the museums, but I never see Bauer's?" Kandinsky's answer was tact itself. "Perhaps," he said, "Bauer does not wish to sell his paintings."

With the advent of nazism in Germany, Bauer got into trouble with the authorities. The baroness has offered several versions of why this happened. One is that Bauer "must have said something bad about the Nazis." Another is that one day when a Nazi parade was scheduled along his street, he hung out an American flag. Another is that the flag was that of the vanished Weimar Republic. Madame insists that Bauer was speculating illegally in marks and dollars. In any event he was hauled off to a concentration camp, from which, at the baroness' instigation, Solomon Guggenheim rescued him "at much cost" and brought him to America.

In this country the course of the Great Love did not run smooth. Solomon gave Bauer a house in New Jersey. He also made it possible for him to employ a housekeeper. This turned out to be a mistake. Bauer fell in love with the housekeeper and married her. This development displeased the baroness, who in a letter to Bauer spoke of his wife as being something less than a lady, whereupon the wife sued the baroness. Since the Guggenheims' respectable law firm would not touch the case with a ten-foot pole, Solomon hired a New Jersey attorney, who counterattacked with the ancient plea that truth is a defense against libel. Said the baroness to Madame, during the calm-before-the-storm of their last conversation at Neuilly-sur-Seine, "It cost me eleven thousand dollars, but I won the suit."

It would seem that the artist, who died in 1954, had already got in his innings, for, according to Madame, Bauer denounced the baroness, then a German alien, in 1942, to the Federal Bureau of Investigation. The baroness' version of this contretemps is that FBI agents climbed into her linden trees, examined her Greens Farms home with "spyglasses," and accused her of placing her estate at the disposal of the enemy for submarine landing purposes, all of which she snaps aside as "rubbish!" The real story lies buried in classified government files. Contemporary accounts in the *New York Times* and in a Connecticut newspaper reveal only that Federal agents and OPA officials raided Franton Court and confiscated 1,400 pounds of sugar, 500 pounds of coffee, and three cases of tea hoarded in a loft over the garage. They then carted the baroness off to Boston where she was detained at the immigration station until the Grand Old Man effected her release.[4]

The Museum of Non-Objective Painting

At the time of its instigation in April of 1939 the Guggenheim Museum was designated the Museum of Non-Objective Painting, a name it was to retain more or less officially until the opening of its permanent home twenty years later. For almost a decade it mounted its displays—two floors and a mezzanine of them at first, later three floors and a penthouse—at 24 East 54th Street. In 1948 it moved into a five-story stone mansion then standing on the site of what is now its permanent home, and from 1956 to 1959, while the present building was being erected, it occupied quarters at 7 East 72nd Street.

As an art center, its course, like that of the baroness' great love, did not run smooth. There were minor crises. During its first year on 54th Street, the roof leaked for a time, and in July an "article protruding from a passing truck" caught on the awning out front, causing "some damage." Occasionally there was trouble with the phonograph installed in the basement so that music, mostly Bach, could be piped through the galleries. And in 1942 Edith G. Halpert, one of the country's best known art dealers, had the effrontery to point out that "the Solomon R. Guggenheim Foundation does not concern itself with American artists," a statement that brought from the baroness an angry letter in which she asserted that her museum did more than most for native craftsmen, citing as proof its showings of the work of such 100 per cent American artists as Hungarian-born Moholy-Nagy and a Mr. "Dockum"—the former, it should be added, having transferred his residence to the United States in 1937, and the latter being the name of a machine used for projecting color onto a screen.

There were also major crises. The opening of the museum, as had been true of the establishment of its parent foundation two years earlier, created a stir in the art world. In scores of letters to New York newspapers, interested individuals expressed the conviction that the new institution would prove a landmark in the progress of contemporary art. Given this initial enthusiasm, the history of the Museum of Non-Objective Painting from its beginnings until 1952 can only be described as one long disillusionment. From time to time an individual show was well received. This was true of a memorial exhibit of the works of Kandinsky in 1945. It was also true of a similar presentation of those of Moholy-Nagy two years later, but admixed with the praises bestowed on these and other artists were anything but faint damns for the manner in which their creations were exhibited. Reviewing the Moholy-Nagy memorial in the *New York Times,* Edward Alden Jewell said flatly that "in presenting this rich panorama" of an important artist's development, "nothing has been done by the museum in the way of making [it] . . . coherent to the museum visitor. The catalogue, save for its reproductions, is almost a dead loss. . . ." And the *Times'* associate art editor, Aline B. Saarinen, then writing under her maiden name, Louchheim, deplored "the unreasonable ankle-level which this institution favors" in its display of canvasses.

The Grand Old Man was unhappily aware of what was happening, as evidenced by the presence in the files of his Foundation of memoranda showing that on several occasions he urged the baroness to resign. She clung to her position, and by November 3, 1949, when Solomon R. Guggenheim died, his museum had become an object of contumely to many critics and a joke to large sections of the public. "During his lifetime," Harry remarked years later, "I'm afraid that my uncle got more kicks in the pants than kicks out of his collection."

In 1951 matters approached a climax with the publication in the *Times* of an earnest and detailed critique by Mrs. Saarinen. Pointing out that the museum was a tax-exempt institution with obligations to the public, she set forth a series of complaints.

One was that because of the baroness' "addiction to nonobjective art," many of the finest works in Solomon Guggenheim's collection—flawed, in the baroness' eyes by the presence of more or less recognizable objects from nature—had so far never been placed on display.

Another was that most of the museum's exhibits had been "dominated in a somewhat immodest fashion with paintings by the museum's own director . . . and by those of her once close friend, Rudolf Bauer. Though hers are spirited," the *New York Times* expert conceded, "and his obviously competent, it is the consensus of most qualified critics that the work of neither would receive this emphasis in any other museum."

Still another was that over "a period of years the museum has invited the antagonism of many of the ablest American artists whose works it has courted or displayed." One reason for this was that artists were averse to being associated with the manner in which the baroness discussed art in her museum's catalogues—a style of writing that Mrs. Saarinen described as "mystic double-talk," citing such jewels from the baroness' pen as "To see such a picture often results in the elevating influence which this important art [nonobjectivism] brings to humanity with the development of its intuitive capacity for personal leadership, and cosmic reaction," or, "Genius is a special gift of God—to the elite of the nation." The museum had further alienated artists by tampering with some of the canvasses accepted for exhibit. One picture by a young American, for example, had been partly repainted and then ruined by a clumsy attempt to remove the alterations before being returned to its horrified creator.

Mrs. Saarinen concluded her bill of particulars with the devastating suggestion that the Museum of Non-Objective Painting turn over its collections and its funds, including those set aside for the erection of its permanent home, to one of New York's established museums specializing in modern art.

In the light of these strictures, it can be assumed that a sigh of relief wafted through the higher echelons of the Foundation when in 1952 the baroness resigned for reasons of health.

Her successor, appointed by Harry Guggenheim on October 15, 1952, was James Johnson Sweeney. Under his informed and tasteful direction, the Guggenheim Museum rapidly acquired stature. "We are indebted to Jim," Harry has said. "He has great talent, along with charm and a sense of humor. He was of major importance in helping me save the museum from the fantastic antics of the past. The museum had become ridiculous, and Jim came just in time to reverse that conclusion in the art world." Sweeney rid the museum of the stigma of cultism that had afflicted it during the baroness' regime. He saw to it that the public had an opportunity to view the finest items from Solomon Guggenheim's collection, irrespective of the "schools" of painting to which they belonged. He strengthened the museum's holdings, eventually adding some 250 items, among them one of Picasso's best paintings and Cézanne's magnificent *The Clockmaker* or *The Man with Folded Arms*. Many critics praised his exhibiting methods and, all in all, his regime was an esthetic success. It was also marked, as will become clear in the next chapter, by a series of further crises.

X

The Guggenheim Museum

On June 18, 1956, Frank Lloyd Wright, living temporarily at the Plaza Hotel in New York City, got off an impassioned letter to Harry Guggenheim.[1]

"Lieber Harry the Guggenheim, lend me your ears," it began. Its subject: a proper name for the museum the celebrated architect had designed and was about to build on New York's upper Fifth Avenue for the late Solomon Guggenheim, Harry's uncle. Its purpose: to persuade "Lieber Harry," then board chairman of his uncle's Foundation, that "museum" was too "shopworn" a term for the proposed building with its unique concrete tower, 28 feet wider at top than at bottom, its delicate spider-glass dome and cantilevered interior ramp spiraling about a great hollow core of a room, so ingeniously wrought that the present director of the museum, Thomas Messer, has described it as seeming "to defy the laws of gravity." For such an architectural innovation, Wright insisted, "some discriminating slang" should be coined, and it was his suggestion that the building be known as the "Archeseum."

There was no need for the eighty-six-year-old architect to define his term. This he had done many times, once saying to Robert N. Cohen, youthful president of the contracting company chosen to translate his plans into concrete and steel, "Arch means 'great' like in 'archduke,' 'archangel' or, as a matter of fact, in 'architect,' the great man, the designer, the boss."[2]

Certainly the term was not new to Harry. He had encountered it a dozen times in as many letters. "Querido Francisco," began his answer to Wright, mailed from the lower Manhattan offices of the Solomon R. Guggenheim Foundation at 120 Broadway on July 2, ". . . please lay off for all time this 'Archeseum' stuff. The family do not want it. They want to honor my uncle." And once more, as in a previous letter, the head of the Guggenheim family decreed that Wright's building was to be "designated, inscribed, and known as the 'Solomon R. Guggenheim Museum.' "

Four days later Wright's capitulation was in the mail. "MU," he wrote, "has already firmly taken the place of ARCH. AMEN."

So ended one of the many arresting exchanges brought to light by an examination of the extensive files of the Solomon R. Guggenheim Foundation. Hundreds of communications in these packed folders are on the outsized notepaper of "Taliesin," Wright's famous architectural school, with branches in Wisconsin and Arizona. Many are over the signatures of other well-known personalities—of Robert Moses, former New York City park commissioner, now president of the 1964 New York World's Fair; of the Baroness Rebay, of James Johnson Sweeney, and of Solomon R. Guggenheim himself, to mention only a few. Supplemented by contemporary press stories and by the memoria of participants in the events covered, the contents of these files present a colorful picture of the tribulations incident to the construction of the present Guggenheim Museum, of the widely publicized quarrel between Wright as its architect and Sweeney as its second director, of the tremors that seized the art world when Sweeney resigned in 1960 after what was euphemistically described as "a split over ideals" with his trustees, and of the progress of the museum since it came into its own as an art center in the 1950's.

A Tribute, a Dissertation, and a Question of Taste

Since the archives of the Foundation record almost three decades of intensive activity, they touch on a diversity of topics. One finds in them, for example, Wright's picturesque tribute to the Grand Old Man. Solomon Guggenheim, according to a letter written by the architect shortly after the former's death, "was the only American millionaire of whom I knew or had heard who died facing the Future. All the others cuddled up to the past."

There is the Baroness Rebay's impenetrable dissertation on her favorite topic, contained in a letter of September 5, 1946, in which she chides the architect for accusing her of being "jealous" of the projected museum. "I feel," the baroness wrote, "I must explain more clearly just what I mean." What she meant was that great paintings "are not a materialistic reference to God's creation of infinitely changing illusions called 'earthly matter' but . . . direct expressive tokens of the Creator's mind itself." It was the baroness' belief that if such paintings were displayed with "loving care" they could uplift even "the irreverent, once his intellect is off guard and his soul free to receive the message portrayed." To make sure that the viewers got the message, care must be taken "to see that the museum building does not swallow all of the attention. . . . Painters do not count, architects do not count, the building counts as a frame, but only as a candlestick to light." The baroness ended by saying that all she wanted from Wright was respect for the *"Source"* and by declaring that "God does not . . . want your brain (as His is far superior); He wants your love."

And there is a sprightly three-way correspondence—carrying the signatures of Wright, Commissioner Moses and Harry Guggenheim—written in 1955 when efforts were being made to bring Wright's unusual plans for the museum in line with the New York City Building Code's more conventional requirements. Wright and the former Mary Louise Sims, Moses' wife, were distantly related, and the two men opened their letters with such salutations as "Cousin Frank" and "Dear Bob the Moses." It is plain that they regarded each other with affection, equally plain that the crusty and outspoken commissioner's fondness for "Cousin Frank" did not extend to Cousin Frank's museum. Throughout the correspondence Moses is on record as disliking the proposed building, comparing it to "an inverted cup and saucer with a silo added for good luck," and contending that its airy façade had no place on New York's grand and essentially nineteenth-century Fifth Avenue.

Throughout 1955 many of Wright's letters were appeals to Moses either to exert his influence to persuade the New York City Building Commission to approve of the plans or to desist from ridiculing them in official circles. On October 11 he was asking Moses "to disabuse the mind of the . . . commission that you are opposing the construction of this building." Moses' answer, written the following day, assured him that he only wanted to be helpful, and if Cousin Frank needed "more money to carry out under the ablest engineering and contracting auspices your bold original plan as modified to meet the [building] code, the Foundation should give it to you."

It was at this point that Harry Guggenheim, having been supplied with copies of the correspondence between Moses and Wright, stepped into the picture. "I see," he wrote the commissioner on October 13, "that you two geniuses can only agree on one thing, that is—how to spend the Solomon R. Guggenheim Foundation's money."

"Not in the least interested in spending the Guggenheim Foundation's money for the museum," was Moses' rejoinder. "I don't personally like either the museum or what's going into it. . . . I have simply tried at their request to help some good friends in a dubious enterprise because they *are* good friends. . . . If the Courts would let you divert the money to the Metropolitan Museum or to an indoor recreation center, I would be positively enthusiastic."

Sites, Fiscal Problems and Delays

Ramified though the Foundation files are, it is possible to detect running through them a handful of major themes. One such theme, accounting for considerable correspondence between Wright and Solomon Guggenheim in 1943, has to do with the problem of finding a site for the building. Typing his message on a beige-colored Taliesin letterhead folded into three vertical panels, Wright on July 14 was describing with relish an "entire afternoon, until 6 o'clock" spent with Commissioner Moses "going over the city [of New York], viewing various sites."

Moses' favorite, among those considered, was a hilltop at Spuyten Duyvil on the western edge of the Bronx overlooking the Hudson River. What interested the park commissioner about this site, he later confessed, was its size: 80 acres. Its purchase and cultivation by the Foundation, he reasoned, would have the effect of giving New York City an additional park, somewhere along whose fringes a place could be found where Cousin Frank's museum could be "neatly and not too conspicuously tucked." Wright also favored the Spuyten Duyvil property; nevertheless he was pleased when, early in 1944, this choice was vetoed, and Solomon Guggenheim bought instead what was then an empty corner lot at Fifth Avenue and 89th Street in the heart of Manhattan. Subsequently two adjoining lots, each with a building on it, were acquired, giving the Guggenheim Museum its present site, a full block-front on the Avenue, 201.5 feet long and 127.8 feet at its deepest, between 88th and 89th streets, across from the Central Park reservoir.

Another theme, giving rise to a flurry of correspondence at intervals, was the architect's recurrent dissatisfaction with his fees. Under his original contract, he was to receive $75,000 in stipulated gradations. As the years rolled on, as building costs soared, and as the amount of land available for the museum increased, impelling the architect to revise his plans, he put in bids for more money.

His arguments ran the gamut of persuasion, from sugar to vinegar. On one occasion his reasoning was that if the trustees of the museum were willing to "pay for great paintings by a painter, why not pay for great plans by an architect?" On another he stated that he had no wish "to enter litigation except as a last resort." Again, he declared that he had made no less than "seven sets of plans . . . for Uncle Sol's memorial," adding that he had brought these to New York "to let them speak to the trustees for themselves, because I do not want to have to close Taliesin because I have stubbed my toe against the Guggenheim fortune in a loyal, unprecedented endeavor to keep . . . faith. . . ." And to a 1957 letter to trustee Albert Thiele he appended an "N.B.," the abbreviation he consistently employed in place of the conventional "P.S." "And Albert," it read, "if the cupidity with which the administrators of Solomon R. Guggenheim's great fortune became evident to his beloved New Yorkers, his friends would be amazed and his enemies delighted."

Sooner or later, on the heels of nearly every demand, the

trustees authorized an adjustment so that in the end the architect's fees came to $240,000, less some agreed-upon deductions.

Solomon Guggenheim was vacationing in New Hampshire when Wright brought him his original plans to be examined. According to a letter written by the architect almost a decade later, when the Grand Old Man "saw the first sketches I made . . . he went over them several times without saying a word or looking up. Finally when he did look up there were tears in his eyes. 'Mr. Wright,' he said, 'I knew you would do it. This is it.' "

It was Solomon's prompt and enthusiastic acceptance of his architect's plans that caused the New York newspapers, in 1944, to predict the early erection of the building. Their forecast, of course, was premature. Thousands of words in the Foundation files are devoted to what might be called the "delays theme," the obstacles that arose to create an almost sixteen-year hiatus between the original plans and the completion of the building.

During the war years the chief obstacle was shortage of materials. After the war it was rising costs, a development the Grand Old Man watched with growing alarm. In the summer of 1949 he dictated what were to be his last words to Wright, a letter that was never sent but which still reposes in the files, a startling reminder that although the tough-minded old millionaire may have died, as his architect put it, "facing the future," he did not like what he saw there.

"You will recall," a section of this letter reads, "that before the recent wars both Germany and France were prosperous countries, but today their currencies are valueless. . . . My great fear is that unless we in this country are most careful, the politicians will bring the United States to the same pass. While I have provided liberally for both the museum building and its endowment it could be that, when the time comes for materialization of our plans, money in this country will have much less value than today."

This letter was prepared on July 5, 1949. Three months later Solomon R. Guggenheim was dead. His original grant to his Foundation had been $3 million and in his will he had set aside another $10 million, $2 million of it earmarked for the museum building.

The Solomon R. Guggenheim Museum: two views of the exterior.

Now came another long delay, the nature of which is illuminated by an exchange of letters between Wright and Albert Thiele, acting as spokesman for the trustees. On February 9, 1950, the architect was writing to Thiele that a museum official "tells me that the reluctance on the part of the trustees to go into action on the building is due to their fear that they may incur a debt beyond the sum named. . . . This natural timidity on the part of these gentlemen . . . is aggravated because . . . gossips inform them that my buildings usually cost more than desired and often more than expected." The architect described himself as indignant that the trustees should be taken in by idle chatter. He pointed out that during the last fifty-six years he had erected over 550 buildings "with not one dissatified client. . . .

"Were it not for my promise to Mr. Guggenheim several weeks before he died that I would build this building for him . . . for two million dollars," he continued, "I would be quite content to withdraw and leave the matter to the trustees. But I do have a conscience in this matter whether they have any or not. . . ."

On the following February 23, Thiele was imploring Wright to withhold criticism of the trustees, pending consideration of the facts. These, he pointed out, were that the executors of Solomon's estate had not yet paid over any sums to the Foundation, and the trustees could not spend the money provided for the building until they received it. "So far as I know," Thiele added, "the trustees have never discussed . . . the assertion . . . that your 'buildings cost more than desired and often more than expected.' "

Wright, responding by return mail, thanked Thiele for clarifying the situation and blamed his own misunderstanding of it on the "museum official" who had misled him as to the attitudes of the trustees. He was further mollified the following summer after a session at the Sussex home of Countess Castle Stewart, whose husband had assumed the presidency of the Foundation following his father-in-law's death. The Earl Castle Stewart's account of the meeting, given in a letter to Harry, is revealing.

"Eleanor and I," the Earl wrote, "had Mr. and Mrs. Frank Lloyd Wright to lunch yesterday . . . both a little unwell, owing to having eaten something the day before, as Mr. Wright is now

80 years of age and had already cancelled one engagement because he felt a bit weary and had been overdoing it. . . . At the opening of our meeting, he was a little bit stiff but . . . as the discussion developed, he became much more easy and friendly. . . . I daresay that some of his opening attitude was due to the fact that he had been told that the Museum was not going to be built after all, and that that rumor was going around New York. After I had explained to him how I thought this rumor had arisen, he became much more affable, and I think you can take it from me that he has a pretty good understanding of Miss Rebay's ways."

Considerable time was required to administer Solomon's estate, and it was not until April 3, 1952, that the Foundation was able to file a formal request for a building permit. The application was promptly turned down by the New York City Department of Building and Housing on the grounds that Wright's plans transgressed the metropolitan building code in thirty-two ways. Throughout the summer Wright reworked his plans, and the number of transgressions had been reduced to eleven when, in the fall, the application was referred to the New York Board of Standards and Appeals, a body empowered to issue permits on exception.

Wright's initial contribution to what was to become the drama-of-the-permit was a "preface" to the Foundation's petition to the appeals board, a draft of which he submitted to Harry Guggenheim. In his covering letter the architect explained that his preface was intended to be merely a "calm and objective" presention of the case for his building. It can be assumed that board chairman Guggenheim was not surprised to find it about as calm as a 100-piece orchestra executing the final crescendo of a symphony.

"Architecture, may it please the court," Wright's proposed preface began, "is the welding of imagination and common sense into a restraint upon specialists, codes and fools."

There was more. Harry read it all and returned the manuscript with the comment that it was very good, although "if I were writing it, I would leave out the word 'fools.' " To this, Wright's reaction, coming along a few days later, was that " 'fools' is out."

Some newspaper reporters, keeping tab on the drama-of-the-permit, cast Wright and the Board of Standards and Appeals in the roles of the Immovable Object and the Irrepressible Force, respectively. The record as given in the files softens this picture. A number of letters, dealing in the main with such technical matters as floor payload and the relative fire-resisting properties of glass and plastic, show that New York's "bureaucrats," as Wright labeled them, viewed the architect with respect and were at least moderately eager to see his building come to life. Wright himself emerges from this part of the correspondence as a man capable of flexibility, willing to make numerous alterations so long as his basic design remained intact. At the branches of his architectural school, Taliesin East in Wisconsin and Taliesin West in Arizona, he and his assistants labored to revise the plans. They widened stairways, added fire exits, completely redesigned the dome, and eliminated an entire wing of the building. As for Commissioner Moses, he turned out to be a friendly enemy, making generous use of his influence and his telephone to expedite matters for "Cousin Frank" and the Foundation.

Despite good will on all sides, the permit hearings dragged on for almost four years. It was not until March 13, 1956, that Wright was in a position to dash off a triumphant note to Moses. "Dear Bob—thrice cousin!" he hailed the Commissioner. "We thank you and we thank you for being mystified, scared and devastated by 'the Tower' . . . building permit issued but so far this turns loose on us an avalanche of art directors, attorneys, committeemen-watchdogs, all scared well wishers, contending, fearful of erection. Harry Guggenheim has his sporting hands full. Harry doesn't like controversy. Harry likes to win. I guess he will. Whatever happens, I am for him."

As Wright's letter suggests, the granting of the permit did not clear all hurdles. Still to be completed was the business of finding someone to put the museum up. Several large construction companies, making note of the engineering problems presented by Wright's sketches, refused to bid at all or insisted on a cost-plus arrangement. Eventually Wright found his man in George Cohen, president and general manager of Euclid Contracting Corporation of New York City.

Cohen was so taken by his first impressions of the architect that he lost little time in reducing them to writing. "I first met Frank Lloyd Wright," he wrote, "in August of 1954 in his apartment at the Plaza Hotel in New York. . . . 'Young man,' he said, 'here are the plans for . . . a GREAT museum. We have two million dollars with which to build it. If your price is higher than that, then don't bother to come back.' "

Cohen's price was higher, but he did come back. In 1943, Solomon R. Guggenheim had proposed spending $750,000 for the museum building and $250,000 for its site. A decade later such figures for such a building had become foggy. Cohen's base contract bid, officially accepted in May of 1956, was $2,609,742.00. Changes made during construction elevated this sum, bringing the grand total for constructing the Guggenheim Museum to $3,733,924.21, to which must be added the $478,544.31 previously carried on the Foundation books for the land on which it stands.

The grand total would have been larger if Wright had had his way. No sooner was the construction contract signed than the architect was shipping off to Cohen thirteen sheets of revised tracings calling for fifty changes in the building, many of them of major proportions. Cohen respectfully demurred, and in the summer of 1956 the delays inherent in this development were scotched by Harry Guggenheim.

During the summer of 1956 demolition began on the two old buildings on the site of the Guggenheim Museum, and the first steps were taken toward actual construction. The drama-of-the-permit was over, but a more spectacular one was under way; had been under way since 1952, when a new note crept into the Foundation files—a faintly risible, often pungent, and occasionally cantankerous note—as increasingly the correspondence revolved around the quarrel between Wright as the designer and builder of the museum and James Johnson Sweeney as its director.

The Wright-Sweeney Quarrel

Those sections of the Foundation archives dealing with the Wright-Sweeney quarrel speak for themselves. Even so, a few prefatory words should be said about the principals.

When Frank Lloyd Wright died in 1959, two months before his ninetieth birthday, he had long since established himself as the foremost architect of his time. Tomorrow's historians will assign him his rightful place in the total scheme of things. Today's observer can only be impressed by his architectural innovations (among them the ranch house, the reinforced-concrete house, the split-level living room, the picture window, and the carport), his productivity (some 640 finished structures, several of them rated as among the all-time greats of American architecture), his fecund imagination (as evidenced by some 8,000 drawings produced at his school, most of them pertaining to novel structures as yet unborn), and his tireless determination to leave the world more beautiful than he had found it.

Born in a small Wisconsin town, he was brought up by a father who fluctuated between preaching and music teaching and deserted his family when his son was in his teens, by a mother who from prenatal days was bound that her boy should be a builder, and by an uncle on whose farm Frank learned what it was to "work from tired to tired." After three years at the University of Wisconsin, he served his apprenticeship under Louis Sullivan, the great skyscraper builder, worked for a time at the drawing boards of various companies, and then struck out on his own.

Eventually he settled on his ancestral acres near Spring Green, Wisconsin, where he gathered a group of young students around him and set up the school to which he gave the name of Taliesin, a Welsh word meaning "Shining Brow." There were three marriages and seven children. Two of the marriages ended in divorce. The third and longest lasting was to the former Olgivanna Lazovich, a native of the Balkan country of Montenegro, who now administers her husband's school with the assistance of her architect-son-in-law, William Wesley Peters.

Wright loved the country, taught his students to build as nature builds—and hated the city, once remarking to Robert Moses that New York was "fit only for cockroaches," indeed was inhabited "only by cockroaches" and well on its way to becoming so crowded that soon the cockroaches—meaning the people—would have to walk "on the tops of the taxicabs." In his way of life he was inclined to be Puritanical and autocratic. In appearance he was slight and small, but he "walked tall," bearing himself with dignity to the end of his days, and, according to Moses, there was always a twinkle in the eyes that dominated his wonderful face.

Less well known than Wright to the general public but highly esteemed in his own field, James Johnson Sweeney—currently director of the Houston Museum of Art, a post he has held since January of 1961—is a tall, compactly built man with a rolling voice that occasionally booms. Admiring friends have described him in various ways. A French associate once termed him "a tranquil man, isolated in his museum as in a lighthouse." An American associate, taking note of his endless lecture tours and active participation in more than fifteen professional societies, found this appraisal wide of the mark and likened him to "a mammoth wheel with terrific physical endurance."

Born in Brooklyn and educated at Georgetown University with graduate work in England and Italy, Sweeney first achieved fame as a poet. For three years he served as assistant editor of the monthly literary magazine, *transition,* founded and first published in Paris and one of the most famous of the "little magazines" of the 1920's. In the 1930's he turned to art criticism, shortly becoming, in the words of Alfred Barr, Jr., of the Museum of Modern Art in New York, "a most respected American authority upon the art of the avant-garde. . . ." In 1945 and 1946 he was director of the department of painting and sculpture of the Museum of Modern Art, resigning with the announcement that his contract of employment had been violated. Married and the father of five children, he was in his early 50's when in 1952 he succeeded the baroness as the director of the Guggenheim Museum.

His appointment was only a few days old when it became apparent that what Harry Guggenheim called "a conflict of personalities" was in the making between the new director and Wright. "I have come to the conclusion," Lord Castle Stewart wrote to Harry in November of 1952, "that the uncalled-for letter, written by Mr. Frank Lloyd Wright, on the subject of a director, he is now rather ashamed of." Wright's "uncalled-for letter" does not appear in the Foundation files, but some idea of its contents is furnished by a later letter in which the architect complained, "Dear Harry—I find that in order to use our precious VIOLIN [his building], we have a man who can only play the PIANO!" In still another communication on the subject of the director, Wright further indulged his penchant for the mangled metaphor with the statement that "too many cooks always did upset perfection."

As the quarrel took shape, Harry Guggenheim found himself in the role of referee. Referees, umpires, and other keepers-of-the-peace are seldom beloved. In the torrent of press comment agitated by the dispute during a seven-year period beginning in 1952, there was a tendency to paint Harry and his fellow trustees as the Philistines. News stories and editorials, especially those in the organs of the art world, generated the impression that in some vague way lay members of the Foundation board, denounced by one commentator as "the Bonds," were laying profane hands on the Temple of Art. Nothing in the Foundation files bears out this black-and-white interpretation of an episode, the villains of which, if any, were not sitting at the trustees' table.

What was it all about? Like many ruckuses in the art world, where tempest-in-teapot is the meteorological norm, this one had its ins and outs, its innuendoes and allusions, its misunderstandings and irrelevancies, its low blows and high comedy, its branches, sub-branches, twigs, and tendrils. It boiled down, however, to two major points of difference.

One had to do with the amount of space that must be set aside in the forthcoming building for such things as offices, storage and workrooms; the other with the manner in which the contents of the building, the painting and sculpture, should be displayed to the public.

Sweeney, of course, was asked by the trustees to furnish the architect with his space requirements, and when he came up with a few inquiries and preliminary suggestions, Wright was irritated by the inquiries and appalled by the suggestions. On April 10, 1954, he wrote "Meine Liebe Harry" that he saw no reason why he should have to bother with queries from the director as to the "disposal of management space." His argument was that the de' Medicis, having commissioned Michelangelo to do the statue of *David*, had not required the great Renaissance sculptor to supply them with the circumference of David's "biceps, area of belly, number of inches around diameter of calf . . . etc., etc." On October 13 of the same year, "Dear James: S.O.S.!" he wrote to Sweeney, "it is now apparent that we cannot build Solomon R. Guggenheim's Memorial and at the same time build whole big buildings for carpentry, photography, storage, conservation, etc., etc." It "seems to us," the architect went on, that "your experts want about the entire area of the Guggenheim lot or about 23,000 square feet, *ex*cluding any building for exhibition purposes whatever, and allowing only a reasonable amount for the corridors, circulation, etc. . . ."

With the passage of time, Wright's animadversions on Sweeney's space demands sharpened. By 1956 he was charging that not only were the demands unreasonable but that the director had delayed so long in making them known that to honor them would "ruin all."

Evidently this complaint was justified, for two years later, with the museum nearing completion, Harry was writing to the director that although "a great many of the functional requirements of the building have been decided, after much controversy and a great deal of trouble to all concerned, there still remain certain functional features that should be decided, if possible by a meeting of minds between the architect and the director . . . but should that be impossible, the final decision will be made by me, with the authority of the trustees." To which Harry added that all of Sweeney's "operational requirements and interior structural needs, which have not been provided for, must be requested at this time," as the trustees were "not disposed" to spend any money for "such things after the completion of the museum." Apparently Sweeney complied with these requests, for this letter, dated March 6, 1958, put a quietus on the space-requirements aspects of the quarrel.

To turn then to those portions of the Foundation files concerned with the argument over the use of the building: Harbingers of this storm had appeared as early as 1952 when, to a June 6 letter to Albert Thiele, Wright attached an "N.B."

reading, "The architect should be 'looked to' for suggestions and veto powers on all furnishings and the installation of pictures." Naturally Sweeney, charged with the responsibility of running the new museum, once it opened, dissented from this position, and the issue was joined. More exactly, three issues were joined.

One had to do with the placement of the paintings with reference to the museum walls. In designing the Guggenheim, Wright departed radically from previous museum construction. Ordinarily museum walls are straight and so arranged that a viewer can step close to the paintings. At the Guggenheim, as visitors are aware, most of the exhibiting space is along the exterior walls of the spiraling ramp. Because of the shape of the tower many of these are curved. Moreover, there is at the bottom of most of them an inclined jog. Wright's plan was that the paintings—all of them frameless since he intended his building itself to frame them—were to be so placed on this incline that they would slant away slightly from the viewer.

In his opinion the curved walls with their sloping feet presented the director with an opportunity to exhibit contemporary art in a "natural way." In Sweeney's opinion they merely presented a problem to be got around, and on April 1, 1958, he proposed three methods for doing so in a letter to Harry.

"In view of the fact," he wrote, "that the incline at the outside wall would force the viewer to remain approximately five feet away from the paintings, it is important to bring the picture forward to the viewer. I feel that a normal viewer should be able to come within two feet at least of the picture, should he wish to distinguish the details." Sweeney then offered his alternative proposals for solving the difficulty. He wrote that his favorite among them—the one he eventually employed—"would be a tripod to be fixed to the rear wall, which would be invisible to the observer in front of the picture, but which could hold the painting by a plate placed in the center of the painting's back."

Another point at issue was the color of the museum walls. To achieve the feeling of unity suitable to organic architecture, Wright wanted the exterior and interior of his building to be variations of the same light tan or ivory. Sweeney wanted all exhibit walls to be white, a color that Wright insisted, in a 1958 letter to Harry, would make the interior look like "the toilets of the Racquet Club."

The third major point at issue was summarized in 1957 by William H. Short, the young architect employed as clerk-of-the-works during the construction of the building. "Mr. Wright's lighting scheme," Short explained in a letter to Harry, "includes natural light from the continuous wall skylights, controlled by adjustable louvers, and artificial incandescent spotlights, energized by the continuous 'trolley duct' on the ceiling. Mr. Sweeney intends to black out the ramp skylights and to install continuous fluorescent troughs to 'wash' all hanging surfaces with full light."

The lighting controversy incited Wright to one of his most outspoken letters. He had been informed, he wrote Sweeney on November 5, 1955, that "the director-fraternity . . . wants a painting to be shown in a fixed artificial light and this is the dream of the common or garden variety of 'museum-men.' . . . Ye Gods and Little Fishes! Here we spend all our good donor's resources, and our own, too, as creative architect, to produce . . . a place where the painter's opus may be seen as he saw it from day to day now only to find that these professional showmen want to show the work artificially." Wright charged that Sweeney's views on lighting put him in a class with those art dealers who display every painting in a blaze of illumination so "that the poor simp who buys it . . . takes it home and is disappointed. . . . What's the word for that subtle kind of shenanigan, Jim? 'Tis a harsh word, me mon! I'll not use it."

In a plethora of letters defending his position, Wright frequently quoted Solomon R. Guggenheim in an effort to prove that his own ideas on the use of the Museum and those of its late donor were as peas in a pod. By 1958 this practice on the part of the architect had put strain on Harry Guggenheim's forbearance. During the early summer he examined the correspondence to ascertain what his Uncle's ideas had been. On July 8 he dispatched to Wright a letter designed to set the record straight.

"Now finally," he wrote the architect, "let me lay once and for all, my uncle's ghost that you exorcise when all else fails. . . . There is not one shred of evidence to support your reiterated appeal to the memory of, to paraphrase you, that good man our benefactor who must not be betrayed. On the contrary, let me refresh your memory of the fear that was always with him about his architect's method of presenting his cherished paintings."

Harry then quoted a letter of August 10, 1946, in which the Grand Old Man had written to his architect, "I have been trying to visualize how our paintings are going to look in the new museum—being installed right in the walls and without frames. Hilla [the baroness] has suggested that you produce a small model, in order to convince me of the merit of this arrangement."

Having called attention to Solomon's request for a demonstration of the architect's ideas, Harry went on. "There is," he chided Wright, "voluminous correspondence from you on the subject, soothing, persuasive, poetically phrased, but only generalities, and no satisfactory reply to his [Solomon's] request." In closing, Harry reminded Wright of the donor's reiterated statement that "the paintings must not be subjugated to the building! Now, Querido Francisco," he concluded, "cease your diabolical manoeuvres because your building is for the angels. Stop causing everyone, including yourself, quite unnecessary bile and labor. Let us finish this job that your cussedness would have killed aborning without our help, and help us dedicate in harmony your beautiful and ingenious pile to an eager world."

Obviously there were intervals when the task of refereeing the quarrel came close to being a full-time one for Harry Guggenheim. Early in 1959 he received a handwritten message of comfort from A. Chauncey Newlin. A member of the Foundation board, Newlin pointed out that in weighing the merits of the dispute, the trustees were going to have "to make a Hobson's Choice," since there was much to be said for both sides.

In an effort to resolve the "Hobson's Choice" Harry took two steps with the backing of his board. He addressed to Sweeney—with copy to Wright—a closely reasoned letter staking out the respective provinces of director and architect. It was in this letter, dated March 6, 1958, that he instructed Sweeney to submit his remaining space requirements. The rest of the letter dealt with the other facets of the dispute. Harry wrote that all decisions patently relevant to the structure and architecture of the building must be made by Wright, subject to approval by the trustees. All those patently relative to the exhibition of art work must be made by Sweeney, with the same condition. Decisions about matters where the two provinces overlapped were to be made by the director and architect jointly or, failing that, by the trustees.

Sweeney's response to this letter, dated March 10, was that "It is very gratifying."

Wright's response consisted of two letters. The first was short:

> Lieber Harry! By your perspicacity and good judgment a great load is lifted from fears for the building. The heartache of a long lingering doubt is put aside and I thank you. You will have saved the memorial for the great cultural value the bequest should have. Uncle Sol's bequest is in safe hands. I had Sweeney in to lunch last week in order to see what could be done—eager to "make up" with him. Not much use because he is not honest with me. Something in his nature makes it impossible for him to be frank—to tell the truth about anything. You do not see this in line—as I see it—but in that lack of his lies real danger. He will dissemble to get what he wants.
>
> But you reassure me. The memorial is still safely on its way to the glory it deserves.
>
> Affection . . . heartfelt (you are wonderful!)
>
> Frank
>
> N.B. "The House of Guggenheim" is what your uncle told Oglivanna that it was.

Wright's second letter was longer. "I understand from your letter to Sweeney," it read in part, "that his function

> is concerned with the selection and direct presentation of the contents of the museum and does not extend to the violation of the architecture and the building. . . .
>
> This type of structure has no inside independent of the outside . . . Separate these beautiful quiet forms of this sculptural architecture from the whole ensemble and the whole building is rendered impotent. I am sorry to believe this might gratify Sweeney. But as I understand it, he should not interfere with the high style and purpose of our building either inside or outside. But to argue these matters with him is like trying to persuade a New York policeman that St. Patrick was English. . . .
>
> The true relationship between inside and outside of a sculptural-

building must be preserved. Great sculpture work seen half natural and half painted white invites derision. White—a devastating color under daylight . . . is a makeshift or a menace."

Having digested his architect's dual response, referee Guggenheim tried again. "Many thanks for your letters of March 11th and 17th," he wrote Wright. "In the former, you express relief and satisfaction. . . . In your later letter, you argue to invade the duties and rights of the Director of the Museum. . . . You seem to have an unpleasant association of ideas with white. Why conjure up the toilets of the Racquet Club? Why not let your fancy image the snows of Kilimanjaro or the breast of the Trumpeter Swan? Now, Querido Francisco, cooperate with me as I have with you to build the most beautiful and functional museum for a living and growing art Foundation."

Harry's second step was to agree to the same arrangement that his uncle had suggested years before. Wright was to prepare and install in the soon-to-be-completed museum a demonstration of his exhibiting ideas. Sweeney was to do the same, with the understanding that the trustees would witness both demonstrations and express a preference which the director could heed or not as he saw fit. Both architect and director assented to this proposal, but once again there was to be a great deal of correspondence and no action. The matter of the demonstrations would be still hanging in air, never to materialize, at the time of Wright's death.

Meanwhile the feud continued. Sweeney did not like Wright's building. No direct inkling of this appears in his correspondence with the Foundation, but he mentioned it to enough people on a sufficient number of occasions to prompt *Time* magazine in its issue of August 1, 1960, to speak of it as "no secret." One of his objections was that the building did not provide sufficient wall space for hanging paintings. Those acquainted with the Guggenheim know that its upper ramps are lined with alcoves whose partitions are designated as "webs." According to George Cohen, whose company put up the museum, the webs not only contribute to the building in an aesthetic sense but also are structural devices, installed to help stiffen the cantilevered ramps.

Without them the ramps would be perfectly safe, but they would jiggle a little, a condition visitors might find disconcerting. When Sweeney, seeking more wall space, suggested extending the webs to within six feet of the ramp parapet, Harry vetoed the proposal on the ground that the partitions, as designed, were integral to Wright's basic concept. When Sweeney proposed blocking up the skylights, Harry issued another veto for the same reason.

In the summer of 1958 Sweeney precipitated a crisis when, during a conference with Harry at the downtown offices of the Foundation, he handed over a letter, concluding, "I find myself . . . obliged . . . to tender . . . my resignation, effective July 15, 1958." This action distressed the trustees who, with the museum not far from completion, did not relish the sound and fury that would emanate from the organs of the art world if its director were to step down on the eve of the opening. Once more Harry sought to pour oil on the troubled waters with a letter dated June 23, dispatched to Sweeney by messenger and reading in part:

> I told you I would reply to your letter of resignation, although dated May 29, 1958, that you handed to me at our conference on June 15th.
>
> At that conference, you said that you felt you no longer had the confidence of the Trustees and myself....
>
> I replied that you had the confidence of myself and the Trustees, that you had at times caused me and the Museum Committee [a group of the trustees] unnecessary difficulties of administration, for which you expressed regret, and that we had no intention of impairing your duties as director....
>
> You then told me that word was being passed about in the art world, humiliating to you, that Frank Lloyd Wright would light and hang the opening exhibition, and that he was writing articles that were appearing in respected publications to that effect. I pointed out that I could not control the statements of Frank Lloyd Wright, that he had been employed by my Uncle, our benefactor, solely as Architect for the new building, that his and your functions had been carefully spelled out by me in my letter to you of March 6....
>
> I then told you that Frank Lloyd Wright had appealed for fair play ... for an opportunity of presenting his proposals for lighting and hanging paintings....
>
> At this point at our conference, you asked me what the Committee would determine, and when I told you as long as you were Director,

it would not ask you to present exhibits in a manner you disapproved, you handed me your letter of resignation.

I further said that no member of the Museum Committee is impressed with Frank Lloyd Wright's stated method of lighting and exhibiting paintings, but no member . . . would deny him an opportunity to present his case. . . .

If I understood your view correctly, it is that the examination of new methods in this field is your function, and you deny the Committee the right of investigation. . . . If this is your view, you must be judged wrong, and if this is your considered proper relationship toward your trustees, I must accept, with deep regret, your resignation. Your stated position analyzed is that . . . so long as you are Director the trustees are prohibited from investigating to determine if there is any better method of presenting art. The logical conclusion would be to make you Director for life because the Trustees would never be allowed to determine if there are other or better methods than yours.

The resolution of the resignation crisis was described in the minutes of a meeting of the Museum Committee on June 25. "Mr. Guggenheim," the record read, "informed the members . . . that he had just finished a telephone conversation with Mr. Sweeney . . . regarding the letter Mr. Guggenheim had sent to him on June 23rd; that it dispelled some false rumors, and that it confirmed he had the confidence of the Committee. Mr. Sweeney said he wanted very much to continue as Director in full conformance with the conditions set forth in Mr. Guggenheim's letter."

Frank Lloyd Wright never abandoned his conviction that, having designed and built the museum, he should prescribe the manner in which its future occupants were to run it. In January of 1959 he undertook a complicated maneuver in one last effort to persuade the trustees to accept his, rather than Sweeney's, art-exhibiting methods. At this time Harry was convalescing in Florida from a broken back suffered on the day before Christmas when he fell down a short flight of steps in his hunting lodge at Cain Hoy plantation.

As Harry said later, "While I was unable to move, Wright moved in on me." The trustees had instructed Short, clerk-of-the-works at the construction site, to set up two mockup bays, one for demonstrating Wright's ideas, the other for demonstrating Sweeney's. With Harry temporarily absent from the scene, Wright functioned with alacrity. In a bombardment of letters he first ordered Short to do nothing for the time being about Sweeney's exhibit and to concentrate on Wright's only; he then endeavored to summon a meeting of the trustees for the purpose of convincing them of the correctness of his methods.

The outcome of these stratagems was covered in the last letter ever written by "Lieber Harry" to "Querido Francisco," a letter that, like most of Harry's reprimands to his architect, seems to have been composed more in sorrow than in anger.

"Word reached me, while recovering from my accident," he wrote on January 16, "that you have countermanded my instructions. . . . Also, that you wish to supersede my authority as President of the Solomon R. Guggenheim Foundation. . . . My dear Frank . . . why don't you gracefully and graciously show us what you have in mind, see what Sweeney has in mind, find out what the Museum Committee concludes, and work out a solution? If this were an architectural matter, we would bow to your genius. We can't accept you as a universal genius who can put on superior art shows and administer our Museum. We respect your views and want to have them demonstrated. We do not propose to have you interfere in museum administration and will not accept your countermanding our orders."

If there was a reply to this letter, it never reached the Foundation files. On the following April 4, a Saturday, Wright, then at the winter quarters of his school near Scottsdale, Arizona, was rushed to a Phoenix hospital. On the following day he underwent an operation for the removal of an intestinal block, after which he showed signs of recovery for a time, only to relapse into coma. In the predawn hours of Thursday, April 9, 1959, the great architect broke his silence with a deep sigh and died.[3]

The Opening

The opening of the Guggenheim Museum, during the next to the last week of October, 1959, was a gala. More exactly, it was a succession of galas. On Monday, October 19, the building was

Harry Guggenheim with Henry Cabot Lodge, Robert Moses and Bernard M. Baruch at the opening ceremonies of the Solomon R. Guggenheim Museum, October 21, 1959.

The Solomon R. Guggenheim Museum: two views of the interior.

thrown open for a preview to members of the press and art critics, and on Tuesday evening there was a reception for personal friends of the trustees and prominent people in the art world.

Wednesday morning was given over to the formal ceremony of opening. A ribbon was cut and speeches were delivered by such notables as Secretary of Health, Education and Welfare Arthur S. Flemming, who brought greetings from President Eisenhower; Henry Cabot Lodge, American Ambassador to the United Nations; Robert Wagner, Mayor of New York; and Commissioner Moses, who disqualified himself as a critic of the building or its opening exhibit on the grounds that he was "an ex officio trustee with janitorial privileges at the Metropolitan Museum of Art," and declared that "We need not debate how much of Cousin Frank was genius and how much was, let us say, showmanship. Genius even in small proportions is very rare indeed and we should always greet it with a cheer."

Seeing that each of these preliminary events featured a different coterie of celebrities, a reporter for a national magazine declared that the opening of the Solomon R. Guggenheim Museum—or rather the openings—had "established a new stairway of status," the particular "round" to which an individual was invited determining his place on the local social graph.

Those who came were aware of two notable absences. Solomon R. Guggenheim wasn't there. Nor was Frank Lloyd Wright; his handsome, black-haired widow, who was present, told reporters that had her husband lived, he would have stayed away rather than have to look on the superficial but noticeable interior alterations effected by director Sweeney. Apparently no one, no reporter at any rate, spotted two equally striking absences from the list of speakers at the official ceremony: Mrs. Wright and Sweeney. This was referee Harry's doing. "I was afraid to let either of them talk," he said later, "lest one or the other, or both, present their extreme views all over again and hold the museum up to ridicule."

When at two o'clock Wednesday afternoon the doors were opened to the public, there was a queue more than four blocks and 2,900 persons long. On the following Sunday the queue was a crush—10,000 persons; only 6,039 got in. As the Sunday closing hour neared, people still in line began offering bribes up to $20 to the guards and feigning emergencies in an effort to crash the gates. "Must use the telephone," was one; "wife's pregnant and can't stand in line," another; "baby has to go to the bathroom," a third.

It was the impression of reporters that, by and large, these early throngs were willing to let the professionals pass judgment on the opening art show. They came to see the building, to exclaim at its beauties or reel back before its eccentricities, according to their tastes. "Fantastic . . . wonderful . . . unique . . . thrilling . . . a thing of beauty . . . a monstrosity . . . a work of art . . . a trash can!" So ran a roundup of expletives gathered by newsmen.

Published reaction to the building was not confined to the American press. It expressed itself in a score of languages around the world. The Yugoslavian newspaper *Politika* of Belgrade had nothing but praise. "Conquers the soul by its aspect and pride," it wrote of the building. The *Standard* of Benclea, Australia, called it "a thought-scraper," and the representative of London's *Art News and Review* found it "fascinating in broad daylight, while at night a surrealist element is introduced by the rivers of light that flow between the curved darkness of the spiralling ramps." Moscow's *Izvestia* gave only passing attention to the building, concentrating instead on the opening exhibit, a brilliantly arranged display of slightly more than a hundred paintings from the museum's permanent collection. "The art of the fat ones," the Communist newspaper sneered, ". . . soiled with lines and blotches that do not express anything."*

In this country published reaction cut an even wider swath. Robert Coates, *The New Yorker* magazine art critic, conceded that it was "a daring and adventurous building" but complained

* In the light of these remarks by the Russian press, it becomes of interest to point out that during the preparation for the 1963 retrospective of the works of Kandinsky, three Soviet museums were persuaded to lend seven of the artist's important paintings to the Guggenheim. The showing of these paintings, all dating back to a crucial period in Kandinsky's development, marked their first appearance in the United States.

that it had "serious drawbacks as a museum." On the other hand Emily Genauer, art critic for the New York *Herald-Tribune,* judged it not only "the most beautiful building in America" but "excellent" as a museum, declaring that the pictures were "immensely improved by a setting so exhilarating that visitors, immediately they enter the front door, are conditioned to enjoying an art whose major virtue is its excitement."

Newspaper editorials ranged the spectrum of opinion from the New York *Mirror*'s suggestion that the museum itself be put in a museum to show posterity "how mad the twentieth century is" to the San Francisco *Chronicle*'s "Heavenly!" Architects, generally, were laudatory. "Mr. Wright's greatest building, New York's greatest building," said Philip C. Johnson, one of the two architects responsible for New York's Seagram Building and then director of the department of architecture and design at the Museum of Modern Art. Of the interior of the main building, "One of the greatest rooms created in the twentieth century," he stated.

Everybody commented. Sports columnist Joe Williams of the New York *World-Telegram* was "thrilled by the structure, bewildered by the art" and quoted a horsey friend as noting, with disappointment, that there was "not one Paddy Barrie" in the place, Paddy being identified as a "superlative artist," well known for his "chemical artistry in transforming platers into stakes horses." And from Eugenia Sheppard, women's feature editor of the *Herald-Tribune,* came a column headlined "Museum Flatters the Public." Her argument was that in Manhattan where "you hardly ever get a good look at people" because they "are too damn close . . . really seeing people is one of the sharp excitements of the new Guggenheim Museum. . . ." Mrs. Sheppard related that on the afternoon of her visit to the building "there was a semi-sun coming through the skylight," and "stopping in front of canvasses, leaning on white parapets," the people, whether beatniks in black stockings or socialites in tweeds and minks, "looked like inspired and meaningful paintings. . . . Let the experts go on arguing about whether or not the Guggenheim Museum is good for paintings. It's the most soulful background people have had in a long time."

More Growing Pains

In the summer of 1960 James Johnson Sweeney once more resigned as director of the Guggenheim, this time for keeps. His action, effective August 15, was made public on the previous July 20, when the Foundation released to the press a brace of letters, signed by Sweeney and Harry Guggenheim, respectively.

Sweeney, in a forty-two-word statement, said he was leaving the post he had occupied for eight years because of a "difference between the ideals held by the Board of Trustees with reference to the aim and use of the museum and my own ideals, which I feel I have a responsibility to follow." Harry, in a somewhat longer response to Sweeney's letter, said the retiring director had done a splendid job, expressed the "gratitude" of himself and the trustees, revealed that since the opening of the Frank Lloyd Wright building less than a year earlier, three-quarters of a million people had visited the museum, and added that "in view of this the trustees believe the time has come to develop a series of activities that will be interesing, informative and educational to an ever-widening number of art lovers."

When reporters, finding these letters wondrously opaque, sought clarification, they discovered, if one may trust their reports, that Sweeney and Harry were not talking. This, of course, did not prevent the reporters from writing. Considerable newsprint was covered with shrewd and on the whole accurate guesses as to what had happened; and the magazine *Art News* once again raised the specter of "the Bonds," reading into what it termed Sweeney's "forced" resignation a glaring example of the "trustee oligarchy . . . presently affecting American museums."

The remarks in Harry's letter, forecasting an expanded educational program at the Guggenheim, sparked a number of thoughtful discussions by editorial writers and art critics, dealing with the perennial question of how far a museum can go in trying to educate the public before it ceases to be an art center and becomes merely an artsy-crafty one. In the eyes of the *New York Times* the quantitative argument, apparent in Harry's delight at the popularity of Wright's building, cut no ice. In a sedate editorial the *Times* reminded the president of the Solomon R.

Harry Guggenheim with Dark Star, winner of the 1953 Kentucky Derby.

This cartoon appeared in the *Morning Telegraph,* May 25, 1963, when both the Guggenheim Museum and Harry Guggenheim's horses were in the public eye.

Guggenheim Foundation that his museum was not a sporting arena, and that its "contribution to the cultural life of its visitors" could not be measured by counting the number of heads passing through its gates, the implication being that if the heads walked in empty they would probably walk out the same way. A similar vein was explored by art critic John Canaday, also writing in the *Times,* by Katherine Kuh in *The Saturday Review,* and by "G.W." (George Wildenstein) in a French publication.

To all observers it was obvious that Harry and Sweeney were of two minds concerning the educational role of the museum. *Progressive Architecture News Report* pictured the outgoing director as of the opinion that a museum's educational responsibilities began and ended with the acquisition and display of first-class works of art. The magazine quoted Sweeney as having written that ". . . museum trustees or perhaps even museum directors are ambitious to embrace the broadest possible public and, in our democratic age, have not the courage to face the fact that the highest experiences of art are only for the elite who 'have earned in order to possess.' "

Harry's chief public contribution to the argument, the statements in his response to Sweeney's resignation, was misleading in that it left the impression that the argument dated only from the opening of the new museum. As a matter of fact, it was an old dispute. As early as 1953 Harry was writing his director that the "need for help in the approach to modern art by intelligent and well-meaning people is apparent, and I think it's one of our jobs to find a way to give it to them." In the same letter the foundation executive sought to disabuse Sweeney of the "erroneous impression that there is implied criticism of the magnificent show that you have put on [at the museum] because there is an educational deficiency. . . . The showing, and the need for education, are two quite separate things. Your fear that anyone wants to spoil your show by submerging it into some form of educational program is ungrounded."

Ungrounded or not, Sweeney's fears persisted, and over the years his and Harry's divergent views concerning the museum-as-educator contributed to a growing complex of tensions.

Another source of trouble, widely bruited in the press both

before and after the resignation, was Sweeney's practice of voicing his discontent with Wright's building to professional colleagues and reporters—a practice that struck Harry as "plain disloyalty." A turning point in this development was reached in the last month of 1956 when the *New York Times* published an open letter signed by twenty-one prominent artists, who characterized the museum, then in the early stages of construction, as unsuitable "for a sympathetic display of painting and sculpture," objected to the sloping ramp on the grounds that pictures displayed on its walls would "look slightly askew," and called on the Foundation to reconsider its building plans.

In public Harry contented himself with a categorical denial of all objections, pointing out, among other things, that the grade of the ramp would be only three per cent, as compared with the "unnoticeable" two per cent from building to curb required of sidewalks under New York City specifications. In private he expressed distress on being told by a leading art critic that the open letter had been inspired by Sweeney. Apparently this allegation was correct for at a later date some of the artists apologized to Harry, explaining that they had signed the letter under the mistaken impression that Sweeney's criticisms of the building were well founded.

The loyalty issue produced another flareup at the time of the opening, when during an interview Sweeney explained his reasons for vetoing the architect's lighting scheme. Wright, Sweeney informed reporters, "put the skylights in, in order to relate the building to the exterior world, but this confronted us with the problem of changing light. . . . I didn't want people to have to wait for the sunshine as though they were photographing a mountain in Ireland." The publication of this interview moved Harry to blunt words. In a letter to Sweeney, dated October 17, 1959, he described the director's remarks as "stepping pretty close to what I consider the precipice. . . . I have been trying," he explained, "to prevent a public Donnybrook about the museum. So far we have succeeded fairly well, but this sort of thing from you is not helpful to that end." Presenting a panoply of comment on the resignation a few months later, *Newsweek* quoted one of the outgoing director's friends as saying that

Sweeney was "so unhappy" with the building "that the trustees felt they couldn't go on working with him. . . . If you are a guest in a house and you don't like the house, you don't stay."

Still another focus of irritation, unquestionably the most decisive one, was that Harry and Sweeney did not see eye to eye on the appropriate scope of a museum director's authority. The crux of this divergence was spelled out in 1953 when, in a letter to Sweeney, Harry objected to some bills which the director had run up without Foundation approval, and reminded him of "the arrangement that I had with you, that all administrative and business matters would be outside of your province so that you would be able to devote your entire time and attention to . . . art matters." Later the same year, Harry was writing the director that until "a few days ago, I knew nothing of the appointment of Miss ——, apparently as the so-called 'Publicity Department' of the Museum. You have not discussed this phase of the Museum's activities with me, nor has there been any authorization for the employment of anyone in this capacity. . . . The change in the by-laws makes it clear that the authority for the creation of jobs rests with the Board of Trustees. . . ."

In the years that followed, the issue of authority intruded itself increasingly. At one point Sweeney objected to placing control of the museum guards in hands other than his own. His argument was that since he was responsible for the art objects owned by the museum, he should exercise direct supervision over the men charged with their protection.

In 1958 the trustees were pleased when Sweeney suggested the creation of a new job at the museum, that of assistant director. Named to this post was Dr. Grace L. McCann Morley, who, prior to her resignation a few months earlier, had been director of the San Francisco Museum of Art for twenty-three years. Dr. Morley assumed her duties on January 1, 1959. A month later Sweeney dismissed her, without consultation with the trustees and without notifying them of his action either before or after it was taken.

Later in 1959 the authority issue came to a head when Harry served notice of his intention of reorganizing the Guggenheim Museum along unusual lines. To understand Harry's plan, the organization that was gradually developed and put into effect at the Guggenheim over a period of years, calls for a few words about the problems of museum administration.

Organizationally, the average museum consists essentially of a board of trustees who serve part-time and usually without pay, and of a paid, full-time director assisted by a paid staff. To use the term once hurled at the Guggenheim trustees, most if not all of the board members are usually "bonds," men and women from the business world. Insofar as art is concerned they are amateurs, whereas the director and his staff are "pros."

Since bonds and pros live in different worlds and speak different languages, cooperation between them is difficult unless at least two devices are built, as it were, into the very fabric of the organization, namely, some means for helping the bonds and the pros to understand each other, and some rule or set of rules precisely and fairly defining the director's area of responsibility. Without such devices, one of two things happens: either the trustees run the whole show, which is bad because they are not full-time employees and as a rule they are inexperienced in the art aspects of museum administration; or the director runs the whole show, which is also bad because he has no immediate responsibility where overall policy is concerned and as a rule he is less than highly qualified in the business aspects of museum administration.

Since the trustees have many other interests, what almost always happens in actual practice is that the director takes over and becomes a little czar. Bent on preserving the integrity of his institution as an art center, bent on keeping the bonds out of his hair, he bites off more than he can chew, insisting on exercising full control over every little aspect of administration including the business end. Sooner or later, of course, he oversteps himself, at which point the trustees intervene and the director resigns in a huff and goes elsewhere, thus giving rise to what is known in the American art world as "musical chairs," the all too frequent movement of directors from museum to museum.

It was in an effort to cope with these problems that Harry, in 1959, began mulling over a plan which he then gradually evolved, with the assistance of Daniel Catton Rich, whom the president of the Guggenheim regards as "one of the most experienced, able and dedicated professionals in the museum world." Harry's overall objectives, as he himself explained them, were: (1) to create "a line organization" so that the trustees, through their president, could administer the museum not only in theory but in fact; and (2) to relieve the director of purely business and other "housekeeping" duties without in any way impairing "those usual functions and that complete authority" which the art world has come to associate with a museum director.

To avoid misunderstanding as between the bonds and the pros, he added to the board of trustees a number of professionals, Rich among them. To clarify the responsibilities of the director and other officers, he effected a distinct separation of the art and business functions of the museum, setting up on the board of trustees a vice-president for art administration and a vice-president for business administration, each of them directly responsible to the president. Under this new setup, to quote Harry, "the director of the museum, carrying on all the usual art functions of this post, collaborates with the vice-president for art and is responsible to the trustees through the president. In the absence of the president, the art vice-president is the former's full-time representative at the museum, acting in accordance with established policies and consulting with the president on all matters of importance and concern. In addition the art vice-president consults with the director, and advises with him on all projects and programs; has a specific responsibility for the development of new projects and programs in the fields of education, publications, research, and membership; and is responsible for continually reviewing with the director the basic policies of the museum on acquisitions and on the permanent collection."

Having conceived this plan, Harry soon discovered that wherever he turned, he ran into danger signals. Associates in the art world and in the business world, alike, urged him to abandon the project, telling him that if he went through with it he would encounter severe criticism from the museum people, a situation that could deprive the Guggenheim of the high aesthetic stature Sweeney had brought to it.

Harry proceeded cautiously. One of his first steps was to solicit the opinions of the presidents of two of the country's largest museums. At Museum No. 1, his plan was not well received. He was informed that if he put it in effect, he would not only lose Sweeney, he would also find it next to impossible to persuade any first class man in the profession to take his place. At Museum No. 2 he received different advice. This museum, he was told, had already installed a plan similar in a limited way to the one Harry was contemplating. Not only had it worked, but in the opinion of the president of the institution, it was the only way a museum could hope to avoid the difficulties inherent in the notable inexperience of most museum directors where business procedures were concerned.

The gist of the advice received at this second of Harry's stops was that he would do well not to let himself be cowed by cries of "trustee oligarchy" in the art world press. This oligarchy business, he was reminded, was a two-way street. True, invasion of the art department by the business department could ruin a museum, but so could invasion of the business department by the art department. The only way to handle the matter was to separate the two, and then provide sensible machinery for taking care of the necessary liaison between them.

As Harry later said, "Naturally I acted on the opinion that coincided with my own," and naturally the imperious Mr. Sweeney was riled. It will be recalled that in 1946 Sweeney had resigned from the Museum of Modern Art after a reorganization there that he regarded as delimiting his authority as director of its department of painting and sculpture. He disliked Harry's projected reorganization of the Guggenheim, and his resignation a few months later was the inevitable outcome of the vexations produced by this and other long-since articulated points of difference.

The Museum Today—and Tomorrow

The reorganization of the Guggenheim Museum, a process which its formulator, Harry Guggenheim, speaks of as "an evolution," took considerable time. The actual separation of the art and business functions was effected in 1959 when supervision of business administration was put in the hands of Albert E. Thiele, vice-president and trustee. Simultaneously Clinton Hunt, who for forty years had been associated first with the Grand Old Man and later with Harry, retired as business manager for reasons of age and was replaced by Glenn H. Easton, Jr. A second major step was taken in September of 1960 when the board created the position of vice-president for art administration. Appointed to this post, at a later date, was H. Harvard Arnason, who prior to assuming his duties at the Guggenheim in January of 1961 had for many years been professor and chairman of the department of art at the University of Minnesota and director of the Walker Art Center in Minneapolis. It was not until the spring of 1961 that the administrative structure of the Guggenheim, as it now stands, was perfected.

To grapple quickly with the bare bones of it: The major officers of the Guggenheim are the president, the vice-president for art administration, the vice-president for business administration, the director of the museum, and the business manager of the museum. In addition there are two working committees: The Art and Museum Committee and the Finance Committee. The president is the chief administrative officer of the Foundation; the trustees determine broad museum policy.

Under the new dispensation, the acquisition of art work for addition to the museum's permanent collection has been carried on since 1961 in a manner that has been closely watched by other museums all over the country. At any museum the discovery of new art work, suitable for inclusion in its collection, is one of the most important functions of the director and his professional staff. Once the director has found an appropriate piece of art, he presents it to his board with the recommendation that it be purchased. At many American museums, the actual decision to buy or reject is made by the full board, most of whose members are usually nonprofessionals. In other words, the selection of art work for most museums is made by laymen, a condition that can cause upheavals.

At the Guggenheim, as now organized, this process does not prevail. The responsibility for approving or disapproving of the acquisition of objects for the museum's permanent holdings is lodged with the Art and Museum Committee, of which the director is a member. However, unless policy is involved—budgetary considerations, for example, or some question as to whether the recommended item conforms to the stated type of art work regularly approved by the museum—only the *professional* members of the committee vote when the time comes to make a decision.

At the time of Sweeney's resignation in the summer of 1960, the Foundation had no successor in mind. For several months, a period spoken of as "the interregnum" by members of the museum staff, the operation of the museum fell entirely on Harry. With an important exhibit planned for that fall, he was fortunate, and as he now says, "mighty relieved," to obtain the cooperation of Gordon Washburn, director of fine arts at Carnegie Institute of Technology in Pittsburgh, who acted as guest director of the show with the able help of the present Associate Curator, Dr. Louise Averill Svendsen. In January of 1961 Arnason joined the staff, and in February young Thomas M. Messer accepted an invitation to take over as the third director of the Solomon R. Guggenheim Museum.

Messer, now forty-three, is a slight, dark, quiet-spoken man, singularly free of the grand manner often associated with museum directors. Born in Czechoslovakia in 1920, he came to this country as an exchange student in 1939, was graduated from Boston University in 1942, and acquired American citizenship in 1944. Following overseas service with the United States Army, he studied at Harvard University, from which he holds a master's degree in Fine Arts. From 1949 to 1952 he was director of the Roswell Museum in New Mexico, and from 1952 to 1956 he was associated with the American Federation of Arts in New York City, first as assistant director, later as director of exhibitions, and still later as director. For the five years prior to his coming to the Guggenheim, he was director of Boston's Institute of Contemporary Art.

Under Messer's gifted and creative guidance and with the aid of veteran Harvey Arnason as vice-president for art administration, the museum has consolidated its pre-eminent position in the art world, and its major shows have attracted the respect and, for the most part, the praise of serious critics. Like his predecessor, Messer has greatly strengthened the museum's permanent collection, adding, among many other items, a masterly painting by Fernand Leger which makes the Guggenheim's holdings of that important artist second only in richness and comprehensiveness to its collection of Kandinskys.* In addition, during the present regime, the museum has inaugurated a dignified educational program, consisting of a yearly series of lectures and an occasional publication designed for the general reader and dealing with the theories and trends of modern art. It has also inaugurated improvements in the selection procedures under which every two years the Foundation makes an award of $10,000 to a living artist whose work is selected by a specially chosen international jury, and it has taken steps toward making its library of more value to art historians and critics.

"All in all," says trustee Carl Zigrosser, vice-director and curator of the Philadelphia Museum of Art, "I would say things are moving along pretty well in view of what we are trying to do. Our major aim, of course, is to acquire and exhibit the best in contemporary art, irrespective of what form that art happens to take. Since we're interested in the jewels, I would say we were in good shape. For one thing, we have a director who has demonstrated not only that he has a good eye for them, but also that he has a fine and sensitive hand when it comes to displaying them. For another, we have the proper building. When your stock in trade is jewels, you need a jewel box to set them off, and that, in my opinion, is exactly what Frank Lloyd Wright has given us."

Obviously Solomon R. Guggenheim's legacy to mankind is in good hands. It would be a reckless chronicler, of course, who attempted to unveil the future of what Harry Guggenheim once called "a living, growing" institution. Presumably as long as the

* In November of 1963 the press reported a gift to the Guggenheim Museum of 75 paintings, including 34 Picassos and the works of other prominent creators of modern art. Under present arrangements these paintings, conservatively valued at $15,000,000, will become the property of the museum on the death of the donor, Justin K. Thannhauser, a New York collector-dealer. An addition to the museum building is planned so that the collection can be exhibited as a unit. In February, 1964, the Museum announced the sale, at auction, of 50 of its collection of 170 Kandinskys.

museum continues growing, it will continue to have growing pains. As Frank Lloyd Wright once remarked, a statement that could readily be extended to all of the Guggenheim foundations:

"Superior things do not come easily or without opposition or we would have none of them."

XI

"*Doctor*" *Murry and the Children of New York*

To thousands of low-income families in the five boroughs of New York City, the name Guggenheim is not necessarily linked with the enterprises that created a family fortune or with the advances in science and culture that fortune has helped to make possible. To these people it is more likely to conjure up a six-story, gray stone building, 100 feet wide, that stands not far from the East River on the south side of Manhattan's East 72nd Street and houses the Murry and Leonie Guggenheim Dental Clinic.

The visitor to this institution, the largest of its kind in the United States, finds himself in a lively world, for all of its "customers" are children, whose varying hues and accents reflect the kaleidoscopic complexity of the most cosmopolitan city on earth. To these youngsters, ranging in age from the preschool years through fourteen, the clinic gives its services without fee provided their parents cannot afford private dental treatment.

Day after day they come, a thousand a day during the school year, six hundred a day during the summer vacation. Day after day they pile out of the big green Board of Education buses that bring most of them to the front door, to trudge up the steps of the arched and deeply recessed entranceway into a roomy and vaulted foyer where colorful murals on buff-colored walls depict such staples of child-land as the capers of the Pied Piper of Hamlin and the curious ways of that country Alice discovered on the other side of the looking glass.

A fantastic place is the Murry and Leonie Guggenheim Dental

Clinic, all the more so when one reflects that its founder was a tough, shrewd and very old-school businessman who enjoyed regaling his associates with the story of the group of children who, entering one of the clinic operating rooms for the first time, gazed at the many dentists working at the many chairs, asked one another, "Now which is Doctor Murry and which is Doctor Leonie?" and decided that "Doctor" Murry was the one with the beard.

Mustachioed but beardless Murry Guggenheim, along with his attractive, Alsatian-born wife, established the clinic in 1929. More exactly, they established the Murry and Leonie Guggenheim Foundation from which the clinic and its associated educational and research programs derive their support. Like some of the other Guggenheim endowments, the Murry and Leonie has a flexible charter. Its trustees may do anything they wish with its funds, anything, that is, which promises to further "the well-being of mankind." At the time of its inception, however, its donors made it clear that they wished the foundation to concentrate on dentistry. It was so run during the remainder of Murry's life, and it has hewn to the same objectives under the guidance of his son Edmond, its president since his father's death on November 15, 1939.[1]

The "No"-Man of the Business

In the Grand Era of the Guggenheims, business, as Herbert Hoover would later put it, was truly the business of America and the successful businessman the national ideal. When the economy faltered, reporters rushed not to the theorists of the universities but to the leaders of the market place for advice and soothing speculation. To examine the newspapers shortly after the turn of the century is to encounter numerous headlines beginning with such expressions as "Guggenheim Finds Economy Sound" or "Guggenheim Sees End of Hard Times." Often the reference was to Mr. Dan, a favorite with reporters. Sometimes the member of the family referred to was Senator Simon or Solomon. Never was it Murry.

"My father," says Edmond Guggenheim, "shunned publicity.

I remember his turning a group of reporters away with a little joke. 'My brothers talk to the press too much as it is,' he told them. 'Why should I compound the crime?' "

A photograph of Murry, taken during the last decade of his life, shows a handsome, full-faced, bald-headed man, with large and prominent eyes under heavy brows. The lips suggest determination and humor, the eyes shyness, integrity, and intensity. The recollections of his son and of others who knew him tend to confirm these impressions.

"Because of my father's dislike for the limelight," Edmond says, "I don't think many people realized the great value of his contribution to the family enterprises. He was the expert in metal sales and financial matters. He worked well with the others. He and his older brother, Dan, for example, complemented one another, each bringing to the business something the other didn't have. Dan had the daring, but many a difficulty was avoided because of a word of caution in the nick of time from my father."

Asked if perhaps Mr. Dan was "too" daring, Edmond shakes his head. "No, no," he says. "You can't say that. He was just daring. The point I'm making is that the finest car on earth needs a brake."

That Murry often furnished the "brake" is brought out also by J. Albert Woods, former chairman of the board of Courtaulds North America, Inc., who during the 1930's directed the sales subsidiary of a Guggenheim company. Woods describes Murry as "the 'no'-man of the business." It was usually Murry, he explains, who when some new project was proposed would say, "All right, gentlemen, we've canvassed the possible advantages of this step. Now suppose we have a look at the possible disadvantages before we act."

"Outwardly speaking," Woods says, "Murry was less expansive than his brothers. Inwardly he was just as large. I remember his asking me once for a financial figure connected with the business. I told him I'd have to look it up and he said that when I did, I would probably find that it was so and so. Sure enough, when I checked, I found that he had hit the figure right on target. When I told him so and expressed amazement, he said, 'Al, if you had several millions dollars in this business, you'd know the figures too.' That made me mad. 'You've no more invested in this business than I have,' I told him. 'You've got your dough in it, but I've got my life!' And I walked out on him." Was the older man annoyed by this behavior on the part of a subordinate? "On the contrary," says Woods. "After that we became the closest of friends. Far from being annoyed, he respected my honest evaluation of my own worth."

Murry had many sides. He loved beauty. "When I heard that rough-and-ready Solomon Guggenheim was collecting art and about to open a museum," says Woods, "you could have knocked me over with a feather. Had I heard the same of Murry, I wouldn't have been surprised at all. He had a passion for lovely things. Flowers, for example. He was forever carrying them home, and I can see him yet in the big partners' room at Guggenheim Brothers, sitting there with his derby hat on and a bright bouquet on his desk."

The man whose generosity was to insure the dental health of thousands of New York school children was a tightwad. According to Woods, "Murry watched those pennies," and Leo Gottlieb, the Wall Street attorney, finds an illustration in Murry's well-publicized tax battle with the Federal government in the 1920's and 30's.

In 1917 Murry established two trusts, later valued at nearly $13 million, for his son Edmond, and his daughter Lucille, now Mrs. Peter P. Summerer. The trusts were revocable. In other words, they were not absolute gifts since at any time during a specified period, the settlor—Murry—could regain title to their principal sums. In 1924 Congress included in the Revenue Act of that year a provision calling for a tax on gifts valued at $50,000 or more. Consequently, when in 1925 Murry decided to make the trusts for his children absolute by revoking his power to cancel them, he called on his law firm. He wanted to know whether his contemplated action would subject him to the recently enacted gift tax. The lawyers believed that it would not. And so Murry made the trusts absolute, whereupon the Federal government demanded and, after a long legal battle that wound up in the Supreme Court, collected a gift tax of approximately $2½ million.

Murry Guggenheim.

Meanwhile an ironic note had injected itself. In 1926 Congress took the gift tax off the books, keeping it off until 1932, with the result that when a short time later the Supreme Court ruled on Murry's case, he was compelled to pay a gift tax that he could have avoided simply by waiting until 1926 to make the trusts absolute.

Viewing this turn of events as having "added insult to injury," Murry was pretty unhappy. Although after paying up, he was still a rich man, he thought of himself as destitute. "That year," says Gottlieb, "he didn't buy a single new suit." And that year he paid another call on the members of his law firm. "I accepted your advice," he told them, "and what with taxes and fees, it cost me five million dollars. That's too expensive for me and I'm taking my legal work elsewhere."[2]

Presents for Every Child

Born in Philadelphia in 1858, Murry, like his brothers, grew up in the Quaker City and attended its public schools. His life as a businessman began when he was in his teens, at St. Gall, the Swiss embroidery center, where Meyer Guggenheim and his partner, then in the lace business, had a number of factories working on commission for them. When the family turned to mining, Murry found himself in Colorado as president of the Guggenheim smeltery at Pueblo. It was the first of a succession of responsible positions.

Romance came while he was still working in Switzerland. There he courted stately, twenty-two-year-old, Alsatian-born Leonie Bernheim on the shores of Lake Lugano, and married her in 1887. Their devotion to each other is still frequently recalled. After Murry's career brought him to Guggenheim headquarters in New York City, he and his family made their home on the ninth floor of 998, the first apartment building to be erected on Fifth Avenue. Their neighbors on the floor above were George T. Delacorte, Jr., founder and now vice-chairman of the board of Dell Publishing Company, his first wife and their six children.

"Mr. Guggenheim," the publisher says, "spent a good deal of time in his billiard room, and after his death his widow, although she did not play herself, kept the room just as it had been, even to having the table re-covered every three years."

Leonie was a pianist of more than ordinary skill. "Naturally," says Delacorte, "she had a sensitive ear, and when my children were young and were taking piano lessons, they made life pretty hard for her. Every now and then she'd send up a note of complaint. The children were always delighted when one of these arrived because they soon discovered that within a few days Mrs. Guggenheim would regret her action and apologize by sending up presents for every child."

Murry was in his middle sixties when in 1924 he began looking about, as Henry Allen Moe would put it, for some way of "doing good with his money," and found it in the discovery that thousands of New York City children were growing up without even the most elementary dental care. It is the belief of Dr. Daniel F. Tobin, director of the Guggenheim clinic, that this need was first called to his attention by Dr. S. S. Goldwater, one-time health commissioner for New York City and, in the late 1920's, director of Mt. Sinai, a hospital of which Murry and his brothers had long been benefactors. Certainly Dr. Goldwater figured large in the initial planning for the clinic, and certainly the need was there. Surveys quoted by the *New York Times* in the closing year of the decade showed that one-half of those New York school children who had reached the age of eight were victims of dental caries, and that at least 600,000 were from homes whose financial status made private treatment out of the question.

Well in advance of taking action, Murry made an on-the-spot inspection of two existing clinics, similar to the one he had in mind: The Rochester (New York) Dental Dispensary, founded in 1915 by philanthropist George Eastman, and the Forsyth Infirmary in Boston. He was impressed by what he saw, especially by figures uncovered in Boston, showing that during the life of the clinic there the number of first-molar extractions among local children had decreased from 33 to 3 per cent.

Public announcement of the forthcoming clinic was made on June 25, 1929, on which day Murry took off on his yacht, thus making himself unavailable to reporters. His absence did nothing to dilute the enthusiasm of the New York press. The *Times* asserted that dental care was the most "generally slighted" aspect of pediatric medicine. In the opinion of the *American* the Guggenheims were "initiating something so far-sighted . . . in its humaneness that to those who have studied the history of the child in human progress it has some of the quality of a dream."

The new foundation pushed ahead in bringing the dream to reality. Within a few months a small pilot clinic had been set up in temporary quarters provided by a Manhattan public school. Meanwhile plans had been drawn up for a permanent home, and workmen had begun demolishing the six old tenements then standing on the site of the present clinic, completed in 1931 and opened on September 14 of that year.

From 1932 to 1944 the Foundation conducted on the fourth floor of its clinic a fully accredited school for dental hygienists, graduating thirty to thirty-three young women every June. The school's discontinuance was dictated by two developments. One was a ruling by the state authorities that henceforth two years of training, rather than one, would be required for a hygienist's certificate. The other was an understanding given to Edmond Guggenheim, as president of the Foundation, that eight such institutions were going to be put in operation by the state of New York. So far, the state has installed only three, a circumstance that leads Dr. Tobin to remark that "if this could have been foreseen, we might have extended our training schedule to conform to the new ruling and kept our school going."

For many years the Foundation sponsored a fleet of mobile units. Hygienists accompanied these units, each of which consisted of the equipment necessary for cleaning teeth, so packed that it could be carried on a van. Since the objective was to alert needy parents to the availability of the clinic's services, this project was discontinued a few years ago when the Murry and Leonie found that the facilities of its clinic were being used to capacity.

Prior to 1954 the Foundation sponsored a variety of research projects, some on its own, some in cooperation with New York hospitals and educational institutions. Since then, except for a training program designed primarily for its own professional staff, it has devoted its clinic exclusively to practical dentistry and confined its research activities to support of the Murry and Leonie Guggenheim Foundation Institute for Dental Research of New York University.

The institute carries on investigations of a basic sort. Its establishment, like that of the clinic itself, received a grateful welcome from members of the profession. Dr. Raymond J. Nagle, dean of New York University College of Dentistry, described it as helping to close a "research gap." Of all the money then being spent on the health sciences, he pointed out, "less than two per cent" was going to dentistry. Currently under way at the institute are studies of the endocrine system as it relates to general and dental illness and of the relationship of oral pathology to rheumatic heart disease and bacterial endocarditis.

Also under way is an investigation of nutritional factors in dental disease. Dr. Tobin deems this project as of "special interest" because of a discovery made at the end of World War II when American soldiers began returning from prison camps in Japan. "Army dentists," he says, "found that the teeth of these men were relatively free of decay. Furthermore they showed little stain or tartar." These findings, the doctor notes, provided evidence for a widely held theory that to some extent "our teeth are what we eat," since during the soldiers' imprisonment in Japan they had lived exclusively on boiled fish and rice. A tall, slight man with a bony face and clear blue eyes, Dr. Tobin punctuates this revelation with a flashing grin. "Mind you," he cautions, "I don't expect any denitst to recommend that diet to American patients. It might improve their teeth, but it would play hell with their dispositions."

At present the Murry and Leonie is handling 53 per cent of all New York school children receiving nonprivate dental care. Its high registration was not reached at a leap. The clinic grew slowly. In 1939, when Murry Guggenheim died, it was treating a relatively small number of children—about 350 a day—and using only two floors of its building for practical dentistry. The first period of expansion began in 1940 when the fifth floor, previously used only for storage and by basketball-playing interns, was equipped with twenty-five chairs, acquired with money provided by Leonie Guggenheim. There was a further expansion four years later when closure of the dental hygiene school freed the fourth floor for clinic purposes.

Later on there were more spurts. One came in 1953 with the addition to the first floor of what is now the 40-by-50-foot main waiting room, along with a new central desk—actually three counters fitted into the archways of a spacious alcove; another in 1955 when the sixth floor, previously used primarily as a laboratory, was equipped for practical dentistry. Throughout the 1930's the clinic averaged 60,000 patient visits a year. By the late 1950's this figure had more than tripled, and in 1962, the last year of record, 39,388 children came to the clinic for a total of 223,537 visits.

Most of the clinic's patients are from the city's schools and are brought to the building in buses provided by the Board of Education. Some come from day nurseries, and are transported in vehicles supplied by those institutions. Some come on their own and are spoken of as "walk-ins." Each busload from a school or nursery is accompanied by a teacher. Younger walk-ins, usually preschool children, are accompanied by adults or older brothers and sisters. Older children come alone.

Since 1958 the clinic has been host to a group consisting of the children of enlisted men stationed at Fort Jay on Governor's Island. In 1962 this special arrangement brought thank-you notes from the commandant and the dental officer of the post, who pointed out that without the Guggenheim clinic many of the children at Fort Jay would not have had the much needed dental care.

Admission to the clinic is limited to children of preschool age and to those in the first four grades. Once a child has been registered, however, he is encouraged to return at regular intervals until he has been graduated from grade school.

Another rule is that before treating any child, the clinic must have the written consent of one or both of his parents or guardians. Also, parental consent is obtained for extracting one or more of a youngster's permanent front teeth. "There's no law which requires this supplemental permission," says Dr. Tobin, "but we find it good procedure. It braces the parents against the sight of Johnny or Mary suddenly arriving home looking like a Halloween pumpkin."

The third rule is that the parents or guardians must give the clinic assurance of their inability to afford private treatment. "The last thing we want to do," says Edmond Guggenheim, "is compete with the profession. On the contrary, one of our aims is to demonstrate the importance of regular visits to the dentist to children who otherwise might never go near one short of their first toothache."

Each parent is required to fill out a brief form showing income, rent paid, and certain data about the child. The Foundation maintains no social department to check on the information given. For one thing, most of this paperwork is handled by the schools whose teachers usualy have a pretty good idea of the financial status of their students' homes. For another, most people are honest about this sort of thing. Occasionally discrepancies appear, as when a form shows income of $50 a week and rent of about the same amount. Then a check is made and the child admitted or not, as findings warrant. Attempts at cheating are rare. A far more frequent occurrence is the arrival at the office of Robert Vitarelli, the clinic's bright young administrator, of a letter from a mother, proudly stating—as did one such letter recently—that "my husband has a better job now and we are sending our boy to a neighborhood dentist. Thank you for past services."

During its first decade the clinic limited its services to the children in only two of the city's school districts. As its facilities grew, however, it extended them gradually, and today it is treating children from all sections of the city. In 1962 most of its patients came from 104 public schools, 37 parochial schools (including 7 Yeshiva [Jewish parochial] schools), and 4 day nurseries.

The staff comes to about 200, including at the moment, 23 supervisors, 9 attending dentists, 70 interns, and 32 dental hygienists and assistants. Because of a work load which requires the presence of dentists at prescribed intervals, no volunteers are used. Most members of the professional staff are full-time, and all are paid. Offers of free service are refused as a matter of policy. So are gifts. Even small presents from grateful parents are returned with a polite note of explanation.

Associate director of the clinic and head of the operative (general reparative) department is Dr. Maurice Edward Low, a short, stocky bachelor with graying hair, hazel eyes, and a pleasant pixie face. A spare-time artist, Dr. Low has exhibited his paintings in several New York galleries and in one of the salons of a large Fifth Avenue high-fashion shop. Head of the special services (primarily surgical) department is genial, dark-eyed, silver-haired Dr. John A. Barratini, who speaks of himself as "the man who came to dinner." Agreeing to "help out temporarily" when the clinic first opened in 1929, Dr. Barratini has remained on—in his present position—ever since. Winter and summer he takes time from a large private practice to work at the clinic all day Monday and on Wednesday and Friday mornings.

The bulk of the dental work is carried on by the attending dentists and interns, or rather "externs," as Dr. Tobin prefers to call them since they do not live on the premises. Prior to 1952 most of these dentists were recent graduates of American schools. Since then all but a few have been graduates of foreign schools.

Brought to the clinic on ten-month fellowships underwritten by the Foundation, the externs from abroad—60 in 1962—represent almost 30 different countries. Their presence adds to the clinic's cosmopolitan atmosphere. Looking around an operating room, one is likely to see at one chair an attractive young woman dentist in the kimono of the Orient, at another a turbaned Hindu, his beard in a hairnet for sanitary reasons. Each fellow, on his arrival, receives three weeks of orientation, during which he performs operations only on metal mannequin heads (spoken of as "phantoms" abroad). During the remainder of his stay, he works in various departments and attends the clinic school, where sixteen courses are offered, for a total of 250 lecture hours a year, by instructors from New York University, Cornell, St. John's, Bronx Hospital, and the clinic staff.

The clinic maintains a few small laboratories and 78 dental chairs. Sixty-two chairs stand in the big, brightly illuminated rooms of floors four, five, and six. Together these comprise the operative department where the most common services are performed, the preparation of cavities and the restoration of teeth. The third floor is given over to the special services department. Of its 16 chairs, 13 are devoted to root canal work, extractions and other surgical procedures, 3 to oral diagnosis, including X-ray, which is employed in all examinations. On the second floor are the executive offices, lounge, library, school and record rooms; and on the first, the foyer, the waiting room, the cloak room, and the drillroom where the children are instructed in caring for their teeth and gums at home.

Except for three weeks in the early fall the clinic is open weekdays from nine to five during the school year, from eight-thirty to three during the summer vacation. Frequently it is open also on holidays and Saturday mornings for special appointments. Winter or summer, it is always a busy, humming place, as demonstrated by a count, made at the end of 1962, which shows that during the preceding three decades the staff of the Murry and Leonie Guggenheim Dental Clinic took care of at least 750,000 children for a total of 3,930,808 visits, wrote "completed" on 554,208 cases, relieved their young patients of 429,379 teeth, and provided them with 3,728,014 permanent fillings![3]

The Worst Boy His School Ever Had

Chatting in the offices of the Murry and Leonie Guggenheim Foundation, its president speaks of the dentistry practiced at the big clinic next door as "protective." It can't be called "preventive," Edmond Guggenheim explains, "because the profession hasn't yet found a way of preventing the decay of teeth. Our main objectives," he goes on, "are to safeguard the health of the child and inculcate in him the good habit of going to the dentist, a habit we hope he clings to when he leaves us."

At seventy-five Edmond is a tall and strong-looking man, with granite, chiseled features and hazel-colored eyes. Like his father, he evinces little interest in publicity. "I haven't talked this much about myself for years," he confessed when finally persuaded to speak of his career and work.

He was born in 1888, in the Swiss town of St. Gall, "at the stroke of midnight." Given a choice between the nineteenth and twentieth of January, his parents decided to celebrate his birthday on the earlier date.

He grew up for the most part in New York City where he got his secondary education at Dr. Julius Sachs' Collegiate Institute. In Dr. Sachs' opinion he did not get enough. As graduation day drew near, the head of the school made this clear to the boy's father during a visit to the Guggenheim offices in lower Manhattan. By prearrangement, Edmond was present at the interview.

"Your son," Dr. Sachs informed Murry, "is the worst boy I have ever had in my school. During his time there he has managed to exert the worst influence on the other pupils. I understand now he wishes to go to Columbia University, and I am here to tell you he won't. He can't. He will fail the entrance examinations."

Dr. Sachs then departed, leaving Edmond to face his father alone. "Well?" queried the elder Guggenheim, "of what I have just heard, how much is true?"

"All of it," replied Edmond, "except the part about the examinations. Let me have a tutor, and I'll pass them."

A tutor was employed for three weeks, and sixteen-year-old Edmond passed them. "Very well, as a matter of fact," he says now, obviously enjoying these memories of an early-emerging talent for orneriness that was to crop up frequently in later life.

He remained only two years at Columbia. Restless "because, living at home, I really had no college life," he told his father he wanted to learn the family business. Reluctantly, Murry packed him off to Utah to work at the Guggenheim holdings there. In Utah he discovered that he knew nothing about mining, and so informed his father, who enrolled him in The Sheffield Scientific School at Yale. There Edmond stuck it out for the full three years, receiving his degree in 1911. From Yale he went to the Baltimore Copper Refinery, a subsidiary of ASARCO at Canton, Maryland, where for a time he worked in overalls, stoking, plugging and tapping the furnaces. His next stop was the Perth Amboy refinery, and his next New York, where his initial job was to look over the Equitable Building at 120 Broadway, then nearing completion, and select the space—four floors in the beginning, half of one now—that has been Guggenheim headquarters ever since.

The years preceding the First World War found Edmond and his cousin Harry charged with overseeing the operations of the family's South American properties. As America prepared to enter the conflict Harry volunteered, but Edmond remained at his job until drafted a couple of months before the war ended. Assigned to the Motor Training School at Camp Meigs, Washington, he looked around, decided that the post was badly run, and conveyed his complaints and suggestions to an old friend of the family, Bernie Baruch, then directing the War Production Board.

This action did not set well with the Camp Meigs commandant. "It's overseas for you, Guggenheim," he said. The prospect was not unpleasant to Edmond, but the war ended too soon for it to materialize. After the war he returned to his work in South America until his resignation from the family enterprises in 1923.

Since his retirement, Edmond has maintained an active interest in Kennecott Corporation, of which he is a director, and has devoted much time to amateur golf and speedboat racing. Honors have come to him in both sports. Among them is the President's Trophy, won at the twenty-fifth Annual Autumn (golf) Tournament at Pinehurst, North Carolina, in 1929. For a few years he served without pay as Special Deputy Police Commissioner for New York City, in charge of police matters in the Bronx. He has also financed some philanthropies of his own.

In marital matters, he has adhered to the formula common to fourth-generation Guggenheims: Three marriages in all. His first took place on June 12, 1910. It was to Marron Price, the mother of his only child, Natalie Price, now Mrs. Frederick Talbert of San Francisco. Edmond's first marriage ended in divorce in 1936; his second, to Jeanne Russell on June 29, 1946, also ended in divorce in 1952. The third and present Mrs. Edmond Guggenheim is the former Marion Kaufman; they were married on June 27, 1955. During the winter months the Guggenheims live in Phoenix, Arizona; during the summer at Saranac Lake in upstate New York, where Edmond owns an extensive camp called

Rock Ledge, which he is now in the process of giving to a Catholic college.

In his work as president of the Murry and Leonie Guggenheim Foundation, he has the assistance of a board of consultants, comprised of eminent New York dentists. It is evident, however, from the comments of the clinic staff, that Edmond runs the show, that he regards the preservation and enlargement of his father's benefaction as an obligation calling for his close and sustained personal attention.

The Folklore of Group Dentistry

When little Johnny arrives at the Guggenheim dental clinic, he stops first at the big cloakroom off the first-floor foyer. There he exchanges his cap and his outer garments, if any, for a numbered tag. If he has come from school or nursery with a group of his classmates, he recives also a red, white or blue tag, whose color informs the dentists upstairs the exact hour when he must return to the first floor to catch the bus back. If the patient is a walk-in, this second tag is always yellow, signaling to the doctors that Johnny need not be out of the building at any particular hour. Both tags are attached to his jacket or shirt with a safety pin, and since the cloakroom tag is metal and the other is rimmed with metal, Johnny for the rest of his stay is like a belled cat. All day long the jingle of his tags and those of hundreds of other children fill the rooms and halls of the clinic with a cheery tinkle.

Johnny goes next to the main waiting room, to occupy one of the long oak benches until his name is called and he can pick up his record chart at the central desk. On the chart is some printed matter and a great many spaces where the dentists can record the services Johnny needs and indicate which have been performed, which remain to be done. There are spaces also for signatures, for after each visit to the dental chair, Johnny must have his chart signed by a supervising dentist before depositing it with the record clerks and making ready to leave the building.

From the desk he goes to the elevator. If this is his first visit, it will leave him off at the third floor for oral diagnosis. If he has been in the clinic before, it will leave him off at third only if his chart calls for special services during this visit. Otherwise it will carry him to one of the floors above, where he will horse around with the other children in a small waiting room lined with murals, until he is assigned a chair by number and told to join the procession wending its way into one of the big operating chambers.

There, in addition to the floor supervisors, he will find a dentist at each chair, an assistant for every six chairs. When the chair to which Johnny is assigned is vacated by its previous occupant, and before he gets into it, the assistant wipes the chair and attached equipment with disinfectant. She also carries away the instruments the doctor has been using and replaces them with a clean batch from the sterilizing room. Ordinarily Johnny will spend twenty-five to thirty minutes in the chair, a shorter period if his colored tag indicates his time in the clinic is almost up. If the work on his teeth calls for novocaine, he will leave the chair with still another object pinned to his clothing—a printed card telling his parents not to worry, explaining that the numbness will disappear soon, and instructing them not to give him anything to eat or drink until the numbness wears off.

When a few minutes later he reaches the second floor, he encounters a road block at the entrance of the long passageway between the executive and clerical offices—a table, so set up as to narrow the opening and discourage Johnny, now feeling pretty good and mighty relieved, from making a noisy dash of it down the hall to the records room. If his current series of treatments are not yet completed, this fact is noted by the records people so that his school authorities can be told when to send him back. If they are completed, he is put on the recall list, with the understanding that he will return for check-ups, every four months if he is a preschool child, every six thereafter. If he is lucky, these checkups will be all, but if later on his teeth need further attention, he will undergo another series of treatments until another "completed" can be written on his chart.

If Johnny is making his first visit, his last stop before reclaiming his outer clothing will be at the first-floor drillroom where he will be told how to care for his teeth a home and given a toothbrush. Chances are, when he gets home, he'll clean his teeth, but

Edmond A. Guggenheim, president of the Murray and Leonie Guggenheim Foundation.

not necessarily with the brush obtained at the Guggenheim clinic. That one, if he's like most of his fellow patients, he'll keep as a souvenir.

As a souvenir, moreover, of what most of the children obviously regard as far short of an ordeal at worst, and something of a lark at best. It is this attitude on the part of the patients that usually strikes the adult visitor to the clinic at once. At times a child takes fright and fills the air with shrill and tearful protest. Administrator Vitarelli sometimes receives a letter from a discouraged mother, reading, to quote a recent one, "This is concerning [the child's name]. It seems that he is afraid to get the work done to his teeth, so he will discontinue. You need not work on him in future." But generally speaking, the youngsters tinkle their way from cloakroom to dentist's chair like troopers.

"There are reasons for this," Dr. Low will tell you. "Going to the dentist here isn't quite like the usual visit. At a dentist's office the child is surrounded by adults. He knows that his yips and yells will get him sympathetic attention. Here he is surrounded by his peers. He knows that all his yips and yells will get him is the raspberry either here or when he gets back to school. Then, too, he's getting a vacation from school, so he arrives here determined to make the most of it."

Standing near his glass-walled office in the center of one of the operative floors, Dr. Low points out a double line of children, waiting to be called for their moment under the drill. "Pretty well-behaved bunch, eh?" he says, beaming on them as proudly as if he were the father of the lot. "They help each other, you know. The old-timers reassure the newcomers and set an example for them. Fact is, once a child has been here two or three times, he gets pretty wise to things. Very often when one of our foreign fellows asks me about procedure, I'll say to him, 'When you want to know anything, just ask the children. They'll tell you what to do.' "

Dr. Low is full of the lore of group dentistry, juvenile division. "Novocaine presents a problem occasionally," he reveals. "Sometimes even a youngster who's been here often will flinch the first time he sees a needle. Naturally we've found ways of coping with that. Hour after hour the youngsters file past the door of my office en route to the chairs. I keep the door open. I encourage them to drop in and have a look at the big set of false teeth and other interesting objects on the desk. Then I explain about the needle. I point out that the needle contains magic medicine. It will hurt when it goes in, but after that no hurt at all. This approach usually works. Pretty soon I'll hear one of the older girls bragging to one of the younger, 'I *always* get the needle.' "

Dr. Low lets his eyes roam the big, bustling operative room. "A child," he says, "likes a dentist who permits him to raise his hand when he wants the drilling to stop. He likes to feel that he isn't completely at the dentist's mercy, that he has some control over the situation. We watch our fellows carefully. To handle children takes something over and beyond technical skill. It takes a certain knack. Some of our fellows have it when they come to us. Some pick it up while they're here. Some never get it."

Dr. Tobin is another source of pertinent information. "We never lie to a child patient," he says. "If it's going to hurt, we tell him so. You can't fool children, and it's a mistake to try."

And administrator Vitarelli adds to this folklore of the clinic an account of a conversation overheard in the elevator between two boys en route to the records room to return their charts.

Said the smaller boy to the bigger one, "You cried in the chair, didn't you?"

"Me! Cried!" was the indignant rejoinder. "Did no such thing."

"How come there was tears on your cheeks then?"

"Oh, them! Just got something in my eye, that's how."

Vitarelli's comment on his story is a query: "Quite a place, no?"

Quite a place, yes, this gift from "Doctors" Murry and Leonie to the children of New York.

XII

The John Simon: Open-Hearted Free-Wheelers

The John Simon Guggenheim Memorial Foundation, founded by the late United States Senator Simon Guggenheim and his wife, is built on one of the most spacious and refreshing concepts in the history of philanthropy. When plans for it were announced in 1925, many observers thought Senator Guggenheim was bringing into being an American version of the trust provided by the will of the British empire-builder Cecil John Rhodes—the arrangment under which, since 1902, a small number of talented college men in this country and others are selected intermittently to attend the colleges of Oxford on Rhodes scholarships. As the new endowment took form, however, under the sensitive guidance of Henry Allen Moe, himself a Rhodes scholar, it became apparent that the John Simon Guggenheim Memorial Foundation was not quite like the Cecil Rhodes Trust.

In truth, it is not quite like any foundation of modern times. "This foundation," Moe has observed, "has been flattered by many attempts to imitate it, but I believe I'm correct in saying that so far no one has quite achieved our open-hearted, crazy freedom."

Open-hearted and crazy it is. If the John Simon were not in its thirty-ninth successful year, one could assume that no such organization could function for thirty-nine months. For here is a foundation that says to the artist, the research scientist, the scholar, the composer, the writer—to any man or woman working in the "field of the mind and the spirit" and sufficiently seasoned to have given some demonstration of his ability: "Here is a sum of money to help you do whatever you want to do, in your own fashion, at your own speed. If we can be of any further help, please let us know. And if next year or the year after or fifty years hence, something comes of whatever you tried to do with the help of this money, we'd be delighted if you dropped us a card and let us rejoice with you."

It is in the spirit of those words, if not in the words themselves, that some official of the Foundation hands over the check to every successful candidate for a Guggenheim fellowship. When at the time of the establishment of the Foundation, Senator Guggenheim addressed what was to be the first of three Letters of Gift to its trustees, he expressed the hope that the proposed fellowships would be issued "under the freest possible conditions," and from that day to this his wish has been honored.

Among the successful applicants for a fellowship in 1931 was the now famous short-story writer and novelist, Katherine Anne Porter. Many years later Miss Porter would put in print these words:

> "As to the obligations of the writer to the sponsor, let me . . . cite my personal experience with the Guggenheim Foundation; their grant took me to Europe for a year, and I managed to stay on for five in all . . . the change was a tremendous one for me, full of violent reactions and intense feelings—not unhappy ones, simply unsettling to the last degree. It took me better than a year to settle to work, though I kept enormous notebooks. I wrote to Mr. Henry Allen Moe full of contrition that I hadn't turned out a book in that year. And Mr. Moe wrote that nobody had expected me to! That the grant was not just for the work of that year, but was meant to help me go on for all my life. And this has been true—without that grant, I might have just stayed in Mexico, or here at home! I should certainly not have gone to Europe when I did; and so in the most absolute sense that Guggenheim Foundation Fellowship has helped to nourish my life as a writer to this day . . . The writer owes his sponsor to write, as well as he is able, in his own time and his own way, exactly what he wishes to write insofar as anyone has ever done that! In fact, he owes to his sponsor exactly what he owes to himself, no more, no less, except thanks!"

"No more, no less"—and the thanks are optional—is all the John Simon asks of its fellows. If a painter finds that he can best

Simon Guggenheim in 1925, the year he and his wife founded the John Simon Guggenheim Memorial Foundation.

further his development by spending his fellowship year sitting and brooding on a sunny beach, he is free to do so. If a week after receiving his fellowship, a scientist discovers that the research project on which his grant was made is taking him off on a tangent, previously unanticipated, he is free to pursue it. If a scholar, having sought and received his grant for the purpose of doing research in Subject A, decides after becoming a fellow that he would prefer working on Subject B, he is free to switch.

In its early announcements, the foundation said each fellow must turn in certain reports. Little or no attention was ever paid to this provision, and for three decades no reports have been required. In the beginning it was unspoken policy to confine most grants to individuals between the ages of twenty-five and thirty-five. Since 1949 no age limitations have been considered, and grants have been made to individuals ranging from twenty-two to seventy-seven, although the average age remains at thirty-five. All along the line flexibility has been the keynote of Foundation procedures. During World War II a number of post-service fellowships were made available; in other words, grants were authorized for men and women then in the Armed Forces, to be used upon release from the service.

Ordinarily each grant covers one year. From the start, however, fellows have been permitted to seek one or more renewals. Several such renewals have been authorized, and in recent years the Foundation has made some grants for more or less than a year, the less-than-a-year grants going as a rule to individuals in need of a little money to finish jobs already begun. At the start, too, it was expected that a Guggenheim fellow would spend most of his fellowship period abroad. That policy no longer prevails. Today many grants are made to Americans whose work can be best accomplished in their own backyards.

Such rules as the John Simon can be said to follow are those dictated by its purposes. Brainpower, Moe believes, is America's "most critical need," and he describes the underlying purpose of the John Simon as an effort to help "stockpile" this precious commodity for the future. Obviously a John Simon grant is seed money; it is reserved for the person who has arrived at a stage in his field sufficiently advanced to justify the assumption that, given a "leg-up," he can scale the further heights on his own. Grants are never made to college students seeking money to obtain their degrees, partly because money of this sort is abundantly available from other sources, chiefly because the average graduate or undergraduate has not yet arrived at that maturity of accomplishment associated with a Guggenheim fellowship. To put this another way: In choosing its fellows the Foundation utilizes guidelines dictated by its objectives and by the realization that liberty and order, freedom and limitation, are two sides of the same coin, neither viable without the other; but to the fellowships themselves there are no strings attached—a fact which makes the success of the Foundation a living justification of the faith of its founder that it is the free man who produces most and best.

That the Foundation has been a success is attested to by the respect public opinion has attached to its fellowships, by the accomplishments of those who have received them, and by the judgments of informed observers.

It is now universally recognized that the recipient of "a Guggenheim" has received not only a monetary award but a title. The money runs out but the title remains: Once a Guggenheim fellow, always a Guggenheim fellow.

Every issue of the Foundation's biennial report carries an index of living fellows. Down through the years this list, currently some 5,000 names long,[1] has always read like a *Who's Who*. The visitor to the Foundation offices in Manhattan finds himself staring at shelves groaning under hundreds of books, scores of music and scripts of plays—all, save for a few standard reference works, the product of Guggenheim fellows. Seven fellows, as has been mentioned, have received the Nobel Prize, thirty-one the Pulitzer.

There has been no end of favorable comment. People all over the world, people eminent in the disciplines of interest to the Foundation, have praised the intelligence with which it has carried out its founder's wishes, making its grants available only to individuals—never to groups: a procedure that has been described as far-sighted by those who agree with the words of poet Ezra Pound—words penned to Senator Guggenheim many years ago—

that the "only way to make a civilization is to exploit to the full those individuals who happen to be given by nature the aptitudes, exceptional aptitudes, for particular jobs. By exploit I mean that they must be allowed to do the few things which they and no one else can."

Memorable among the commendations bestowed on the Foundation is a statement by Gian-Carlo Menotti, Pulitzer-prize winning composer and Guggenheim fellow. In common with a few other organizations similar in aim, Menotti has written, the John Simon has become a "father of America's outcasts." It is a regrettable truth that American society has never been overwrought with solicitude for the welfare of its creative individuals —of its serious writers, composers, and artists; of its scientists seeking new discoveries as distinct from those seeking practical application for the old ones; of its original thinkers. For these toilers in "the field of mind and spirit," support has always been hard to come by. Noting that American parents often look with horror on a son or daughter who wishes to embark on a creative field and that a well-to-do father will seldom give financial aid to such a son, Menotti adds that in "a certain sense, the Messrs. Guggenheim and Pulitzer are playing the part of the ideal father to these American outcasts. Without them, I really do not know what many young American artists would do."

Notwithstanding this state of affairs, America's contribution to the arts, to science and to scholarship has been extensive and glorious, but without the John Simon Guggenheim Memorial Foundation it might have been measurably less so. Like the Daniel and Florence and the Aeronautical Fund, the John Simon is not just another foundation; it is a unique social institution with a unique history, the opening "chapter" of which, for obvious reasons, revolves around the man who made it possible.[2]

Thousands of Sons and Daughters

Harold Loeb, speaking as a fourth-generation member of the American Guggenheims, offers an interesting recollection concerning his Uncle Simon. "When as a youth," he says, "I used to visit him and Aunt Olga, Simon would always hand me a hundred-dollar bill. Well, I was very young and very aware of being a blood relative, and the smallness of the sum hurt my pride. So one time when Simon pulled out a crisp new bill to give me, I just waved it aside with a 'no thanks.' I thought he would get the idea and give me more, but he didn't. He took me at my word and never offered me another cent. I guess you might say I misread what was going on in his mind."

At other times, under other circumstances, other men were to misread what was going on in Simon Guggenheim's mind. Bernard Peach of Duke University and Paschal Reeves of Florida Southern College, in a recent appraisal of the John Simon Guggenheim Memorial Foundation,[3] relate how in 1910 the editor of a Richmond newspaper wrote to the senior U.S. Senator from Virginia asking him to appeal to Senator Simon Guggenheim of Colorado for aid to a small college. The reply of the Virginia Senator, Thomas S. Martin, was that "Mr. Guggenheim . . . does not, so far as I have been able to observe, take any broad view of educational or other public interests. . . . I will say very frankly that I do not think it will be possible to get any generosity for the cause of education from the Guggenheims. I do not know of an instance in which they have shown any interest in institutions of learning or in any charitable or benevolent undertaking."

Since as of 1910 Simon Guggenheim had already given a building to the University of Colorado and another to the Colorado School of Mines and was soon to enlarge the scope of his benefactions, it must be assumed that Senator Martin, a man noted for his judgment, had misread his colleague for the same reason that others often did. The Senator from Colorado was not given to revealing his inner self to strangers or, for that matter, to friends. A small, dark man—"tender, soft and sweet," to quote Loeb—Simon, in both his mode of speech and his way of life, was unspectacular. As a rule only close friends and acquaintances, and only the more perceptive among them at that, were aware of the broadness of his personal culture, of the depth of his interest in things of the mind and spirit—of his having, in short, the caliber of mind able to conceive a foundation like the John Simon.

Simon and Robert, the latter being the twin whose early death was to reduce the brothers to seven, were born in 1867. At the time Meyer and Barbara Guggenheim and their enlarging brood were living in the Philadelphia suburb of Roxborough, and Meyer was engaged in one of those numerous business coups that were to constitute the rungs on his ladder to fortune. Primarily a spice merchant at this stage of his career, Meyer, always on the outlook for new worlds to conquer, had discovered in England a cheap caustic alkali then widely used by American housewives for making soap. Obtaining an option on the English product, he had processed, packaged and placed on the market a lye which sold so cheaply that soon the Pennsylvania Salt Company, holder of a monopoly on American lye, was tearing its hair. Shortly this maneuver came to its not unexpected denouement. Pennsylvania Salt bought Meyer out, with the result that in 1867, the year of Simon's birth, the head of the House of Guggenheim added a substantial sum to an already respectable bank account.

As befitted a man of means, the Roxborough house, at 443 Green Lane, was spacious with a large piazza in front and a large orchard behind, full of trees of the sort boys delight in climbing. Simon and his twin were not to enjoy them, however, for soon after their birth, and shortly before that of brother Will, the restless Guggenheims moved back to Philadelphia proper. There Simon grew up with his brothers and sisters, survived Meyer's efforts to make musicians of all of them, got his preliminary education in the public schools, attended the Pierce School of Business, successfully resisted his father's efforts to enroll him in a university and, in 1888, took off for Spain where he lived for two years, rounding off his education and acquiring a fluency in the language.

Over the years there developed among the Guggenheims a marked split between the older and younger brothers. The older sons—Isaac, Daniel, Murry and Solomon—tended to gang together. The surviving younger ones—Benjamin, Simon and William—did the same. For Ben and Will the split was permanent. As time wore on, both drifted away. Simon, on the other hand, threw in his lot with the older sons. Indeed the suspicion arises that one of his most persistent motivations was a desire to earn their confidence and respect.

By the time he returned from Spain, New York had become the family home and mining and smelting its major enterprises. Ben and Will were already working in the West and soon Simon was on his way to Colorado. There he was to make his headquarters for the next twenty-two years, serving the family business as its Western representative and as its principal ore buyer both in the American West and in Mexico, where his knowledge of Spanish was helpful. Home, for a short time, was Pueblo; then Denver, where in 1898 he brought his bride, the former Olga Hirsch, after a honeymoon in Japan, the two living first in a suite at the Brown Palace, later in a mansion belonging to Otto Mears, the railroad magnate.

In 1896 Simon edged into politics. It was a move off the beaten path for a Guggenheim but an understandable one in view of his eagerness to shine before his older brothers. In the 1890's American politics were chaotic. The entire country was agitated by what historians would come to regard as a grass-roots struggle to win a greater share of political and economic power for the worker, the farmer and the small businessman.

In Colorado there was no straight-away Republican-Democratic cleavage. On the one hand were the "Silver Republicans," consisting essentially of big-business conservatives perversely and short-sightedly addicted to soft money because of the state's silver-mine interests. On the other was a loose fusion of old Democrats and new Populists, ranging in political coloration from Grover Cleveland hard-money men to William Jennings Bryan silverites. In 1896 the Silver Republicans gave Simon the nomination for lieutenant governor, and then snatched it away, since at twenty-nine he was under the legal age. Two years later the National People's party, a hastily put together aggregation of conservative Silver Republicans and so-called middle-of-the-road Populists, ran him for governor in a furious campaign. Nothing came of it because, toward the end, Simon withdrew in deference to the wishes of his older brothers, who had found that his outspoken support of silverism was making trouble for them in the hard-money climate of the New York financial market. Success came finally in 1907 when Colorado sent him to the United States Senate.

In 1907, senators were still being named by state legislatures, rather than by direct vote of the people, and given the shabby condition of Colorado politics at the time, it would be a thankless task to argue with the charges, coursing through the state press, that Simon had "purchased" his seat by playing what one reporter called the "good angel" to his party. In the Denver *News* Albert Damon Runyon, later to drop the "Albert" and become a short-story writer of distinction, speculated that the senatorial toga had cost Simon a million dollars. It is undeniable that he did not go to Washington as the "people's choice." Eight years later his brother, Mr. Dan, testifying before the Federal (Walsh) Commission on Industrial Relations, would earn the epithet of "Socialist" by endorsing the right of labor to organize and by calling on the state and Federal governments to help workers achieve their legitimate demands.

"The working man," the then head of the famous mining family told the commission, "does not only want higher wages. He wants something higher—comforts for himself and family. He will get them and he should get them." Such were Mr. Dan's words in 1915, but in 1907 he and his brothers were neither more nor less concerned with the welfare of labor than were the general run of American industrialists. In the West, just before the turn of the century, the Guggenheims had won a temporary respite from labor criticism by honoring and giving support to Colorado's first eight-hour-day law. They had taken this position, however, at a time when they could embarrass their smelting competitors by doing so. Later, having bested their competitors by seizing control of ASARCO, they had won the undying enmity of the Western Federation of Miners by helping to thwart an attempt by the legislature to implement an amendment to the state constitution that authorized eight-hour-day legislation and had been voted by the people in 1902 after the previous law had been declared unconstitutional by the state supreme court.

On the eve of Simon's election William Jennings Bryan, writing in his Nebraska magazine, *The Commoner,* predicted that while "Guggenheim may not intend to represent the smelters and other corporations, he is so accustomed to look at the interests of the people through corporation spectacles that he will be quite sure that what is good for the corporations is good for the people."

On taking office the new Senator gave up his job as Western viceroy of the Guggenheim interests, but generally speaking his meager senatorial record was to be in line with Bryan's prophecy. On economic legislation, as a rule, he went along with the highly conservative leadership of a Senate then often described as "America's best millionaires' club." His only progressive action of consequence was to cast a favorable vote for the popular election of senators. His only sensational one was to lead an unsuccessful filibuster against the bill that established a department of labor in the presidential Cabinet.

So abundant was the Republican membership of the Senate in the early 1900's that Guggenheim and several other Republican newcomers were seated on the extreme right of the Democratic half of the chamber. Among the occupants of this overflow enclave were Robert La Follette of Wisconsin and William Borah of Idaho. Because of the presence of these young reformers and other so-called Republican "bolters," the section came to be known as the "Cherokee strip." It amused reporters to point out the presence in the "strip" of "Simon Guggenheim, the most conservative man in the Senate." One reporter noted that he was the only man in the chamber whose feet, when their owner was seated, did not reach the floor.

The junior Senator from Colorado was energetic in seeing to it that his state got its share of well-heeled Federal construction projects; showed special diligence in taking care of constituents' requests, however insignificant; ran his office with business-like efficiency; served conscientiously on two standing committees; got along splendidly with the press; and handled with dignity a brace of anonymous poison-pen letters, scurrilously attacking his race and his private life and widely circulated back home. He made no important speeches, lent his name to no important legislation, and on the whole his senatorial career is fairly summarized in a 1908 article in the *Pueblo Chieftain*.

"That Mr. Guggenheim would receive a popular majority for

the position he holds," the newspaper editorialized, "is hardly to be claimed; and it is scarcely more probable that he would be the choice of the Republicans of the state at a general primary election. But for the political customs . . . that made Senator Guggenheim's election possible, the people of Colorado, and not this occupant of the Senatorial office, are responsible, and . . . Senator Guggenheim is a far more respectable and worthy representative of the people . . . than some of those that have preceded him in this position."

In Washington the Guggenheims occupied a handsome red brick mansion on Scott Circle. There was no entertaining in the beginning because of a recent family bereavement. There was a good deal thereafter, and as a capital hostess Mrs. Guggenheim—a beauty, a linguist, and an accomplished musician—was a success.

In 1911 Simon announced that he would not stand for re-election. The announcement appears to have surprised no one; presumably one of the Senator's reasons was that insofar as he had sought to impress his older brothers, one term would serve his ends as well as two* Obviously the brothers were impressed. When Simon left the Senate in 1913, they created three top executive positions for him in their New York headquarters, and in 1919 he succeeded Mr. Dan, then in the process of retiring, as president of powerful ASARCO.

The climactic action of the Senator's life, the creation of the John Simon Guggenheim Memorial Foundation, was conceived

* It will be recalled that in 1911 young Harry Guggenheim, then at Cambridge, was giving thought to a career in politics, and that his father was seeking to dissuade him. One of the older man's stratagems was to cite his brother's vicissitudes in Washington. "Your Uncle Simon," he was writing to Harry on April 12, "has been reasonably successful in the political life; he has worked hard and faithfully for his party and for his state. It is conceded generally that he has accomplished more for his state than almost any other Senator . . . This is conceded by his worst enemies . . . And still he is dissatisfied with his constituents because there is a great lack of appreciation on their part; and he is tired of political life. He wants to get back to the financial arena again. He says . . . thousands [of voters] are trying continually to tear him down . . . hundreds . . . abuse him orally and in print; not because they are dissatisfied with him, but because they are after his position. . . ."

in tragedy. Two sons were born to the Senator and his wife: John Simon in 1905, George Denver in 1907. Neither was to live long. A victim of ill health, George was thirty-two when in 1939 he took his life in a room of the Paramount Hotel in New York City. John, the older son, was a promising lad. He had made a good record at Exeter and was on the verge of entering Harvard, with a business education in mind, when death came in his eighteenth year, following a siege of pneumonia and an operation for mastoid. Three years later his parents founded the John Simon, the Senator explaining their motives in a touching Letter of Gift—a document addressed to the original Foundation trustees and bearing the date of the third anniversary of John's death.

> The name John Simon Guggenheim embodied in the title [the Senator wrote] is that of a dearly loved son who was cut off by death on April 26, 1922, just as he had completed his preparation for college. In this great sorrow, there came to Mrs. Guggenheim and myself a desire in some sense to continue the influence of the young life of eager aspiration by establishing a foundation which in his name should, in the words of the charter, "promote the advancement and diffusion of knowledge and understanding, and the appreciation of beauty, by aiding without distinction on account of race, color or creed, scholars, scientists and artists of either sex in the prosecution of their labors."

Decades later the Senator's words would be echoed in a comment on the John Simon by Brand Blanshard, Sterling Professor of Philosophy at Yale Universty and a Guggenheim fellow. "The Foundation," Blanshard wrote, "is the Socratic midwife of American scholarship. It has helped bring to the birth all sorts of insights, theories, and systems, scientific hypotheses and works of art. I cannot think how anyone could have made a more imaginative or decisive contribution to American scholarship than Senator Guggenheim did in his memorable letter of gift. He was moved to make the gift because he had lost a son. He gained some thousands of sons and daughters who will always think of his name with thanks and honor."[4]

"We Aim . . . to Provide that Room"

The birth of the John Simon was preceded by a period of gestation, during which the Senator leaned heavily on the advice of the late Carroll Atwood Wilson, tall and personable general counsel for the Guggenheim enterprises, a Rhodes scholar and a student in the field of bibliography. On Wilson's suggestion the Senator engaged two other Rhodes scholars to assist in formulating plans.

One was Frank Aydelotte, who for several years had been secretary of the Rhodes Scholarship trust in this country. Born in Sullivan, Indiana, in 1880, and educated at the University of Indiana and Harvard, Aydelotte for some years taught English at MIT and elsewhere. From 1921 to 1940 he was president of Swarthmore College, and from 1939 to 1947, director of the Institute for Advanced Studies at Princeton, New Jersey. Having helped set up the John Simon, he became closely associated with it for the rest of his life, which ended in 1956. He served principally as chairman of the Advisory Board, a frequently changing committee of experts who play an important role in the selection of Foundation fellows.

The other man was Henry Allen Moe, who at the time of his recent resignation to take over directorship of an important study for the National Science Foundation had been with the John Simon for thirty-nine years, serving first as secretary, later (1938-1954) as secretary-general, still later as secretary-general and vice-president. In 1945 he became a member of the Board of Trustees and during his last two years with the Foundation he was its president, assuming this title following the resignation of the Senator's widow, Mrs. Simon Guggenheim, who at eighty-six holds the title of president emeritus.

Newspaperman, mathematician, lawyer, author, retired naval officer and holder of a ship's mate's license, Henry Allen Moe is a scholar's scholar. Now in his sixty-ninth year, he is a rather large man, with a small white mustache, ragged eyebrows, a cap of light brown hair deeply receded from a very high forehead, a round head, and the face of a poker-playing cherub. In conversation his faded green eyes brim with humor, otherwise they tend to be noncommittal. Some attribute this trait to his Scandinavian ancestry. Others believe that Moe's "deadpan" was deliberately cultivated, since one of his jobs for many years was to play the role of listener—and "sizer-up"—in interviews with fellowship candidates.

He is a hard worker, often during his years with the John Simon putting in from ten to twelve hours a day, either at the Foundation office on the twenty-third floor of 551 Fifth Avenue or at his home in the Riverdale section of New York City, a Dutch-style house that Mrs. Moe describes as "furnished mostly with bookcases." Vacations are not to his liking. "The trouble is," he says, "you have to earn them before you go and make up for them when you come back. It's really more restful to just keep on working." He does enjoy travel but during his administration of the John Simon his only extended stay away from his long, horseshoe-shaped desk at Foundation headquarters was back in the early 1930's when the organization first began making grants to Latin Americans and Moe went to Spain for three months to acquire the language. Mrs. Moe, who accompanied him, could speak French and had no difficulty learning to speak Spanish. "But Henry was not content with that," she says. "He also taught himself to write the language properly, principally by translating the whole of Charlotte Brontë's *Jane Eyre* into Spanish."

Henry Moe wears his learning lightly. "The most modest man I have ever known," Mrs. Simon Guggenheim has been quoted as saying, and staff members of the John Simon cherish the recollection of the young lady who, barging into the reception room one day, asked how to apply for a fellowship and was ushered into Moe's cluttered office. On the following day the lady was on the phone, pouring apologies into the ears of one of the secretaries. "When you took me in to see that Mr. Moe yesterday," she explained, "I got the impression he was just a nice elderly gentleman you kept around the place to talk to stray visitors. It wasn't until I got out on the street and ran into an old friend that I learned that he is the director of the whole shebang!"

To the questioning reporter the reluctance of the one-time "director of the whole shebang" to talk about himself is in one way a handicap; in another it is an advantage, since on those rare occasions when Moe's modesty gives way, one learns which of his accomplishments he values most. He takes pleasure in the

Dr. Henry Allen Moe, who served the John Simon Guggenheim Memorial Foundation for thirty-nine years in every capacity from secretary to president.

judgment of an eminent scholar that one of his own scholarly papers contains an original contribution to history. The paper, "The Power of Poetic Vision," was originally published in *Proceedings of the American Philosophical Society* (CII, iv., Aug., 1958). In his opening paragraphs Moe called attention to a television program on which two distinguished poets, asked to cite "an instance of a poem directly affecting history," were unable to do so. Dr. Moe's comment was that "they muffed it," and the remainder of his paper dealt with an English reform law, passed during the reign of Elizabeth I, which not only drew its spirit but many of its provisions from William Langland's *The Vision of Piers the Plowman,* a poem written and widely read in England two and a half centuries before.

Well over two-score of pithy and thoughtful papers have come from Moe's pen, and his biennial "Reports of the Secretary" of the John Simon are choice examples of the personal or familiar essay. Graceful, aphoristic and free of jargon, they are highlighted by the recurrence of themes dear to their author's heart.

One is freedom. "We," he was writing of the Foundation in his report for 1945-46, "have not undertaken to say what ought to be done as useful or most useful to the state of society; we have erected no design of inquiry. And it is our intent to remain the stronghold of free enterprise in things of the mind and the spirit that we have been since our beginnings. . . ." And in 1947-48, "The history of America, in its main stream," he was writing,

> is a history of the guarding of the ramparts of freedom. Of no other part of the world can this be said with equal truth. In one aspect, the history of freedom in America is a history of the proper line dividing the functions and operations of government and of private enterprise. Every shift of that line, to enlarge the functions of government, has involved a hard-fought fight. We did not like it and we do not like it; but the judgment which now controls is that the size of internal and international social and economic problems—problems become too great to be dealt with by private enterprise or individual or local action—has made it necessary.
>
> Collectivism starts from another direction—a state proclaiming benevolence to its people, which is a concept that Americans, at least

historically, will in no way admit to be valid. And it is perfectly clear that collectivism has triumphed over a large part of the world only because the peoples thereof had not the American concept of freedom, nor the American conception of government.

Another recurrent theme is the importance of the individual. "It seems to be the accepted doctrine," he wrote in 1955-56, "that no man is indispensable. Perhaps this is true if the objective is . . . mere survival; but, clearly, the doctrine has no basis in truth if the objective is something more. . . . All of the great breakthroughs, to what we call progress, have been made by men who were, indeed, indispensable . . . we [the Foundation] are determined to continue our search for indispensable men. . . . When we find [them] . . . we shall continue to let them know that they, not we, are indispensable, and that our conduct toward them will be warm and friendly, helpful and understanding. We understand that if they knew what they would create, it could not be creative: we understand that what they need is room for the exercise of their trained imaginations. *We aim, quite simply, to provide that room.*" (Italics added.)

As these words eloquently indicate, Moe always proceeded on the principle that as head of the John Simon he should not merely sit at his desk and let applicants come to him. It was his practice to move about in the world of the mind and spirit, to mingle with its members, to seek out the "indispensable" men and women. To this end he served on numerous bodies, including the boards of other foundations. Occasionally the John Simon, having turned down a fellowship bid only to discover later that the applicant was worthy, has deliberately sought out the unsuccessful applicant and urged him to apply again. Occasionally, too, individuals who have not applied, but whose work has been recommended to the Foundation by fellows, are the recipients of "feeler" letters urging them to make application.

Moe's attainments have not gone unrecognized. He has been the recipient of many honors. Not the least of them was his election in 1943 to membership in the American Philosophical Society, oldest of this country's learned bodies. Since 1959 he has been the twenty-seventh president of this organization, of which Benjamin Franklin was the first president and, in 1743, the founder.

Senator's Choice

According to Mrs. Edith Monroe Moe, her husband's name is the Norwegian equivalent of the English "moor" or "field," which suggests an out-in-the-open environment for his ancestors, one of whom was Norway's great folklorist, Jorgen Moe, who wrote lyrics set to music by Grieg. There was a time when Moe's forebears lived in a big Gothic house on a Norwegian country place called Gaustad. His father, Christian Moe, however, was born and brought up in Christiania (Oslo), where for generations his family had been in the business of importing and exporting furs. In the 1880's Christian and his wife, Sophia Gaustad, came to the United States, where in the Mississippi River village of Monticello, Henry Allen was born on July 2, 1894.

At Hamline University in St. Paul from 1912 to 1916 he majored in mathematics, and from 1916 to 1917 he worked on the editorial staff of the St. Paul *Dispatch and Pioneer Press*. At our entrance into the First World War he enlisted in the Navy. He wanted sea duty, and was on a training ship when he made the mistake one morning of picking up a sextant on deck to "shoot" the sun. The captain, seeing him, detached him, and all other enlisted crew members competent in mathematics, to officers' training school. Off went Moe, protesting, and came out at the head of his class.

After officers' training school he taught navigation at Annapolis and then was sent to sea as commander of a submarine chaser, a tour of duty that was cut short on August 15, 1919, by an accident on board which left him with several broken bones. Confined for almost eighteen months in the U. S. Naval Hospital in Brooklyn, he gave thought to his future and decided to apply through his home state for a Rhodes scholarship. He was turned down, but Carroll Wilson happpened to see his application papers, visited him several times at the hospital, was impressed by him and subsequently succeeded in having him named a Rhodes scholar-at-large.

At Oxford, moving about at first on crutches and later by bicycle, Henry Moe studied law, took first class honors, became Hulme lecturer in law at Brasenose and Oriel Colleges, and was called to the bar at the Inner Temple, London, becoming a barrister-at-law in 1924. Later, after his return to the United States, he was admitted to the New York bar and from 1927 to 1929 was a lecturer in law at Columbia University.

Running parallel with some of these events was a romantic interlude which reached its conclusion on December 18, 1924, when Henry Moe and the former Edith Louise Monroe were married. Their son, Christian Hollis, a Ph.D. from Cornell, now directs plays and teaches playwriting as an associate professor at the University of Southern Illinois in Carbondale, where he lives with his wife and two small sons.

Henry Moe had left Oxford and was on the verge of joining a New York law firm when Senator and Mrs. Guggenheim asked him to assist in drawing up the plans for the projected Foundation. Months of intensive work followed, during which Moe, under the guidance of Aydelotte, studied the amounts and sources of scholarship and fellowship funds then available in this country, and with Aydelotte interviewed scores of scholars, creative artists, college presidents, professional and business men, seeking their advice, as Moe would later phrase it, "as to the most useful area, from the point of view of the country, in which a foundation such as that which Senator and Mrs. Guggenheim had in mind . . . ought to function." On the basis of this research, Moe drew up a set of plans which he then talked over with Aydelotte and others. This phase of the work involved travel, and Moe combined it with a visit to his mother, who today, having survived her husband by forty-one years, lives in the Hamline section of St. Paul, a frail little lady of ninety-five. According to Dr. Moe's wife, she "picks and jells her own currants and keeps a watchful eye on Henry's doings."

Back again in New York, Moe accepted Senator Guggenheim's luncheon invitation on the top floor of 120 Broadway where Guggenheim Brothers have their offices. It was during this meeting that the Senator asked Moe to run the Foundation. "At that time," Moe says, "I was still planning to join a law firm, so naturally I had to consider the proposition. As a matter of fact, I thought about it for half a second before saying yes." Two days later, to quote Moe further, "we threw a couple of desks and a secretary into a room on the thirty-fourth floor of 120 and got going." Still later the Senator opened the hall door one morning, popped in his head and said, "Any idea of how to get started?" Moe replied, "No, none." And the Senator, preparing to close the door and retreat, said, "Well, keep at it, and no doubt you'll have an idea."[5]

Gripes, Frugality and Freedom

Henry Moe kept at it. It pleases him to recall the beginning years when he worked side by side with Senator Guggenheim. "Sanguine, constructive, liberal . . . kind, generous and appreciative," so runs his published tribute to the founder of the John Simon. "Always interested, always helpful, never obtrusive," is his spoken description of the Senator as president of the Foundation from its incorporation till his death on November 2, 1941. "One of the things I often recall about him," Moe says, "is his memory. I once told him I'd do this or that, somehow never got around to it, and salved my conscience by assuming that he'd forgotten all about it. I never made that mistake again!"

During its first year the Foundation left 120 Broadway. For two years headquarters were a little office at 100 East 42nd Street, and in 1927 the present quarters on Fifth Avenue were taken over. An impecunious scholar or artist who visits the Foundation would not be overwhelmed by the plushness of its six small, modestly furnished offices—seven if one counts a connecting hall that also does duty as a library. A few years ago the Foundation acquired additional space across the corridor from its main quarters, a relatively large room used partly as a gathering place for such Guggenheim fellows as happen to be in town, partly for meetings of the Board of Trustees and of other Foundation bodies, including a committee recently set up by the fellows themselves to act as a combination observation and clearinghouse through which the work of the Foundation can be kept under surveillance and suggestions channeled for its improvement.

Such suggestions, incidentally, are always considered by the Foundation leadership, and from time to time changes have been made in policy and procedure in response to gripes from fellows.

The dollar value of a Guggenheim fellowship varies. The amount awarded is adjusted to the objectives and needs of each fellow, a procedure that sometimes involves conferences between the newly appointed fellow and the Foundation. No Guggenheim fellowship, in other words, carries a fixed stipend. Over the years the average amount has moved upward with the decreasing value of the dollar. In the forties it was $3,000, and in the fifties, $3,750. Today it is close to $5,000. Some large grants have been double the average; some small ones, only half.

About the only general statement that can be made concerning fellowship stipends is that they tend to be minimal, as such things go these days. There have been criticisms of this practice. Some fellows contend that in these inflationary times it would be wiser for the Foundation to make fewer awards and to attach more money to each. So far the Foundation trustees and officers, having wrestled at some length with the problem, have stuck to their guns. Commenting on this decision, Peach and Reeves note that "the Foundation recognizes that people need more dollars now; [but] it questions whether they should expect more, or manage less well just because that happens to be the spirit of the times."

Another gripe vouchsafed from time to time has to do with the manner in which the Foundation fellowships are distributed among the intellectual and creative disciplines. A survey made some years ago showed that in 1953 almost one-half of the John Simon's expenditures for fellowships went to the support of scientific research. Some fellows argue that since nowadays large amounts of money for this type of investigation are obtainable from other sources, the John Simon should either eliminate or reduce such grants so as to bestow more of its largess on the financially neglected humanities. Again, after careful consideration of the proposed change, the Foundation authorities have seen fit to stick to their guns. Their decision to do so is readily understandable. True, a great deal of money is now available for scientific research, but more often than not its recipients are required to pursue objectives previously established either by the bestower of the money or by some unit of the institution to which it has been given.* The John Simon remains one of the few organizations which makes gifts to scientists under conditions that leave them free to pursue objectives they themselves have set up.

The freedom of movement allowed to Guggenheim fellows became a newspaper-headline matter in 1950 when the United States Commissioner of Internal Revenue ruled that the Foundation's grants were not gifts, as the government had previously held, but were taxable income in that they constituted "compensation for personal services." The Foundation denied the government's assumption, awarded additional sums to all affected fellows—so as to make it easier for them to meet their unanticipated tax obligations—and sat back to await the outcome of one of several attempts to contest the ruling in the Federal courts. In 1953 a test case brought by a fellow, Dr. George Winchester Stone, Jr., was argued, and on the following November 17, 1954, the tax court ruled that a Guggenheim fellowship grant was a gift pure and simple and therefore not taxable as income.[6]

Pursuits That Dignify, Ennoble and Delight

As the assets of the Foundation have grown, it has increased its benefactions proportionately. In its first year of operation it awarded fellowships to fifteen men and women. In its second it increased its awards to thirty-eight. In 1936, to pick a later year at random, there were fifty-nine fellows; in 1946 there were sixty-nine (plus a number of "delayed" or post-service fellows), in 1956 there were 277, and in 1961 there were 286. Notwithstanding these increases, the tendency has been for the number of awards to remain small relative to the number of applications. As of 1961, the Foundation had received at least 50,000 applications,

* See, for example, W. H. Whyte, Jr., *The Organization Man,* p. 233. Where grants are given to institutions, Whyte observes, "the money has a way of accumulating direction as it gets passed down the line. Eventually, of course, individuals have to do the work but the work is apt to be what a committee or a department or a center thinks should be done, and while this may be worthwhile it is not the kind of independent non-directed work under discussion."

had granted 4,035 fellowships (4,794 if renewals are included in the total).

To these statistics a few others, of a general nature, may be added: Fellowships have been granted to individuals working in eighty-nine different aspects of intellectual and creative work. So far as any large division is recognized in the Foundation's records, it is between those engaged in research in science or the humanities, on the one hand; and those engaged in creative work, on the other. Of the 4,794 fellowships and renewals granted from 1925 to 1961,* only 809 went for creative work, a proportion of 17 per cent. Moreover, the percentage of fellowships for creative purposes has shown a sharp decline over the years. There has also been a decline in the percentage going to "non-academics" (people not associated with schools) and to independent or free-lance researchers and creative artists. The significance of these shifts is difficult to read. Obviously they are rooted in a complex of social factors. Just as obviously economics can be assigned a heavy role, since under inflationary conditions the problem of making ends meet becomes severe for the creative artist and especially severe for the free-lancer, whatever his field.

Originally the grants of the John Simon were made available only to citizens and permanent residents of the United States, including its territories and some of its possessions. Over the years, however, the Foundation has expanded its scope, a process initiated by Senator and Mrs. Guggenheim in June of 1929 when they presented the organization with a million dollars to enable it to extend its benefactions to the republics of Latin America. Pointing out that he and his wife had had these republics in mind from the beginning, the Senator, in his Second Letter of Gift, set forth the motives.

> My brothers and I [he wrote] have long been engaged in commerce with many of the republics to the south of the United States, and we know that there are no longer any important factors of economic isolation separating us. But a similar commerce of things of the mind, of spiritual values, is yet to be accomplished. . . .

* Exclusive of renewals, the total of fellowships granted through 1963 was 5,181.

...It is our conviction, based on our experience with the present Fellowships of the Foundation, that this may best be accomplished by aiding scholars and artists of proven abilities to carry on research and creative work in contact with the scholars and artists of other lands. Such aid should be afforded under the freest possible conditions to men and women devoted to science and liberal studies, great teachers, creators of beauty, and generally to those devoted to pursuits that dignify, ennoble and delight mankind.

The exchange fellowship program, as it is usually called, was not actually put under way until 1931, when grants were made for the first time in Mexico, Argentina, Chile and Cuba. In 1933 Puerto Rico was added; and in 1939, Brazil, Peru and Uruguay. By 1950 coverage had been extended to all Latin American countries, and by 1952 to the British Caribbean. Earlier, in 1940, Canada and Newfoundland had been added, so that today the Foundation's fellowships are available throughout the Western Hemisphere and also in the Philippines, originally included as a possession of the United States and retained following its assumption of independent status.

On the Selection of Fellows

Since the inception of the Foundation no changes of consequence have been made in its basic structure. Organizationally, its major units are:

1. *The Board of Trustees,* originally consisting of seven, now of eleven members, all of whom are also members of the Corporation. The trustees have the last word on the appointment of fellows, but since the actual selection of fellows is carried on by other bodies, this amounts to a power of veto which, according to Moe, has been exercised only on rare occasions.

2. *The Advisory Board* (originally known as the Educational Advisory Board), consisting at present of thirty-six men and women, so appointed that every year approximately one-fourth of them retire. The advisers assist the trustees by making suggestions concerning policy and procedure and by passing on the qualifications of fellowship candidates.

3. *The Committees of Selection,* each consisting of seven men and women drawn from the membership of the Advisory Board.

As the name indicates, these are standing committees and their members do the bulk of the work involved in passing on the qualifications of fellowship applicants. In the beginning only one such committee was necessary, but to take care of the Foundation's expanded program, there are at present two—one for the United States, Canada and the British Caribbean; the other for Latin America and the Philippines.

4. In addition the Foundation utilizes a number of *juries and referees.* Each jury consists of men and women competent to pass on applicants in a specified discipline. Since 1928, for example, paintings, sculpture and other work samples submitted by artist-applicants have been judged by a jury of established artists, museum directors and other professionals in the field. The identity of some juries is kept secret. This is true, for instance, of the jury which passes on material submitted by composer-applicants. "New York is the center of the music world," Moe points out, "and we discovered long ago that if the names of that jury were revealed, its members would be subjected to intolerable pressures." Year in and year out the Foundation makes use of at least a hundred referees culled from the various disciplines and qualified to pass judgment on the books and other materials submitted by applicants.

Dr. Moe places a high value on the labors of the Foundation's advisers, selectors, juries and referees. "If our choice of fellows has been pretty uniformly good, and I think it has," he once said, "it's because of them. Every year applications come in from people working in almost a hundred different intellectual and creative disciplines. No one man can be acquainted with all of those fields; certainly I'm not; and since I put no trust in amateur opinion, not even my own, I conceive my principal job to be the finding of men and women qualified to give us professional appraisals on our applicants."

For approximately nine months of every year, beginning in the fall when the applications come in and ending in the spring when the fellows for the following year are announced, the selection procedure absorbs the energies of Moe and a small staff consisting of some twenty people. Since it is a search for "indispensable" men and women, it is not a cut-and-dried process;

nonetheless, for purposes of description, it can be treated as embracing four major steps.

Step One consists of the accumulation by the Foundation staff of a dossier on each applicant. Each fall brings to the Foundation applications from approximately 2,000 persons. For every one of these the Foundation staff compiles a file that in many cases runs to hundreds of pages.

Into this file goes, among other things, a good deal of correspondence. Every applicant is asked to supply a list of references. The average number is seven, so the Foundation staff's first job is to write to these seven references, whose replies go into the dossier. Next, appraisals of him are solicited from known experts in the field—from experts other than those mentioned by the applicant. Occasionally correspondence is supplemented by legwork, Moe or some other official of the Foundation calling on the staff of some institution engaged in work within the applicant's field.

A story from Henry Moe illustrates the care with which Step One is carried out. Some years ago a scientist applied for a fellowship to undertake research in immunology. Since his name was unfamiliar to the Foundation staff, Moe made inquiries by phone at the university where the applicant was teaching. One of the things he learned was that the applicant had only one arm.

"This gave me pause," he confesses. "Here was a man who did his research in a laboratory where a fellow certainly needs two arms, and could use three. Moreover one of the referees submitted by the applicant had written us that his ideas were old hat. To resolve the matter I got hold of some of his papers and took them up to Rockefeller Institute to be looked over by their top men in immunology. They reported that the scientist in question was doing research far in advance of anything they had yet attempted. So we gave him a fellowship and about twenty years later he received the Nobel Prize!"

A sigh escapes Dr. Moe at this juncture. "That's how it goes," he says. "We hooked that one and he did us proud, but I get nervous when I think how close we came to losing him. We make mistakes. We're not the Almighty. Mistakes of appointment, of course, are irrevocable; but mistakes of nonappointment can be rectified and each year since the first, we have made grants to persons whom we had declined to appoint in previous years."

Eventually all dossiers are filed in specified categories. Originally dossiers of the most promising applicants were filed in category A, the others in B, C and D. This system is no longer followed. At present the dossiers are simply filed according to subject matter.

Step Two consists of obtaining the judgment of juries and of referees other than those listed by applicants. Midway of the selection procedure, most applicants are asked to submit samples of their work. Artists send in photographs, paintings and sculpture, and these are sent to a warehouse where in due time they are put on display in an improvised gallery and examined by the art jury. Musical compositions are submitted to the music jury, and manuscripts, books, papers and the like to appropriate referees.

Step Three consists of obtaining the judgment of the Committees of Selection. To this end Moe prepares a digest of the contents of all dossiers. This digest, Moe wrote some years ago, comes to a volume "of from 1,500 to 2,000 pages [longer now] which contains my information, compiled under the pressure of a thousand letters a week, for the Committee of Selection [actually for the committees, since there are now two]. Applications in the higher groups [those of the most promising applicants] are presented in greater detail than applications in the lower groups; but in each case there is included enough information to enable the Committee of Selection to make a sound decision. . . . One copy of the digest is made for each member of the Committee and is mailed out to them in installments over a period of a month before the Committee meets for the first time that year. The members of the Committee study that digest; they know all about it when they come to the meeting; they come . . . with a thousand questions from fresh points of view; they ask them of me, and if I can't answer them I find out. For two or three days we discuss, and sometimes debate, questions arising from the applications. Then there is a lot of work to be done in the interval between the time the Committee adjourns and the second Committee meeting a month later. We have no set, standardized procedure; if an interview with a responsible scholar seems likely to yield the information needed for a sound decision, or if the applicant seems merely in need of advice, I arrange that."

Further insight into what happens at these meetings is supplied by Dr. Marjorie Hope Nicolson, only recently retired as chairman of the Department of English at Columbia University, who since the conclusion of her own fellowship year (1926-27) has frequently served the Foundation as a member of the Committee and as a referee. "We usually meet," she says of the Committee of Selection, "over a weekend. It's terribly hard work—Henry Moe sees to that; and terribly satisfactory—he sees to that, too. He fairly drives us to dig in and do our utmost to see that the best people get the appointments. When he sends his digest along, he also sends a list of the candidates. On this he indicates his own ratings. The names of those he considers tops are typed in upper-case letters and material about them is double-spaced. The names of those he considers secondary are also in upper-case letters, but the material about them is single-spaced. All the other names and material are in lower case. One of our jobs—and Henry never fails to remind us—is to see if we can't rescue some of the applicants from their lower-case or upper-case single-spaced status, and as a rule when the dust of battle settles, some of those names have found their way to the top.

"Except for the rated list," Professor Nicolson continues, "Henry never indicates his own preferences by word or gesture. Many a time, with the argument revolving around this or that candidate, I've glanced at him, hoping to find in his manner some clue to his own opinion. All I see is that noncommittal face. It's only afterwards—after the recommendations have been made —that he sometimes comes to me and says, 'Marjorie, if you folks hadn't selected Candidate X, I swear I would have gone to the nearest body of water and jumped in.' He's a wonderfully objective man, and I've never known him to hold rancor. The John Simon Guggenheim Memorial Foundation is erected on a great idea. Under any circumstances it would have proved an important institution, but I believe that it's because of the way Moe has run it that its fellowships now carry the distinction that so unquestionably belongs to them."

Step Four follows logically from what has gone before. The recommendations made by the Committees of Selection are passed on to the Trustees for final approval. Then the Guggenheim fellows for the following year are announced—and that with a little biographical material is about all that is announced. The mountain of data assembled and sifted during the selection procedure is treated as forever confidential. Members of the Foundation staff say agents of the Federal Bureau of Investigation, calling at the office in search of information about fellows, go away empty-handed.

It is plain from the care with which fellowship applications are handled that a determining element in the success of the John Simon is hard work. This attribute has not gone unnoticed. W. H. Whyte, Jr., in his widely read study of a modern American phenomenon, *The Organization Man,* takes some of the bigger foundations to task for failing to make any large percentage of their resources available to the lone scholar or creative worker. According to Whyte, the reasoning of the big-foundation executives is that it takes as much work and money to make a grant of $5,000 to some individual researcher as it does to make one of $500,000 to some school or other institution.

"But need it?" Whyte wonders. "Instead of cutting down on the number of individual grants, a better solution might be to cut down on the amount of staff work involved. It's been done, and quite successfully," he adds. "Henry Allen Moe, the wise old bird who directs the [John Simon] Guggenheim Foundation, manages to give a million dollars to some 200 to 250 individuals each year. He uses advisers liberally (and gets their advice free), but his basic apparatus consists of no more than himself, two assistants, nine clerks, and a passion for excellence."

Whyte's words appeared in 1956. At the time of his resignation in 1963 the "wise old bird" was distributing more money among more individuals with an only slightly larger staff—and a still burning "passion for excellence."[7]

Moment of Truth

The last six months of 1952 brought additional labors to the John Simon's hard-working staff, following the appointment by the United States House of Representatives of a committee, headed by Eugene E. Cox of Georgia, to investigate "tax-exempt foundations and comparable organizations." Objectives of what the press headlined as the "Cox Probe" were "to determine which such . . . organizations are using their resources for purposes other than the purposes for which they are established, and especially to determine which . . . are using their resources for un-American and subversive activities. . . ."

It was not the first governmental inquiry into the practices of foundations. In 1915 the Commission on Industrial Relations, created by Congress two years earlier and headed by Senator Frank P. Walsh of Missouri, examined the then newly established Carnegie and Rockefeller endowments, along with a number of large American industries, as possible foci of power concentration. At that time and for some decades to come the chief criticism of foundations was that their activities promoted what were spoken of as "the forces of reaction." Basil M. Manly, director of research for the Walsh Commission, saw them as instrumental in extending "the power of the big corporations to the control of the education and social service of the nation." Samuel Untermeyer, at that time counsel to United States Steel, put a similar charge on the record. The Knights of Columbus castigated the foundations as "a menace to democracy," and in the early 1920's Mayor Hylan of New York, whom we last surprised in the act of poaching on the Guggenheim-Goldman band preserve in Central Park, turned down an offer from the Rockefeller Foundation to erect a hospital for the city's drug addicts. "The money," Red Mike said with a shudder, "is tainted!"

Subsequent to 1930 criticism veered off in the opposite direction. Throughout the depression decade and the World War II era the foundations were repeatedly accused of giving aid and succor to the advocates of socialism and communism. By 1950 such criticisms had become rife, fueled by certain developments of the period. In 1950 Alger Hiss, one-time official of the State Department, was convicted of perjury in connection with charges that he had transmitted confidential government documents to the Russians. For a short time, beginning in 1947, Hiss had been employed as president by the Carnegie Endowment for International Peace. Also, along about 1950, came revelations that the Institute of Pacific Relations had been instrumental in misleading the American public as to the true objectives of the so-called "agrarian reformers" in the civil war that placed most of China under Communist control. For twenty-five years the Institute had received generous support from the Rockefeller and other large foundations.

On August 1, 1951, Representative Cox introduced in the House a resolution calling for an investigation. The Georgia Democrat singled out the John Simon for special attention, charging that its money was being used "to spread radicalism throughout the country to an extent not excelled by any other foundation." With the same brush he tarred the Rockefeller Foundation, the Carnegie Corporation, the Rosenwald Fund and other endowments. Cox's resolution was referred to the Rules Committee and reported out by it on August 15, but for some reason was never called up for action that year. On March 10 of the following year Cox introduced an identical resolution, which after an acrimonious debate was passed by the House. At this point the members of the John Simon staff, along with those of many other foundations, began digging into their files in preparation for the moment of truth.

The Cox Probe of 1952 was conducted with fairness and objectivity. American history yields examples, notably in the Reconstruction period, of misuse by Congress of its investigative powers. Fortunately remedies exist for these abuses, and their occasional occurrence leaves intact not only the right but also the obligation of the representatives of the people to conduct inquiries consonant with their legislative functions. The general effect of the Cox Probe was to clear the air, then noxious with ungrounded suspicions and troublesome half-truths regarding foundation practices. In the course of the proceedings Congressman Cox, who died before the final report was drawn up, admitted to "some change of heart." Brief and judicious, the Committee's report, released in January of 1953, was that in the area covered by the investigation a few of America's thousands of foundations had made a few mistakes—principally in the employment of Hiss and in the support of the Institute of Pacific Relations. On balance, the Committee concluded, the foundations had done a good job of resisting communist infiltration.

As to the specific charges against the John Simon, these crumbled before the facts. Both in a lengthy written communication to the Cox committee and during his personal appearance before it on Thursday, December 11, 1952, Moe pursued a policy of forthrightness coupled with a closely reasoned exposition of the importance to a free society of permitting its citizens to hold views contrary to prevailing majority opinion and to give voice to such views "subject to prohibition of those abuses of expression which a civilized society may forbid."*

In detail in his written communication and in a more condensed form during his appearance before the Committee, he set forth statistics obtained from a perusal of "80-odd" publications issued by the Un-American Activities Committee of the House and the Subcommittee on Internal Security of the Judiciary Committee of the Senate. He revealed that of the 2,190 individuals who had so far received Guggenheim fellowships, only 57 had been "mentioned" or "cited" in one or more of the 80 government publications. Of these 57 individuals, 51 had received their fellowships "before there existed any mention of them by either of the referred-to committees." Moreover, of the total sum so far expended on fellowship grants—$7,019,993.25—only $152,065 or 2.1 per cent had gone to these 51 individuals. As for the other six individuals named by the two committees, the Foundation had been unaware of any "citations" against them at the time they were given their fellowships—and their share in the total expended came to only $21,825 or 0.3 per cent.

Moe contended that this was a good record, especially good

* The words in quotation marks here are part of a statement by Mr. Justice Frankfurter in *United States v. Dennis,* 341 U.S. 494 (1951), which, as quoted more fully by Moe, reads: "The soil in which the Bill of Rights grew is not a soil of arid pedantry. The historic antecedents of the First Amendment preclude the notion that its purpose was to give unqualified immunity to every expression that touched on matters within the range of political interest. . . . Free speech is subject to prohibition of those abuses of expression which a civilized society may forbid. . . ." (Moe, "Answers," 185)

since during World War II the State Department had urged American institutions to encourage a friendly feeling toward the Soviet Union in the area of cultural relations and the Foundation at that time had been under "pressures from that general atmosphere" in that regard. The John Simon, Moe informed the Committee, had resisted those pressures. He set forth several instances in which the Foundation had turned down otherwise acceptable applicants on learning that they were not interested in the "pursuit of truth" but only in "the pursuit of better methods for disseminating their political views." It had always been Foundation policy, he declared, that a Guggenheim fellow should be a "good citizen."

He should also be a truth-seeker. "The purpose of this Foundation," Moe asserted, "is to give financial help to men and women who, it is judged, will be, by that assistance . . . assisted toward leadership in science and liberal studies, in all scholarship and in all the arts—which leadership is what makes our country strong. We know that no man or woman can have a part in making our country strong unless he is a good citizen, devoted to the principles which are basic to our strength. For workers in the fields of . . . scholarship and the arts this means—quite simply—that they shall be free to go to the conclusions to which the facts and their own thinking take them. If they are members of any movement, organization, group which does their thinking for them or which indicates what their conclusions must or ought to be, they are not free to follow their evidence and their own thinking; and they get no money from us."

In his written communication to the Committee, Moe listed by name all of the fifty-seven "cited" or "mentioned" fellows, adding that he did so "under protest . . . and only because we judged that we are required to do so. . . ." Both in this statement and during his appearance before the Committee, he said the Foundation deeply regretted having made grants to at least two individuals, both of whom had subsequently been revealed to be Communists. As for the other "cited" or "mentioned" fellows, he argued that the evidence set forth in the congressional lists was not clear. Most of these cited individuals were mentioned as being members of organizations designated as "subversive" by the

Attorney General, and Moe reminded the Committee that under a ruling of the U. S. Supreme Court mere membership in an organization cannot be regarded as a "determiner" of a person's political leanings.

During Moe's appearance before the Committee, a definitive question was put to him by a member. "Where a man is an avowed Communist," asked Congressman Simpson, "or known to be to your satisfaction a Communist sympathizer, you would not consider him for a fellowship?"

Moe's answer: "We wouldn't have any truck with him at all."

Another interesting question came from Harold M. Keele, general counsel to the Committee. "Isn't it a fact, Mr. Moe," he inquired, "that among the groups whom you seek to promote in their interests, that is, those with artistic abilities particularly, there is apt to be a greater risk of their embracing a foreign ideology?"

"Well, I don't know about that, Mr. Keele," was the reply. "The artist, contrary to popular impression, is likely to be a pretty sensible fellow"—an answer that if Moe had never said or written another word would entitle him to immortality. Having taken a manful swipe at the vulgar prejudice that the creative worker is by definition a "kook," Moe conceded:

> What I think you can say on the basis of history is that the great artists, and writers, and composers of all times have never been exactly cozy members of society. And if you look back at your history from that point of view, you can start back, certainly as far as Dante, and you can come up through John Milton in England, and Goya in Spain, and Cervantes in Spain and Baudelaire in France, and our own Edgar Allan Poe. These people live in a world that isn't the world of reality to you and to me.
>
> And . . . you take a calculated risk that they are not going to be conformists in any sense, and in my view, it is a good thing they are not, too. They are the people that, when they are really good, carry the ball for the progress of civilization.

The official report of the Cox probe hearings offers evidence that as a one-time journalist Moe brought to the committee room a canny sense of what newspaper men regard as "good copy." "After all," he remarked toward the conclusion of his hour and forty-five minutes of testimony, "it's a free country and from my point of view everybody has a right to make a damn fool of himself in his own way if he wants to." Mrs. Moe, who was in the audience when this statement rang out in Room 1301 of the New House Office Building, remembers the reaction with a wince. "The reporters rushed for their telephones," she says. "That I didn't mind at all and I thoroughly agreed with Henry's sentiments—but oh my goodness his *language*!"[3]

Modestia Nos Programas

In the early phases of the Cox probe the Committee submitted to the larger foundations a twelve-page questionnaire, consisting of eighty-nine main questions subdivided so as to bring the total to 130. So extensive was the information requested that several foundations employed legal firms, at fees ranging up to $100,000, to do the necessary research and writing. Moe, with his customary frugality, did his own work with the aid of his regular staff. Today he confesses that "when that questionnaire arrived, the thought of the work demanded—work that would have to be carried on in conjunction with the everyday tasks of the Foundation—terrified us. In fact, in prospect the whole investigation was terrifying. But in retrospect, it seems to have been good for us. It has made us more aware of our responsibilities insofar as keeping a record of our procedures is concerned. It did not cause us to change or tighten any of our procedures, only to make a fuller record of them and a better effort to keep it up to date."

Whereas some foundation executives viewed the Cox probe as a costly nuisance at best and an inquisition at worst, Moe appears to have regarded it as an opportunity to present to an arm of the United States Congress a picture of the services to its country which a private-giving organization can perform better than any other unit of the social structure. That such was his attitude is implicit both in the generous manner in which he responded to the Committee's questionnaire and in the efforts he made to see to it that the resulting document was actually read by Committee members.

The Committee asked the foundations to be "brief," and in a covering letter dated November 19, 1952, Dr. Moe was at pains to present his reasons for allowing himself no less than 329 typewritten pages to present his "Answers." To this end he quoted "a great American lawyer, Horace Binney, [who] . . . when he argued the Girard will case before the Supreme Court of the United States in 1844 [said:] 'May it please the Court . . . The great accumulation of business upon the calendar is an unquestionable motive for the recommendation . . . by the presiding judge, to study economy of time, and to aim at all practical condensation and brevity in their arguments. . . . But a very liberal expenditure is at times demanded by the wisest economy: and if it shall be found . . . *from the immense magnitude of the interests at stake, and from the almost elementary manner in which to meet all exigencies, the questions must be discussed* [Moe's italics] that my own outlay offends against the letter of the recommendation, I hope it will also be found that it is in harmony with its spirit.' "

In harmony then with what Dr. Moe conceived to be the spirit of the Cox probe, he was lavish with fact and argument and, where the Committee's questions touched on the great American tradition of liberty under law, painstaking in his efforts to get down to bedrock. "I hold fast," he wrote in answer to a question of this nature, "to what Mr. Justice Jackson of the U.S. Supreme Court . . . wrote in *West Virginia State Board v. Barnette,* 319 U.S. 624 (1943), at page 642, 'if there is any fixed star in our constitutional constellation, it is that no official, high or petty, can prescribe what shall be orthodox in politics, nationalism, religion, or other matters of opinion . . .' I believe that if this Foundation . . . should attempt to prescribe 'what shall be orthodox in politics, nationalism, religion,' natural science, social science, art, or in any other manifestations of the mind or spirit, it had better not be in existence."

In effect one of the Committee's questions required information as to what safeguards the Foundation utilized to make certain that grants to individuals in other lands did not allow undesirables to enter this country. Moe's reply was that before awarding fellowships to "citizens not resident in the United

States," the Foundation consulted the Department of State and the Department's cultural relations officers in the countries from which the applicants came; that it always first made certain that the individuals under consideration were eligible to receive visas for the United States.

In a series of questions the Committee asked Moe to give his estimate of what impact the activities of the John Simon had had on education, United States foreign policy, economics and other aspects of the social structure. Moe prefaced his replies with the statement that all such effects were "manifestly those of the individual fellows and not of the Foundation as such." He then outlined what appeared to be the "indirect" impact of the Foundation on the fields listed.

On education: "Our fellows [including many teachers] . . . constantly write us that we are of great assistance to them in their development."

On foreign policy: "Some of the fellows . . . by their researches contributed substantially to our country's development of the atomic bomb, which in turn doubtless has affected the foreign policy of the United States. . . ."

On economics: In March of 1941, Moe informed the Committee, the Foundation granted a fellowship to Dr. Merrill Kelley Bennett of the Food Research Institute of Stanford University, to assist in furthering his studies on diet in the Hawaiian Islands "with special reference to the competition between wheat and rice.

Dr. Bennett [Moe continued] was in Honolulu carrying on his studies when the Japanese struck on December 7, 1941. By that date the statistical data he required . . . were practically complete: tabulated evidence of food imports, local production, outshipments and consumption, and his data were usable at a moment's notice. Dr. Bennett at once, with our approval, volunteered to serve without pay in the Territorial Office of Civil Defense, Division of Supplies and Finance, and later was, by official military appointment, made Chief Statistical Officer of Food Control, Office of Military Governor, Territory of Hawaii. This appointment also was without salary; for the foundation agreed that his fellowship grant should be available for his support while Dr. Bennett made his training, his data, his studies available to the Military Government of Hawaii. . . Later the Executive Officer in the Office of Food Control, T. H., wrote us of "the importance of Dr. Bennett's work . . . for the Territory . . ."

Once Moe had completely his "Answers," he made personal visits to three members of the Cox Committee, General Counsel Keele, Congressman Simpson and Chairman Cox. "My impression," he says, "was that Representative Cox was a little surprised to see me, but he was the soul of courtesy and we had a pleasant chat. For a time, as a young man, I was secretary to a United States congressman. When I called on Mr. Cox in Washington, I mentioned this experience, explained that as a result of it I was keenly aware of how very full his schedule must be, but expressed the hope that he would somehow find time to study my 'Answers.' "

To this day Moe's unpublished "Answers" to the Cox Committee questionnaire remains a remarkably thorough and vivid picture of a remarkable foundation at work. On the whole the tone of it is dispassionate. Only at one point does the author's voice rise, so to speak. This occurs in connection with Question G-2.

"In your opinion," the Cox Committee inquires at this point, "could the functions of foundations be effectively performed by government?"

"In my sharp opinion," begins Moe's answer, "the question as stated is an improper question in our free country. It is no proper question," he continues, "that suggests, even in the form of question, that government might do what private goodness—religious goodness, indeed—wishes to do and does and, by and large, does well. *It violates the spirit of philanthropy—the desire to do good with one's money—which has been one of the most powerful motivating forces of good men throughout all recorded history.** It violates the essentially religious motives of donors."

There's more, and Moe winds up his understandably indignant answer with the unkindest cut of all. "And I shall add," he finishes, "as the final part of my answer to Question G-2, that you may ask anybody who has a basis for judgment, whether or

* Italics added.

not I, as this Foundation's principal executive officer, can get, or cannot get, more of social value per dollar of Guggenheim Foundation money, with less overhead, than any government agency could possibly do."

At this writing, Dr. Henry Allen Moe is devoting most of his working day to the National Science Foundation, having assumed the directorship of a commission charged with conducting a study of the large grants for science now being made by the Federal government to institutions of higher learning. His successor as president of the John Simon is Dr. Gordon Norton Ray, Guggenheim fellow, authority on William Makepeace Thackeray and H. G. Wells, former provost and vice-president in the University of Illinois. When Dr. Moe stepped down on July 1, 1963, he left behind a record whose high qualities are feelingly reflected in a motto inscribed on a plaque which for many years hung above one of the doors of his private office at the John Simon.

Its Portuguese words—attributed to the late Henrique da Rocha Lima, one-time director of the Institute of Biology in São Paulo, Brazil—read:

Modestia nos programas.
Imodestia nas realizacoes.

In translation:

Modesty in our programs.
Immodesty in their realization.[9]

Reaching for the Moon: A Postscript

During its brief and busy career the Daniel Guggenheim Fund for the Promotion of Aeronautics maintained a small library at its New York headquarters, and one of its early purchases was a volume published in 1927 and entitled *The Great Delusion.* The major proposition of the author, who wrote under the suggestive pen name of "Neon," was that men would do well to leave the air to the birds. According to Neon, aviation had no future; even if a practical plane could be developed, the cost of doing so would far outweigh its value to mankind. Deploring what the author termed "feverish propaganda" in the interests of aviation, Neon contended that the people of his generation were being called on to witness a "terrible race" among the nations for "air supremacy."

His words have a familiar ring in view of current criticism of the so-called "moon race," the effort to land a human being on the moon. "Is it worth it?"—Whenever men strike out for unknown goals, this question arises. It is an inevitable query, reasonable, human and challenging. But it is also academic, for progress is not made by men who insist on guarantees; it is made by gamblers, by men willing to reach for the moon without having much more than a highly general idea of what they will find when they get there.

This venturesome spirit is readily discernible in the record of the Guggenheim foundations. As has been noted, the potentialities of aviation were a matter of serious concern to only a handful of men when in the nineteen-twenties Mr. Dan came to its support. To the American press Dr. Robert H. Goddard was still the "moon man," a faintly amusing visionary, when first Mr. Dan personally and later his permanent foundation, the Daniel and Florence, undertook to support the classic experiments with rockets that were to open the door into the still unexplored realms of interplanetary travel. The Guggenheim Museum exists today as one of the most influential art centers in the world because in his old age Solomon Guggenheim deserted the sure and safe as an art collector, turning away from the old masters to the work of living artists, of men who are famous now but whose names at that time were unknown outside of the inner circles of the world of art. Dental science was the stepchild of the healing arts when Murry Guggenheim, with the establishment of his dental foundation and clinic, held out a helping hand to it. And although Senator Simon Guggenheim's creation of the John Simon Guggenheim Memorial Foundation was greeted with peans of gratitude by leaders in the world of the mind and spirit, their approval was diluted by grave skepticism concerning the durability of a fellowship-granting program based on a policy of no strings attached.

Today aviation is an accepted and important world enterprise. For this reason we can speak in the past tense of Mr. Dan's fund and of his other efforts on behalf of the airplane. We cannot, however, speak in that tense of any of the four existing Guggenheim foundations. All of their major programs look to the future. The university centers for the development of the aerospace sciences, sponsored by the Daniel and Florence, are engaged in research and experimentation aimed at revealing what are now the great unknowns of space. Year in and year out the John Simon continues to issue fellowships to scholars and scientists, to writers, artists and composers; and there is no telling when one or more of these gifted, these "indispensable" individuals will provide us with yet another advance in human knowledge, another victory in our endless battle with ignorance. At New York University the study program financed by the Murry and Leonie Guggenheim Foundation continues its search for a means of preventing dental decay, a part of the current movement of dental science away from a primarily mechanical

James H. Doolittle, Harry Guggenheim, and Charles A. Lindbergh on the terrace of the swimming pool at Falaise. The three men, friends for many years, are discussing plans now underway for a "Man's Relation to Man" project.

approach to its problems to a broader and essentially biological approach. At the Guggenheim Museum the hunt goes on for the best products of the painters and sculptors of today, for ways of encouraging the development of the artists of tomorrow. And at this moment, true to his family's philanthropic tradition, Mr. Dan's son is plotting the general lines of a relatively new endowment, the Harry Frank Guggenheim Foundation, whose chief concern will be with man's relationship to man, with a search for those sources of disaffection which so wastefully pit human being against human being.

It is no accident that a sense of the future and a certain daring are characteristic of the Guggenheim foundations. These attributes adhered also to the men who founded them. Indeed, to give further emphasis to points already made, it can be said that the story of the Guggenheims in America is at base a study in daring.

Less than a century and a half have elapsed since its inception —since Simon Guggenheim brought his second wife and their combined families out of the confinement of a Swiss ghetto into the freedom of Philadelphia. By the time Simon's son Meyer was forty-five years old, he had worked himself up from peddler to proprietor of a thriving lace-importing business. Had he settled for that, he could have died a rich man, content in the knowledge that his children were provided for. But Meyer would not settle; his eyes were on the future, on the world in which his sons would have to live. Because he wanted to leave them a business sufficiently expansive to hold their interests and absorb their energies, he took a chance. He put some money into a couple of holes filled with water in Colorado. Fortunately the holes turned out to be filled also with silver.

After that the Guggenheims were in mining. What the father had built, the sons greatly expanded, often taking large risks to do so. Given this background it is not surprising that throughout their now extensive history the foundations founded by Meyer's sons have been marked by a spirit of daring, by a faith in the future of the country to which they were given as a token of gratitude for the opportunities that country had given to the Guggenheims.

Notes

CHAPTER I. IN SWITZERLAND'S GREEN GHETTOS

1. (Since there is no bibliography, references to publications are given in full except where full references are obviously unnecessary.) Florence Guggenheim-Grünberg, *Beitrage zur Geschichte und Volkskunde der Juden in der Schweiz,* No. 3, Zurich: Verlag Judische Buch-Gemeinde, 1953, 1-12. German title of Ulrich's book is *Sammlung Judischer Geschichten welche sich mid diesem Volk in XIII. und folgenden Jahrhunderten bis auf 1760 in der Schweiz von Zeit zu Zeit zugetragen* (Collection of Stories about the Jews of Switzerland from the Thirteenth Century to 1760), Basel, 1768.

2. The Surbtal Lengnau rarely appears on atlas maps. What one does find as a rule is a town of the same name in Canton Bern and one called Langnau in Canton Zurich, both often confused by mail clerks and others with the Lengnau of which we are speaking and which, like Endingen, is in Canton Aargau. Lengnau is about 24 kilometers from Zurich.

3. Interviews in autumn of 1961 with Jacques Oppenheim, Rev. Dr. S. N. Gut, Miss Hanna Gut, and Herr Fried of Lengnau; Mr. and Mrs. Sigmund Bloch and Mrs. Rosa Bloch of Endingen; and Mr. and Mrs. Harry Guggenheim, Dr. and Mrs. Georges Guggenheim, Walter Baer, and Alphonse Bollag of Zurich; Nathan Ausubel, ed., *A Treasury of Jewish Folklore,* New York: Crown Publishers, 1948, 731; Isidore Epstein, *Judaism: A Historical Presentation,* Baltimore: Penguin Books, 1959, 161.

4. See, for example, Exodus 22:25; Deuteronomy 23:19; and Ezekiel 18:8.

5. Guggenheim-Grünberg, *Die Juden in der Schweiz,* Zurich: Verlag Judische Buch-Gemeinde, 1961, *passim.;* James Hastings, ed., *Encyclopedia of Religion and Ethics;* William Martin, *A History of Switzerland,* trans. from the German by Grace W. Booth, London: Grant Richards, 1931, 94.

6. This explanation of how the Guggenheims got their name is probably as good as can ever be found. The author's effort to see if the word has any meaning in the German, from which it is apparently derived, has brought out only that the first names of the seven brothers

do have meanings. Daniel is a Hebrew name meaning Judge of God. Isaac, also Hebrew, means laughter; Murry, a Gaelic name, Great Water; Solomon, Hebrew, peaceful—a misnomer in the case of the Guggenheim Solomon; Benjamin, Hebrew, Son of the Right Hand; Simon, Hebrew, hearing and obeying, or attentive; William, Teutonic, shield; and to add the name of the present head of the family for good measure, Harry, in its Teutonic derivation means home ruler, in its Saxon derivation, brave, powerful lord, or wealthy (Nathan Gottlieb, *A Jewish Child Is Born . . .* New York: Bloch Publishing Co., 1960, 145 *et seq.*) and in its Hebrew derivation (Arye), lion. The Jews of the Diaspora, of course, picked up their present surnames in sundry ways. In 1788, for example, Joseph II of Austria issued an edict under which every Jew was required to adopt a "proper recognizable surname" to replace the biblical patronymic then largely in use. When some of the Jews objected, the officers in charge of carrying out the emperor's orders simply imposed names on them, with the result that a number came up with such surnames as "Hunger," "Fresser," "Weinglas," "Pferd," and "Stinker!" (Cecil Roth, *A Short History of the Jewish People,* illustrated ed., rev. and enl., London: East and West Library, 1948, 339-40; *The Jewish Encyclopedia,* New York: Funk & Wagnalls.)

7. Guggenheim-Grünberg, "Die Lengnauer Vorfahren der 'Kupfer-Guggenheim' in Amerika," *Israelitish Wochenblatt,* Aug. 7, 1953; same author, *loc. cit.*

8. An almost complete family tree for the Swiss Guggenheims is in the *All-Families Book,* two copies of which may be examined in Lengnau, one in the office of the town clerk, the other at the home of Jacques Oppenheim, president of the Society for the Preservation of the Endingen-Lengnau Synagogues and Cemetery.

9. Guggenheim-Grünberg, the *Israelitish Wochenblatt* article, and *op cit.,* 13-14; Gatenby Williams (William Guggenheim) and Charles Monroe Heath, *William Guggenheim,* New York: The Lone Voice Publishing Company, 1934 (hereafter cited as Williams), 15.

CHAPTER II. FOR SEVEN SONS, ONE BUSINESS

1. Eric E. Hirschler, ed., *Jews from Germany in the United States,* New York: Farrar, Straus and Cudahy, 1955, p. 65; Harvey O'Connor, *The Guggenheims: The Making of an American Dynasty,* New York: Covici Friede, 1937, pp. 24-25; Williams, *op. cit.,* p. 14.

2. O'Connor, pp. 26-41; Williams, pp. 14-29.

3. New York *Inquirer,* April 8, 1905; Williams, pp. 14, 15; O'Connor,

pp. 39, 48-60; Isaac F. Marcosson, *Metal Magic: The Story of the American Smelting and Refining Company,* New York: Farrar, Straus and Company, 1949, 26-41; Peter Lyon, "The Adventurous Angels," *Horizon,* May, 1959; Matthew Josephson, *The Robber Barons,* p. 12; Gustavus Myers, *History of the Great American Fortunes,* New York: The Modern Library, p. 706; Guggenheim Brothers files (hereinafter cited as GB), Isaac Guggenheim deposition in *Guggenheim v. Guggenheim,* 1913-14; Charles and Mary Beard, *The Rise of American Civilization,* vol. 2, p. 176; Allan Nevins, *Study in Power: John D. Rockefeller. . . ,* vol. 1, vii-ix; Harry F. Guggenheim (hereafter cited as HFG), "Building Mining Cities in South America" (unpublished paper in GB); *New York Times:* Jan. 22, 1915, Sept. 29, 1930. (Although the A.Y. and Minnie ceased to be of much value after the demonetization of silver in 1893, the Guggenheims continued to retain an interest in them until 1941 when they were sold to R. T. Walker, a consulting geologist representing several mining and smeltering firms.)

4. The name Guggenheim Brothers has been applied to three family firms. The first was organized in 1916 by Mr. Dan, and consisted, so far as the family was concerned, of Dan and his brothers, Isaac, Murry, Solomon and Simon; Dan's son, HFG; and Murry's son, Edmond A. HFG and Edmond objected to the sale of Chuquicamata in March of 1923 and six weeks later retired from the firm. The second was formed in 1949 by HFG and Solomon, then the only surviving son of Meyer. The third was formed by HFG in 1951, the other partners being Horace R. Graham, Albert E. Thiele, James F. Doetsch, R. Paul Miller, and Albert C. Van de Maele. Mr. Graham died in 1954, Mr. Miller in 1962, and two partners have been added: John A. Peeples in 1956, and Oscar S. Straus II, a grandson of Mr. Dan, in 1959. The present Guggenheim Brothers consists essentially of the Anglo-Lautaro Nitrate Company, organized April 20, 1931, under the laws of Chile; the Pacific Tin Consolidated Corporation, organized as the Yukon Gold Company on February 28, 1907; the Guggenheim Exploration Company as revived in 1959; and one of the partners is a director of Kennecott Copper Corporation, the world's largest copper producer. The Guggenheim foundations have large holdings in the companies comprising or associated with Guggenheim Brothers.

5. Dante, Purgatorio VII, lines 122, 123 (Cory's translation); Baruch, *My Own Story* (vol. 1 of his memoirs), New York: Holt, 1957, p. 195; GB: Isaac and S. R. Guggenheim depositions in *Guggenheim v. Guggenheim,* M. Guggenheim's Sons, Articles of Co-partnership; O'Connor, pp. 183-89; "The Guggenheims," *Fortune,* July, 1930; Cleveland Amory,

Who Killed Society?, New York: Harper & Brothers, 1960, p. 455; Marcosson, *passim; New York Times:* Jan. 22, 1914, Sept. 29, 1930; Peter Lyon, *loc. cit.;* GB: HFG to Partners, Feb. 16, 1959, minutes of Partners' meeting, Dec. 14, 1961, and press release of April 13, 1959.

CHAPTER III. VICTORIANS, PURITANS AND PLAYBOYS

1. *New York Times:* Jan. 13, 1914; Mrs. Henry Obre (Barbara Guggenheim) to author, March 20, 1962; O'Connor to author, Feb. 20, 1962, and his biography of the family, p. 162.

2. O'Connor, pp. 165, 175, 160, 161; Max W. Javanna to author, 1962; William Lindsay White, *Bernard Baruch: Portrait of a Citizen,* New York: Harcourt, Brace, 1950, p. 35; Williams, p. 164.

3. O'Connor, pp. 153, 471, 146-152; Williams, pp. 166, 13, 14, 21, 26, 27, 22, 30, 41, 67; *New York Times:* Jan. 1, 2, 12, 28, Feb. 8, 25, 27, 28, and Mar. 1, 1913, June 28, 1941, May 1 and July 23, 24, 1941, and Dec. 19, 1947.

4. The number of lives lost in the *Titanic* disaster, as given in different official sources, varies from 1,653 to 1,490.

5. O'Connor, pp. 154, 28, 36, 62-3, 71-3, 80-96, 100, 104, 145, 275; Marguerite Guggenheim, *Out of this Century: The Informal Memoirs of Peggy Guggenheim,* New York: Dial Press, 1946, pp. 2, 3; Amory, *op. cit.*, p. 466; Walter Lord, *A Night to Remember* (Bantam edition), pp. 46, 63, 65, 66, 70; U.S. Congress, Senate Report, *"Titanic" Disaster,* pp. 4, 23-66.

6. O'Connor, pp. 144, 153, 154; *New York Times,* Sept. 29, 1930.

7. Amory, *op. cit.,* p. 457; O'Connor, pp. 154, 158, 167, 168, 364, 365, 465-70; *New York Times:* Dec. 19, 1947, Jan. 13, 1962; Ernest M. Lundell to author, 1962; HFG to author; Mildred Gilman to author; Washington *Evening Star:* Nov. 17 and 19, 1959, and Aug. 11, 1962; Washington *Post:* Nov. 17, 1959.

CHAPTER IV. THERE IS NO GUGGENHEIM FOUNDATION

1. The term "foundation" is used in its limited popular sense. In this sense it is defined by *The Foundation Directory, Edition I* as "a nongovernmental, nonprofit organization having a principal fund of its own, managed by its own trustees or directors, and established to maintain or aid social, educational, charitable, religious, or other activities serving the common welfare. Excludes organizations which make general appeals to the public for funds, are restricted by charter solely to aiding one or several named institutions, which are captive trusts within

colleges, churches, or other organizations, or are small—defined as having neither assets of $50,000 nor making grants of at least $10,000 in the latest year of record."

2. *Register and Tribune Syndicate,* 1938; Wilmer Shields Rich, *American Foundations and Their Fields,* 7th ed., New York: American Foundations Information Service, 1955, XIV, XVI; *World Almanac,* 1962; Bernard Peach and Paschal Reeves, "John Simon Guggenheim Memorial Foundation: Investment in Free Individuals," *South Atlantic Quarterly,* LX, No. 2, Spring 1961; Henry Allen Moe, "Answers" to the Questionnaire of the Select Committee to Investigate Tax-exempt Foundations, 82nd Congress, 2nd Session (unpublished), p. 254; *New York Times,* June 25, 1929.

3. During the fiscal year, 1962, the United States Weather Bureau spent $26.3 million on its Air Weather Service, a figure that does not include communications costs, which are borne by the Federal Aviation Agency.

4. John Simon Guggenheim Memorial Foundation, *Reports of the Secretary and the Treasurer,* 1957-58, pp. 22, 23; Solomon R. Guggenheim Foundation files, Excerpts from Minutes of a meeting of the Art and Museum Committee . . . on Friday, July 14, 1961.

CHAPTER V. HARRY GUGGENHEIM AND THE UNIVERSAL HIGHWAY

1. Jerome Clarke Hunsaker, *Aeronautics at the Mid-Century,* New Haven: Yale University Press, 1952, pp. 11, 12; *Encyclopedia Britannica,* 1962; Lindbergh, *We,* pp. 48-83, and *The Spirit of St. Louis,* p. 41; Dos Passos, *The Big Money* (Washington Square Press edition), p. 238; *New York Times,* Jan. 22, 1915. The quotes from Mr. Dan's correspondence with his son, cited hereafter as the DG letters, are taken from a collection of sixty-two letters written by the older man to Harry between the years 1908 and 1930. The letters quoted in this section are dated Nov. 29, 1912 and January 19, 1913. The Congressional commission referred to was popularly known as the Walsh Commission after its chairman, Frank P. Walsh. Set up in 1912, the commission devoted the next three years to a broad inquiry into the conditions of labor in America's principal industries, including agriculture.

2. (The records of the Daniel Guggenheim Fund for the Promotion of Aeronautics are in the Library of Congress, catalogued as the Daniel Guggenheim Papers. Since much of the information in this and the following chapter is based on these records, citations are made only to other sources used.) D.G. Letters; Williams, *op. cit.,* p. 67; O'Connor,

p. 163; Philip Dormer Stanhope, 4th Earl of Chesterfield, *The Works of Lord Chesterfield,* New York: Harper, 1852, *passim.*

3. HFG and other members of Guggenheim family to author, 1961, 1962; Amory, pp. 458-59; GB: HFG to GB Partners, Feb. 8, 1959; HFG, *The United States and Cuba,* New York: The Macmillan Company, 1934, pp. 150-1, 120, 129, 208, 128, 129, 237; O'Connor, pp. 439-46; Toledo *News,* Sept. 20, 1929; Washington *Evening Star,* Nov. 16, 1930; *Christian Science Monitor,* March 9, 1953; Havana *American-News,* Dec. 22, 1932; HFG Papers at Library of Congress; *Book Review Digest,* 1934; New York *Herald-Tribune,* Dec. 31, 1939; New York *Sun,* Aug. 13, 1936; Garden City (N.Y.) *Newsday,* June 23, 1961; HFG, "Latin American Policy" Correspondence, 1940-1962; HFG Scrapbooks: HFG to LaGuardia, Jan. 10, 1941.

4. HFG to author; Kenneth M. Merritt, "Cain Hoy Stable," *The Thoroughbred Record Magazine,* Nov. 28, 1959; George J. Fountaine to author, Aug. 23, 1962; Alicia Patterson as told to Hal Burton, "This Is the Life I Love," *Saturday Evening Post,* Feb. 21, 1959; "Split in the Family," *Time,* June 20, 1960; Miss Patterson to author, 1962; *New York Times,* Feb. 4, 1923, Oct. 31, 1926, Nov. 3, 1929.

5. Patterson, *loc. cit.;* Edmond Guggenheim to author, Oct. 1, 1962; Detroit *Morning News,* July 2, 1908; Christopher Hollis, *With Love, Peter,* The Declam X. McMullen Company, 1948, p. 16; *New York Times:* June 15, Sept. 18 and Oct. 24, 1925.

CHAPTER VI. MR. DAN'S FUND

1. In this chapter, as in its predecessor, information about the Fund is based on the Daniel Guggenheim Papers at the Library of Congress, unless otherwise indicated.

2. Land, *Winning the War with Ships,* New York: Robert M. McBride Co., 1958, Ch. 10; U.S. Dept. of Commerce, Bureau of the Census, *Historical Statistics of the United States,* pp. 465 *seq.* (A sampling of Harry Guggenheim's addresses on aviation is found in his book, *Seven Skies,* New York: G. P. Putnam's Sons, 1930; and a detailed story of the Fund in Reginald M. Cleveland's *America Fledges Wings,* New York: Pitman Publishing Corp., 1942.)

3. Cleveland, *op. cit.,* pp. 18, 19, 107-10, 119; U.S. Dept. of Commerce, Bureau of the Census, *loc. cit.*

4. W. A. Swanberg, *Citizen Hearst,* New York: Charles Scribner's Sons, 1961, pp. 391-392; U.S. Dept. of Commerce, Bureau of the Census, *loc. cit.*

5. Cleveland, 20; Quentin James Reynolds, *The Amazing Mr. Doolittle,* New York: Appleton-Century-Crofts, 1953, pp. 98-110; *New York Times,* Sept. 30, 1929; Doolittle, "Early Blind Flying" (manuscript of speech delivered at MIT), *passim.*

6. Cleveland, Chapter 3; U.S. Dept. of Commerce, Bureau of the Census, *loc. cit.*

7. Reichelderfer, "The Rossby Memorial Volume," WMO (World Meteorological Organization) *Bulletin,* July, 1960; *Time* magazine, Dec. 17, 1956; Hunsaker, personal files; Cleveland, Ch. VI.

CHAPTER VII. MILLIONS FOR SCIENCE

1. Lee Edson, "He Tamed the Wind," *Saturday Evening Post,* Aug. 3, 1957; Giuseppi Gabrielli, F. N. Scheubel and F. L. Wattendorf, eds., *Selected Papers on Engineering Mechanics: A Tribute to Theodore von Kármán . . . ,* London: Butterworths Scientific Publications, 1955, VII, VIII.

2. Robert A. Millikan, *The Autobiography of . . . ,* New York: Prentice-Hall, 1950, pp. 221, 238, 243-44; *New York Times:* Feb. 1, 1917 and June 17, 1942.

3. Robert Millikan, *op. cit.,* p. 244; The Guggenheim Aeronautical Laboratory of the California Institute of Technology, *The First Twenty-five Years,* Pasadena: Caltech, June 1954, pp. 7, 30, 35, 37; Clark B. Millikan to author, letters of May 17 and June 11, 1962.

4. MIT, *The Technology Review,* XXXIX, no. 4, Feb. 1927, p. 213; Cleveland, *op. cit.,* pp. 152-56; Hunsaker and Prof. Emeritus Shatswell Ober of MIT Guggenheim Laboratory to author, letter of Nov. 21, 1962; Robert Millikan, *op. cit.,* p. 244.

CHAPTER VIII. THE DANIEL AND FLORENCE: SPONSOR OF GODDARD

1. The concerts are not, as has been reported, endowed "in perpetuity." As John D. Rockefeller remarked in connection with his own huge endowment, "Perpetuity is a pretty long time." (U.S. Congress, House, *Hearings before the Cox Committee to Investigate Tax-exempt Foundations*...) Even Plato's Academy, seemingly the longest-lasting foundation known to history, lasted only 900 years, coming to an end in A.D. 529 when it was suppressed by the Christian Emperor Justinian. (Frank Emerson Andrews, *Philanthropic Foundations,* p. 23.)

2. *New York Times:* Oct. 31, 1918, Jan. 27, June 15 and 16, 1924, June 20, 1925, July 10, 1940, June 14, 1942, July 15, 1944; Swanberg, *op. cit.,* p. 310; O'Connor, p. 429.

3. Although the Smithsonian was established by Congressional act in 1846, its original endowment was from a private source and, strictly speaking, it is not an agency of the Federal government. Andrews (*op. cit.,* p. 43) speaks of it as a "ward of the national government." The only Federal tax-supported foundation is the National Science Foundation, set up in 1950 (*ibid.,* p. 35).

4. Soldiers at Camp Devens stole Goddard's equipment, and the neighbors complained of the noise and the danger, one lady writing to Abbot, demanding an investigation and claiming that what she described as a "radio experiment" by Goddard had struck her "near the apex of the heart." (Goddard correspondence: Goddard to Merriam—president of the Carnegie Institution—July 14, 1930; Miss Gertrude A. Cody of Fitchburg, Mass., to Abbot, July 21, 1930.)

5. Arlene and Howard Eisenberg, "The Tragic Case of Robert Goddard," *Saga,* Nov., 1961; Pendray, *The Coming Age of Rocket Power,* New York: Harper & Brothers, 1945, pp. 88, 89, 92; Mrs. Goddard and Pendray, eds., *Rocket Development,* New York: Prentice-Hall, 1948, xi, xv, xvi; Goddard correspondence: Goddard to Abbot, July 26, 1929, to Albert C. Erickson, Sept. 25, 1934, to Alice Strong of Arlington, Mass., Mar. 3, 1930, to Wells, Apr. 20, 1932—Michel L, Theodor V and Victor S (of Ekaterinoslav, USSR) to Goddard, May 26, 1929; Robert E. Molt (fire inspector) to George C. Neal (marshal), July 25, 1929; Abbot to Goddard, Oct. 28, 1929; Worcester *Evening Post,* July 17, 1929; Goddard Diary.

6. Goddard correspondence: Goddard to Mrs. Anna Johnson of Chicago, Oct. 28, 1931, C. Gayette Taylor of MIT to Goddard, Nov. 22, 1929, Goddard to Abbot, Nov. 29, 1929, Goddard memorandum on Carnegie Institution conference of Dec. 10, 1929, Merriam to Goddard, Dec. 19, 1929, Goddard to Abbot, May 28, 1930; *Proceedings of the Institute of Radio Engineers,* vol. 18, 1930, pp. 217-18.

7. Goddard and Pendray, *op. cit.* xiii-xxi; Goddard letter to his wife, April 28, 1935.

8. Pendray "Opinion Survey"; *New York Times:* Dec. 12 and 14, 1948.

9. The composition of the Foundation Committee is: Harry F. Guggenheim, Chairman; General Earle E. Wheeler, Chief of Staff, U.S. Army; Vice Admiral John S. Thach, Deputy Chief of Naval Operations (Air); Brig. Gen. Jay T. Robbins, Deputy Inspector General for Safety, U.S. Air Force; Admiral E. J. Roland, Commandant, U.S. Coast Guard; Dr. H. L. Dryden, Deputy Administrator, National Aeronautics and Space Administration; Mr. Najeeb Halaby, Administrator, Federal Aviation Agency; Mr. Alan Boyd, Chairman, Civil Aeronautics Board;

Dr. Robert M. White, Chief, U.S. Weather Bureau; Dr. F. W. Reichelderfer, Former Chief, U.S. Weather Bureau; Dr. Theodore P. Wright, Ithaca, N. Y.; Lt. Gen. Elwood R. Quesada, Washington, D.C.; Dr. G. Edward Pendray, Consultant, the Daniel and Florence Guggenheim Foundation; Mr. Jerome Lederer, Director, Cornell-Guggenheim Aviation Safety Center; Dr. J. A. Perkins, President, Cornell University.

10. Pendray to HFG, letter of Jan. 14, 1963; Stanojlovic, "Aviation Safety and the Guggenheims," mimeographed manuscript; *New York Times,* Sept. 18, 1950.

CHAPTER IX. SOLOMON'S COLLECTION

1. New York *Sun,* June 29, 1937; *New York Times,* same date; Solomon R. Guggenheim Museum (hereafter cited as SRG Museum), *Vasily Kandinsky, 1866-1944: A Retrospective Exhibition,* p. 11; Michel Seuphor, *Dictionary of Abstract Painting,* p. 106; Solomn R. Guggenheim Foundation files (hereafter cited as SRG Fdn.), résumé of acquisitions for insurance purposes, dated July 1, 1938.

2. Williams, *op. cit.,* p. 21; O'Connor, p. 398; SRG Fdn.: Mrs. Obre to HFG, Jan. 9, 1960, mailed Mar. 9.

3. New York *Sun,* Feb. 27, 1946; *New York Times,* July 4, 1937; SRG Fdn.: HFG to Rebay, Mar. 16, 1961; Rebay to HFG, Oct. 24, 1960, memorandum (dated Sept. 1954) regarding Miss Hilla Rebay and the Solomon R. Guggenheim Foundation.

4. (Interview with Madame Kandinsky took place on Feb. 1, 1963, during her visit to New York to attend opening of retrospective exhibit of her husband's work at Guggenheim Museum.) SRG Museum, *op. cit.,* p. 11; Seuphor, *op. cit.,* pp. 18, 127, 196; *New York Times,* Dec. 8, 1942; unidentified and undated clipping, apparently from Westport (Conn.) *Town Crier,* supplied to author by Mrs. Henry Obre. Résumé of critical appraisal of Bauer's works is based on extensive sampling of reviews of shows at Museum of Non-Objective Painting in New York newspapers and the magazines, *Art News* and *Art Digest,* during decade, 1940-50.

5. SRG Fdn.: Confidential files, and Rebay to Halpert, June 19, 1952; *New York Times:* Dec. 29 and May 25, 1947, April 22, 1951; Mar. 25, May 11 and May 30, 1954.

CHAPTER X. THE GUGGENHEIM MUSEUM

1. During the decade and a half that the Guggenheim Museum was being built, Frank Lloyd Wright carried on a voluminous correspondence, first with Solomon Guggenheim and, after the latter's death, with

Harry Guggenheim as Solomon's nephew and surrogate. That this correspondence would be of value to future historians was not lost on the architect. In a letter to Harry, dated Dec. 27, 1958, he confessed that he often wrote just for the record, adding that the day would come when "these 'definitive' letters to you—the President— . . . will be read in every school and museum in the world." A few months later, Harry—himself far from indifferent to the curiosity of posterity—culled some 700 items from the correspondence and commissioned Miss Mamie Schweppenheiser to compile and index them into four leather-bound volumes. Known as the "Frank Lloyd Wright Historical File," these priceless volumes now rest in the safe of the downtown offices of the Solomon R. Guggenheim Foundation. Except as otherwise indicated, this chapter is based on the Wright historical file, on supplementary material in the general and confidential files of the foundation, and on hundreds of contemporary newspaper and magazine articles.

2. Cohen, "The Archeseum: A Story of the Development and Construction of the Solomon R. Guggenheim Museum," unpublished memorandum, 1.

3. Wright, *An Autobiography,* New York: Duell, Sloan & Pearce, 1943, *passim.*

CHAPTER XI. "DOCTOR" MURRY AND THE CHILDREN OF NEW YORK

1. Except as otherwise indicated chapter is based on annual reports and other publications of the Murry and Leonie Guggenheim Foundation. New York *World-Telegram and Sun,* June 19, 1954.

2. O'Connor, p. 471; *Burnet v. Guggenheim,* 288 U.S. 280, opinion by Associate Justice Benjamin N. Cardoza.

3. O'Connor, pp. 39, 153; *New York Times:* June 25 and Oct. 3, 1929, Jan. 5, 1930, May 20, 1954; New York *American,* June 25, 1929; New York *Herald-Tribune,* Nov. 11, 1931. During its early years the clinic, in its annual report, differentiated between the number of "new" patients registered during the year and the total number, which included patients from previous years. Subsequently this practice was discontinued so that the number of different patients treated by the clinic over the years can only be estimated. Given the other statistics available, the total used here—750,000—is conservative.

CHAPTER XII. THE JOHN SIMON: OPEN-HEARTED FREE-WHEELERS

1. At present (1963) the total number of Guggenheim fellows, living or dead, is in the vicinity of 6,000.

2. (Except as otherwise indicated, this chapter is based on the biennial—originally annual—*Reports to the Secretary and the Treasurer* of the John Simon Guggenheim Memorial Foundation.) U.S. Congress, House, *Hearings before the Committee to Investigate Tax-exempt Foundations . . . ,* 1952, p. 604; Pound's letter is quoted in Dwight Macdonald, *The Ford Foundation: The Men and the Millions,* New York: Reynal & Co., 1956, p. 122; Menotti, "A Plea for the Creative Artist," in Fernando Puna, ed., *7 Arts,* New York: Permabooks, Doubleday & Company, 1953, p. 42.

3. "John Simon Guggenheim Memorial Foundation: Investment in Free Individuals," *South Atlantic Quarterly,* IX, No. 2, Spring, 1961.

4. O'Connor, pp. 29, 30, 227, 231-32, 240; Williams, pp. 26, 30; Denver *News,* July 7, 1908; *New York Times,* Jan. 22, 1915, Mar. 3, 1913, April 27, 1922; Denver *Post,* Aug. 5, 1908; New York *Tribune,* Aug. 2, 1908; Pueblo *Chieftain,* Aug. 7, 1908; sundry clippings in Senator Guggenheim's 1908 scrapbook, penned-in dates and identifications on which are unreadable or incomplete. Blanshard quote is in Peach and Reeves.

5. Moe, "Answers" to the Questionnaire of the Select Committee to Investigate Tax-exempt Foundations, 82nd Congress, 2nd Session—hereafter cited as "Answers"—pp. 26, 40.

6. Moe, *op. cit.,* p. 11; Frank Emerson Andrews, *Philanthropic Foundations,* p. 10n; same author, *Scientific Research Expenditures by the Larger Foundations, passim.* For conditions under which amounts received as scholarship or fellowship grants may be excluded from income, see Section 117 of the Internal Revenue Code of 1954.

7. The foundation, *Charter, Letters of Gift, Constitution and By-Laws;* Moe, "Answers," p. 319; Whyte, p. 232.

8. U.S. Congress, House, *op. cit.,* pp. 1, 519, 617-18, 610, 605-6, 620; same author, *Final Report,* no. 2514, 1953, *passim.;* Rene Albert Wormser, *Foundations: Their Power and Influence,* New York: The Devin-Adair Co., 1958, pp. 328-329; Macdonald, *op. cit.,* pp. 23, 28; *Congressional Record,* April 1, 1951, a-5046; Moe, "Answers," pp. 219, 216, 183-211.

9. Moe, "Answers," pp. v, 53, 62, 183-211, 245, 247, 251, 256-257, 272; Macdonald, pp. 31-33; Wormser, Appendix B. (Wormser was general counsel to the Reece Committee, which carried on a subsequent investigation of foundations, and although his study is critical of most foundations, he has words of praise for the John Simon.)

Appendix

Further data concerning the Guggenheim Five:

1. *The Daniel and Florence Guggenheim Foundation.* Founded in 1924 by the late Mr. and Mrs. Daniel Guggenheim and incorporated under the laws of the State of New York. Purpose: To promote the "well-being of mankind throughout the world." Method of operating: Principally by making grants to other organizations. Emphasis at present: The aerospace sciences. Directors as of May, 1963: Harry F. Guggenheim (president), Mrs. Roger W. Straus (vice president), Robert Guggenheim, Jr., Mrs. Albert C. Van de Maele, Oscar S. Straus, Roger W. Straus, Jr., Albert C. Van de Maele, Dana Draper and George J. Fountaine.

2. *The John Simon Guggenheim Memorial Foundation.* Founded in 1925 by the late United States Senator Simon Guggenheim and his wife in memory of their son, John Simon, who died on April 26, 1922. Incorporated by special act of the Legislature of the State of New York. Purpose and method of operating: The awarding of fellowships, under the freest possible conditions, to individual men and women of "high intellectual and personal qualifications who have already demonstrated unusual capacity for productive scholarship or unusual creative ability in the fine arts." Trustees as of June, 1962: Mrs. Simon Guggenheim (president emeritus), Dale E. Sharp (chairman of the board), Henry Allen Moe, John C. Emison, Medley G. B. Whelpley, Charles Merz, Roswell Magill, Elliott V. Bell, Forrest G. Hamrick, James Brown Fisk and Ernest M. Lundel, Jr.

3. *The Daniel Guggenheim Fund for the Promotion of Aeronautics.* Founded in 1926 by Daniel Guggenheim by means of a letter of intention to Herbert Hoover as United States Secretary of Commerce, and incorporated under the laws of New York State. Purpose: To provide for aviation, at a critical period of its infancy, "immediate, practical and substantial assistance . . . in its commercial, industrial and scientific aspects." Method of operating: By grants to other organizations and by itself conducting promotional and experimental programs. Began operations in January of 1926, ended them in January of 1930. Trustees and officers at termination: Harry F. Guggenheim (president), Emory S. Land (vice-president), H. I. Cone, F. Trubee Davison, W. F. Durand, Charles A. Lindbergh, A. A. Michelson, R. A. Millikan, Dwight W. Morrow, Elihu Root, Jr., John D. Ryan, Orville Wright and J. W. Miller (secretary). Original grant: $2,500,000. Total expenditures: $2,984,209.52.

4. *The Murry and Leonie Guggenheim Foundation.* Founded in 1929 by the late Mr. and Mrs. Murry Guggenheim and incorporated under the laws of the State of New York. Purpose: The promotion, "through charitable and benevolent activities of the well-being of mankind throughout the world." Following the wishes of its donors, the foundation so far has devoted itself to the promotion of dentistry and oral hygiene and to the practical application of these sciences to the children of New York City. Method of operation: By grants to other organizations, principally to the Murry and Leonie Guggenheim Dental Clinic and to the Institute for Dental Research at New York University. Officers and directors as of January 1, 1962: Edmond A. Guggenheim (president), Albert Green (vice-president and treasurer), John J. Duffy (assistant treasurer), Llewellyn L. Thomas (secretary), Charles R. Cox (died January 18, 1962), Marion F. Guggenheim, Robert A. Jones, Natalie G. Talbert, Daniel F. Tobin (director of the clinic) and Neal M. Welch.

5. *The Solomon R. Guggenheim Foundation.* Founded in 1937 by the late Solomon R. Guggenheim and chartered by the Regents of the University of the State of New York. Purpose: "The promotion of art and art education and the enlightenment of the public, especially in the field of art." Method of operation: Principally by grants to organizations, notably to the Solomon R. Guggenheim Museum in New York City. Trustees: Harry F. Guggenheim (president), Albert E. Thiele (vice-president), H. H. Arnason (vice-president, art administration), Eleanor Countess Castle Stewart, A. Chauncey Newlin, Mrs. Henry Obre, Daniel

Catton Rich, Michael F. Wettach, Medley G. B. Whelpley and Carl Zigrosser. Actual assets difficult to estimate since they include the Guggenheim Museum building designed by Frank Lloyd Wright and one of the most valuable art collections in the world.

Picture Credits

(Numbers refer to facing pages of text.)

44: John Simon Guggenheim Memorial Foundation.
74: Louisville *Courier-Journal;* Larry Spitzer.
75: *Newsday.*
86: Mason Studios, Port Washington, L.I., N.Y.
92: Underwood & Underwood.
106: UPI.
148: Mrs. Robert H. Goddard.
188, 204, 205: The Solomon R. Guggenheim Museum.
209: *Morning Telegraph* (N.Y.).
222: The Murry and Leonie Guggenheim Dental Clinic.
238: Underwood & Underwood.
250: Mrs. Henry Allen Moe.

Author's Note

So many people have helped with the preparation of this book that to list them all would require more space than can be allowed. In the book itself, either in the text or in the notes, many of these people have been mentioned, and to those so named as well as to those who have not been named, I want to convey my sincere thanks.

The interviews and conferences with these individuals, well over a hundred and fifty in all, are now cherished memories. I recall with unique pleasure my talks, some of them extending over several days, with Mr. Bernard Baruch, Brig. Gen. Charles A. Lindbergh and his wife, Lt. Gen. Harold H. Doolittle, Commissioner Robert Moses, Dr. Jerome Clarke Hunsaker, the late Dr. Theodore von Kármán, Mrs. Robert H. Goddard, Mrs. Frank Lloyd Wright, Mrs. Henry Allen Moe, and Madame Nina Kandinsky; with such members of the Guggenheim family as Mrs. Roger W. Straus, Countess Eleanor Castle Stewart, Mrs. Henry Obre, the late Mrs. Alicia Patterson Guggenheim, Mr. Harold Loeb, and Mr. Edmond A. Guggenheim; and with such close friends and business associates of the family as Mr. Leo Gottlieb, Mr. J. Albert Woods, and Mr. Medley G. B. Whelpley.

Pleasure also attaches to my memory of the hospitable manner in which I was received in the autumn of 1961 while poking about Switzerland in an effort to penetrate to the European beginnings of the American Guggenheims. In this connection my indebtedness is unusually great to Mrs. Dr. Florence Guggenheim-Grünberg of Zurich, unofficial historian of the family, and to the Rev. Dr. S. N. Gut, who administers the old people's home in Lengnau, an institution made possible by the Guggenheims, and whose then 13-year-old daughter, Hanna, acted as my interpreter on research expeditions in the area.

As for the help I have received from the head of the Guggenheim family, Mr. Harry Frank Guggenheim, this has been provided with such patience and with such largeness of spirit that I can only describe it by saying that what began as a series of formal conferences very rapidly became a case of friend communicating with friend.

Milton Lomask
Capitol Hill
Washington, D.C.
July, 1963

Index